NOT WITHOUT PERIL

NOT WITHOUT PERIL

One Hundred and Fifty Years
of Misadventure
on the Presidential Range
of New Hampshire

by

NICHOLAS HOWE

APPALACHIAN MOUNTAIN CLUB BOOKS
BOSTON, MASSACHUSETTS

Cover Photograph: *Huntington Ravine*, Robert Kozlow
Cover Design: Ola Frank
Book Design: Carol Bast Tyler

Distributed by The Globe Pequot Press, Inc

Library of Congress Cataloging-in-Publication Data

Howe, Nicholas S.
Not without peril : one hundred and fifty years of misadventure
on the Presidential Range of New Hampshire / by Nicholas Howe
p. cm.
ISBN 1-878239-93-7 (alk. paper)
1. Mountaineering—New Hampshire—Presidential Range—History.
2. Presidential Range (N.H.)—History. I. Title
GV199.42.N42 P722 2000
796.52'2'097422—dc21   99-086536

The paper used in this publication meets the minimum requirements of the American National Standard for Information Sciences—Permanence of Paper for Printed Library Materials, ANSI Z39.48–1984.∞

Printed on recycled paper using soy-based inks.

Printed in the United States of America

10 9 8 7 6 5 4 3 2 1   00 01 02 03 04 05

There have been joys too great to be described in words, and there have been griefs upon which I have dared not to dwell, and with these in mind I must say, climb if you will, but remember that courage and strength are naught without prudence, and that a momentary negligence may destroy the happiness of a lifetime. Do nothing in haste, look well to each step, and from the beginning think what may be the end.

— EDWARD WHYMPER, who made the
first ascent of the Matterhorn with six others
in 1865. On the way down, four of
his companions fell to their deaths.

CONTENTS

CHAPTER ONE

IN THE BEGINNING

*M*ountains were invented in the 19th century. There had always been high places, of course, but the ancients usually thought that the gods lived there and avoided them for fear of giving offense. More recently, settlers considered mountains to be a piece of bad luck, a barrier to travel, and a hindrance to farming. One of my forebears was named Jemima Tute and she lived on the western frontier when the frontier was at the Connecticut River. There were two mountain ranges within reach, but no one in her family went hiking. If their eyes were open they were working, and they held off all the Indian attacks except the last one.

The high mountains of New England were approached slowly. They were first reported by a coastwise navigator in 1524, and early news was a mixture of wonder, dread, and confusion. One account was "A Voyage into New England," published in London in 1628: "This River (sawco), as I am told by the Savages, cometh from a great mountain called the Cristall hill, being as they say 100 miles in the Country, yet it is to be seene at the sea side, and there is no ship ariuse in NEW ENGLAND, either to the West so farre as Cape Cod, or to the East so farre as Monhiggen, but they see this Mountaine the first land, if the weather be cleere."

The ecology of the new world was not yet subject to rigorous study and some seaborn observers wrapped themselves in the mantle of whatever science as was available, so they attributed the brightness of that inland "Mountaine" to white moss. Others heard the optimistic accounts of distant sightings and early speculators, and thought it might be the sheen of precious stones. One gazeteer of 1638 brought less promising news; he pushed northwards from the Massachusetts settlements, but the track became difficult and he reported that the regions ahead were "daunting terrible," so he turned back.

If he'd persevered, he would have learned that the Cristall hill was Agiocochook, the highest point in the northeastern quarter of the North American continent. This distinction loomed large in the Indian culture of the region, and those natives dared not tread the heights that were reserved for the gods. When the summit was finally reached, the attempt was not inspired by any sense of adventure or scientific inquiry, it was politics.

That climb was made by Darby Field. He'd been living in the Massachusetts colony, then in about 1638 he settled in Dover, near the bustling docks of Portsmouth in New Hampshire's short coastline. At that time, leaders in Massachusetts were looking northward with a view to extending their realm. Governor John Winthrop and Richard Saltenstall were willing servants of the spirit of expansion that would characterize America, but they had not forgotten the sense of religious propriety that brought them to the New World. This meant that they had to deal with the natives that they found there, but they had to do it properly, with conferences and deeds.

Darby Field was a quick study and he learned several Indian tongues. He also had his eye out for the main chance, and he became a translator for Messrs. Winthrop and Saltonstall in their dealings with the natives. In particular they had to deal with Passaconaway, the principal chief of the Abenaki tribes in the north. It seemed important to impress upon the natives that these European newcomers were not to be trifled with, that they were not afraid of either nature or gods. Darby Field decided that the surest way to do this was to conquer the throne room of their gods. So, in June of 1642 and in the witnessing company of an Abenaki, he found the untrodden top of Agiocochook. The prize was far more valuable than precious stones — this ascent helped convince Passaconaway to treat with the white settlers and trade away his lands.

The expansionist element in the Massachusetts colony lost no time in executing an intricate series of deeds with the Indians living in New Hampshire, but this was not the end of their ambition. They knew that the lands east of New Hampshire were more amenable to farming and better provided with access to the sea, so they looked to the territory that would become Maine.

When the negotiations were held, the delegation from Maine may have been surprised to learn that the men from Massachusetts already had maps of their lands. Darby Field had made a second ascent of Agiocochook in October 1642 and brought back reports of what he saw and gave them to his patrons in Massachusetts. As far as can be determined, that was the extent of high climbing in colonial New England.

It takes security from physical and economic threat before people feel they can take time off; that is to say, it takes vacations to turn daunting high places into something to be enjoyed, into mountains. The first vacationer of record in the hinterlands of New Hampshire was a person who had every right to feel secure in person and purse. This was John Wentworth, the last colonial governor of New Hampshire and probably its first tourist.

When the Honorable Wentworth took office in July 1767 he promised "to preserve the honor of the crown and advance the prosperity of the district." He was also "surveyor of the King's Woods in North America," which meant that he should see to it that a plentiful supply of trees suitable for ships' masts was provided to the king's navy. Two months after the governor took office he provided a further insight into the prosperity business. Portsmouth was the capitol of the colony and a circular advised the people that "John Wentworth gives notice that the General Court having empowered him to receive in demand 10,000 gallons of West India rum from the several towns in the state in lieu of taxes, he is ready for it and requests delinquent towns to hand it over."

This was a wide-ranging job description, and Governor Wentworth sought to escape the burdens of office and the hubbub of city life by building a second home on the shore of Lake Winnipesaukee, which lay at the beginning of the mountain region in the north. He spent his summers there from 1770 through 1775, thereby becoming the first New Hampshire vacationer of record, and he also built a series of splendid roads in the state. His visits were cut short by the stirrings of revolutionary sentiment and in 1778 he fled to a more comfortable situation among the Tories of Nova Scotia, never to reclaim either office or vacation home.

Agiocochook could be seen from the waters of Winnipesaukee and in 1784 it was renamed to honor the general who won the Revolutionary War: Mount Washington. Before long the stage drivers were persuaded to drive on for another day to reach the highlands and soon there were inns and hostelries to accommodate travelers. One prominent visitor was Anthony Trollope, the celebrated English writer who flourished in the years after the American Civil War. He wrote that he was amazed "that there was a district in New England containing mountain scenery superior to much that is yearly crowded by tourists in Europe."

Mr. Trollope spent a night in Jackson, ten miles southeast of Mount Washington, then he went through Crawford Notch at the southern end of the Mount Washington range and met Mr. Plaistead, who spoke in the simple patois of the yeoman farmer: "Sir! I have everything here that a man ought to want; air, sir, that ain't to be got better nowhere; trout, chicken, beef mutton, milk — and all for a dollar a day. A-top that hill, sir, there's a view that ain't to be beaten this side of the Atlantic, or I believe on the other. And echo, sir! We've an echo that come back to us six times, sir; floating on the light wind, and wafted about from rock to rock till you would think the angels were talking to you."

"That hill" was Mount Washington and the peaks and valleys in its range, once daunting terrible, were now stylish. New England was prosperous and this brought wealth, leisure, and rather unpleasant cities. All traffic was horse-drawn and calculations show that one million tons of manure fell in the streets of London each year, with proportional amounts in downtown America. Not only that, but when horses died on the job they were not always removed from the street very quickly. The heat of summer lent emphasis to these conditions and affluent families were easily persuaded to escape.

The security of empire and the leisure of aristocracy sent Englishmen into the high places of Switzerland in the 1830s, and those sons of privilege were the first great generation of mountaineers. Their fame became fashionable and was admired even by those who would not follow them, thus Queen Victoria's husband had a panoramic picture of the Mount Washington summit view on the wall of his study in Buckingham Palace.

The Edenic promise of Mr. Plaistead's oration was not a complete inventory of those echoing heights. He would have known that "the sheen of precious stones" reported by the coastwise navigators was actually rime ice or snow, which can accumulate on the Mount Washington range in every month of the year. Mr. Plaistead could see that, but he probably did not know why winter came to the range even in midsummer.

Mount Washington is 6,288 feet high, and the summit and its buttress ridges lie at the intersection of two jet streams in the upper air. These combine with the upslope on the windward side of the range and the high elevation of the crests to create local weather systems of sudden and extraordinary violence. In later years, scientists would occupy the summit of Mount Washington and measure temperatures of 60° below zero and winds of 231 mph, the highest ever recorded on the surface of the earth.

These lethal conditions would cause more than 200 deaths and uncounted desperate survivals in the years to come, but Anthony Trollope didn't know that. He followed Mr. Plaistead's suggestion and went to see the celebrated view for himself, and all he saw was the inside of a cloud. It was worse for Frederick Strickland.

· FREDERICK STRICKLAND ·
OCTOBER 1849

$\mathscr{F}$rederick Strickland was a gentleman of substance and good prospect, the son of Sir George Strickland of Bridlington, England, who was a baronet and a member of Parliament. Frederick graduated from Cambridge University in 1843, the school that taught Charles Darwin in the previous decade.

There was a lot going on then. Queen Victoria was in the second decade of her reign and Darwin was in the first gestures of his ascendancy. He'd gone from college to his five-year voyage on the Beagle, and upon his return he began to publish the essays that would be collected as *Species and Speciation* and lead to an enthusiastic but mistaken reading of his ideas. [Darwin didn't think evolution is teleological — it has no direction or goal or end, evolution is what comes out in the wash.] But it was convenient for English gentlemen of that era to believe that the whole history of evolution ended at English gentlemen, destined as they were to achieve dominion over palm and pine and to know a good sherry when they tasted one.

Young Mr. Strickland was very keen on science, he would have been attuned to the Darwinian buzz at Cambridge and encouraged by the confident energy of his countrymen. In 1849, he went to see America. Frederick was twenty-nine years old when he sailed in the company of his brother Henry, and they spent several months touring the hinterland of the vast continent. Returning to civilization, the junior Stricklands reached Boston during the first week of October and took rooms at the Tremont House, whence Frederick's brother soon returned to England.

The travels of an English gentleman were dignified and the details were well-understood. Chief among them was the letter of introduction, a sort of pre-packaged reputation, and *The Boston Advertiser* reported that Frederick Strickland was "most respectably introduced

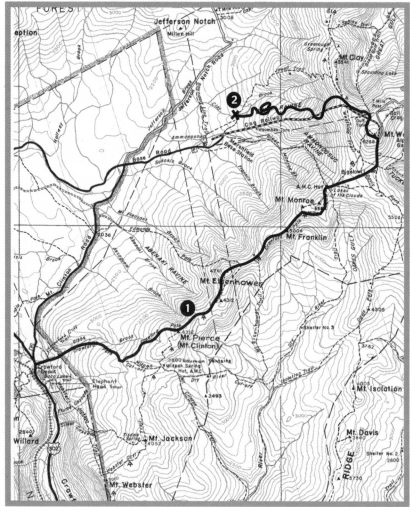

AMC map, circa 1992, by Louis F. Cutter

1 Guide and horses turn back
2 Body found below treeline

(and) had become known to a considerable number of persons in this city and vicinity, by whom he was highly respected as a gentleman of amiable character, ardently devoted to literary and scientific pursuits." *The Boston Transcript* added, "He brought letters to some of our most distinguished citizens and was advised to visit the White Mountains by several gentlemen of science and taste in our community."

History is silent on the names of his new friends, but gentlemen of science and taste would certainly be found at Harvard College, where the faculty included geologist Louis Agassiz, geographer Arnold Guyot, and mapmaker George Bond. They had all been active in the White Mountains that summer, they left their names on the mountains they explored, and they might well have advised the young Englishman to visit the same region. Frederick stayed on in America after his brother went home, and in October 1849 he took the stagecoach north.

A measure of endurance was required to approach the mountains. A road had been built to provide a way for farmers in the upper reaches of the Connecticut River to trade in the markets of Portland, Maine, but it was not a trip that invited the casual tourist. The route led through what they called The Notch of the Mountains, soon renamed Crawford Notch, and the way was so difficult that the first person to make the trip had to lower his horse down one section with a block and tackle. Even after the road was improved, the spur of commerce was barely enough to force the passage; "It was," said one rump-sore hero, "like driving a wagon up a brook bed."

Once Frederick Strickland was in the shadow of the mountains, he stopped in Crawford Notch at Abel Crawford's inn named The Mount Crawford House just south of Mt. Crawford, then he went on to The Notch House kept by Thomas Crawford. Frederick came to the mountains with the intention of climbing the Crawford Path, a density of nomenclature that must have persuaded him that he'd come to the right place. The surroundings would have added to the assurance. Five years earlier, a traveler wrote that "the cavernous descent into which you look from the road is so savagely torn & distracted, so to speak, by the confused mingling of black depths and contending masses of old and young trees, & scattered & monstrous rocks, while the heights above are perhaps higher than anywhere else, that the scene is more imposing that in any other part." Another few hundred yards led to Thomas Crawford's door.

Three generations of this protean family built their hostelries for the convenience of farmers and tradesmen with accommodations that were minimal, but sufficient. Winter was the easiest time to travel because the streams and muddy swales were frozen and the Crawford diaries report that in 1819, "Lucy would many times have to make a large bed on the floor for (the travelers) to lie down upon, with their clothes on, and I would build a large fire in a large rock or stone chimney that would keep them warm through the night. It was no uncommon thing to burn in that fire-place a cord of wood in twenty-four hours, and sometimes more."

The next summer some pleasure-seekers inquired about climbing the mountains and seven of them signed Ethan Allen Crawford's register. He was of the middle generation and, alert to this new commercial opportunity, he and his father Abel "made a foot path from the Notch out through the woods, and it was advertised in the newspapers, and we soon began to have a few visitors." This trail building would have been a prodigy of labor, but the Crawfords were used to hard work and Ethan was a giant of a man. He was over 6'2" in a time that counted 5'6" as well grown and he could lift a 500-pound barrel of potash two feet to the bed of their carrier. In present terms, the Crawford's path led three miles up Mt. Clinton and another 6.2 miles along the ridge to the summit of Mount Washington. Then in 1840 Ethan and his son Thomas widened and graded their path for horse travel, which was considered to be the most reasonable way to ascend a mountain and, for the owner of the stable and the toll gate, the most profitable.

Thomas Crawford was keeping the family's inn beside the small lake at the top of the notch when Frederick Strickland arrived and announced that he'd like to climb Mount Washington. The innkeeper replied that the season for such an undertaking was past, there had been an unusually severe early-season storm and the snow up on the range was too deep for his horses to negotiate. Frederick thought that this country cousin was trying to shake him down for more money.

Thomas Crawford's cautions were rooted in something that he

understood even if he couldn't explain it. Mount Washington is 130 miles north of Boston and this puts the seasons as much as two months behind the down-country metropolis due to an indwelling global imperative. The summit of the mountain is more than 6,000 feet higher than Boston and each 100-foot gain in altitude is equivalent to moving ten miles north. By this formula, the summit is 500 miles north of Boston, about in the middle of Labrador. Frederick Strickland would soon understand the effect of this rule, although he'd probably think that it didn't apply to him.

The English visitor came from a time and a culture that believed man could do anything, that triumph over nature was steady and inevitable and seemed to be confirmed by the recent propositions of the estimable Mr. Darwin. Thus strengthened, Frederick told Thomas Crawford that he was sure he could make the climb, he insisted that he could. Mr. Crawford agreed to provide a guide and horses and told him that if he did reach the top of Mount Washington he should not return by the Crawford Path, he should take the short route down by Horace Fabyan's bridle path, a three-mile route over the same terrain the cog railroad would follow twenty years later, then seven miles out along the Ammonoosuc River to Mr. Fabyan's hotel.

The English visitor seems to have been gaining in bravado, if not in wisdom. He said he didn't need any provisions for the long trip, but his host finally persuaded him to take a couple of crackers. Another Englishman was present, and he joined his countryman and the guide as they started up the Crawford Path on Friday morning, October 19.

Clothing is important here. Man is a tropical animal and nature does not protect him from cold. Darwin argued that the survival of a species depends on successful adaptation to a changing environment and the fittest among them survive best. Mr. Strickland would not have been worried. Consonant with the habits of his class while on a country outing, he would be wearing a shirt with high collar and floppy tie, a vest and hip-length jacket nipped at the waist, and tapered trousers. He'd been traveling with a large steamer trunk and here, facing the snowbound heights in North America, he put on his overcoat.

Ethan Allen had no education past his letters, but he was a natural civil engineer of the highest order and the location of his bridle path brought travelers to the crest of the Southern Peaks by steady and moderate grades. This is a delightful climb. The Crawfords' trail leads up the western slope of Clinton and as the prevailing winds carry moist air up the rising land it cools and the moisture is wrung out of it. This slope is a forest primeval, with moss carpeting the ground and draping every tree.

The same atmospheric laws wring snow out of October air and although the valley weather was fine this day, a storm had just blown through and, as Thomas Crawford anticipated, the snow up on the ridge was deep. The Crawford's trail reached the ridgeline just north of Clinton, a place with scrub spruce from a foot to about eight feet high and far too dense to push through, which means it provides good shelter from bad weather. The small party went on northward along the ridge. The terrain here is gently rolling and it's almost exactly at timberline — on the open rocks for a way, then dipping into the dense spruce, then rising into the open again. On this day, it was also clogged with snow and very heavy going for the horses.

The party got some little way along the ridge from Clinton, but the snow was getting too deep for the horses. The trail would soon leave timberline behind and the climbers would be wholly exposed to the elements. The guide decided they should turn back, he did not want to risk either his horses or his clients on a trip that obviously could not go very much further. Frederick Strickland wanted to keep going and the guide refused. Mr. Strickland was adamant, he said he'd go on alone. The guide implored him to turn back, but he was unmoved. Then the guide and the other Englishman returned to the valley and Frederick Strickland went on alone, heading for the summit of Mount Washington five miles away over increasingly steep and exposed terrain. He did reach the summit, then he found the Fabyan Path and started down the west side of the mountain.

The amenities were being observed in the valley if not on the heights and Thomas Crawford, knowing that Frederick planned to come down the Fabyan Path, sent his trunk on to the hotel kept by Horace Fabyan, near the place where the old Bretton Woods railroad depot now stands. Thomas went over the next morning and learned that Mr. Strickland was not there. He immediately directed that a search be started on the Crawford Path while he and Mr. Fabyan gathered a few more men and started up the Fabyan Path. This second search party found footprints in the snow about a mile up the mountain, well below the last of the difficult terrain and, it seemed to them, safely below timberline. They followed the track and it led to a small brook. They came to a pool and in it they found a pair of trousers and underclothes which proved to belong to Frederick Strickland. By then it was getting dark, so the searchers repaired to the valley. The next morning Thomas Crawford and Horace Fabyan gathered a larger search party and they found the body about a mile from where they'd found the clothes; Frederick was lying face down in a pool of water with his head wedged between two rocks. His overcoat and his gloves were missing, and his torso and his legs were bruised and cut.

He had followed the Fabyan Path down the western slope of Mount Washington to timberline and then he lost the path among the trees. The searchers said that he'd circled around in the woods, crossing his own track and crossing the bridle path twice without realizing it. Finally he found a small stream which shows on modern maps as Clay Brook and leads to the larger Ammonoosuc River, which eventually reached Horace Fabyan's hotel in the valley.

Mr. Strickland was apparently still thinking clearly enough to follow the brook downstream, but blood in the snow indicated that injuries were slowing him until his final fall. The men in the rescue party were puzzled by the clothes they found in the pool. The body was examined by a physician and he suggested that when Frederick fell into the water his pants froze to his legs and he pulled them off so he could keep going, thus explaining the places where the flesh seemed to be stripped away. The doctor's education would not have included studies of hypothermia and the attendant drop in core temperature, but experience would have taught him that the combination of cold and water are lethal.

Frederick Strickland's body was taken back to Cambridge, Massachusetts, and he was buried near Green Briar Path in the Mount Auburn Cemetery, about a mile from the place where he first heard stories of the Presidential Range. He was the first person to climb Mount Washington in winter conditions, and he was the first to die there.

CHAPTER TWO

GENTLEFOLK ESSAY
THE HEIGHTS

*W*hen gentlefolk of the mid-nineteenth century went climbing on the Presidential Range, it was widely assumed that horses would do the work. The Crawford family converted their first trail up the Southern Peaks to a bridle path in 1843 and Nathaniel Davis sought to cash in on the Crawfords' success by building his own bridle path up the adjacent Montalban Ridge to the summit of Mount Washington in 1844. Then the Crawfords built a road to the base of a western ridge of Mount Washington, which provided a shorter route to the summit by way of a bridle path managed by the Fabyan family. Finally the Thompson Bridle Path up the eastern side of Mount Washington was built in 1851.

The Glen House was the only hotel on the eastern side of the Presidential Range. It opened in 1852 and the bridle path already ran from the Glen to the summit of Mount Washington. The path was named for the man who kept the Glen House and it's worth noting that the Canadian Grand Trunk Railroad paid the construction costs. This was an investment to draw tourists to the northern end of the Presidential Range and gain a share of the revenue provided by customers of the popular Crawford Path leading up the Southern Peaks of the range.

The first four miles of the Thompson Path were built on the same location as the auto road of today, then known as the carriage road, and the remainder of the bridle path was abandoned when the carriage road was completed to the summit in 1861. Most of the old location is very difficult to find today, but traces can still be discovered. As the old texts would put it, persevering effort by an attentive tramper will be rewarded.

Just before the present auto road rises above timberline, there's a wide clearing where the Halfway House used to stand. Soon the road starts a large bend of 180 degrees around a conspicuous outcropping of rock known as the Ledge in the early days and, more recently, Cape Horn. Sections of the summit road have always been identified by the markers along the way and the 4-Mile post is near the beginning of this turn. The last of the dwarf spruce are soon left behind, then the road begins a long traverse of the northeast side of the mountain, passing 5-Mile en route.

The bridle path turned sharply left at the Halfway House clearing and went into the woods at the back of what is a rocky gravel pit today. It went up the steep slope here, thus cutting off the loop of road around the Ledge and met the present auto road again a short way above the point where the Chandler Brook Trail departs to drop steeply into Great Gulf. There are two paved parking lots at this point. The bridle path entered the back of the upper lot bearing slightly to the left, looking upslope. A conspicuous winter tractor route begins just above this point and heads upslope to cut off the long loop out to Cragway Turn on the auto road, then it rejoins the road just below the point where the Six Husbands Trail departs right and the Alpine Garden Trail departs left. This tractor route was roughed out directly on top of the bridle path, so no traces remain here.

The bridle path crossed the auto road location at 6-Mile and ran close to the Alpine Garden Trail up the slope toward the top of the ridge. This part of the old location is the easiest to see. The horses followed several switch-backs here to ease the grade and these are quite visible from the Alpine Garden Trail, then the bridle path turned sharply right just before the top of the ridge. The horses continued along a meandering and still quite obvious route up the shoulder of Chandler Ridge, then the path cut across the large right-angled loop the road makes around the flat area known as the Cow Pasture. The stone foundation of a structure used in that windswept animal husbandry can be found in the cow pasture, and a few steps away to the northwest, toward Mt. Madison, there's the old spring and the fragile remains of its wooden framing.

The bridle path ran diagonally up the slope below the road and, from this viewpoint, it disappeared around the horizon just below 7-Mile. It crossed the road location again to cut off the more moderate last bend below the summit, but at this point the terrain was very much modified for the research buildings built in the 1950s and now razed, so the old route is impossible to find. The bridle path crossed the present auto road for the last time and passed under the cog railway trestle near three large fuel tanks of the summit establishment, then climbed the last few yards to the summit.

Seen on a larger scale, the bridle path followed a nearly straight line up the crest of Chandler Ridge from 4-Mile to the summit. Seen on the closest scale, it quickly becomes obvious that a horse could step higher and manage more difficult terrain than we of the post-horse age would probably imagine.

By the same token, Americans were expected to negotiate more difficult terrain than the dress of the mid-nineteenth century would suggest. Most Americans' clothing was not yet diversified according to activity and a gentleman's turnout would not have been very different from what he wore to work: shirt and tie, vest, jacket, trousers, and probably a bowler hat.

Well-placed young ladies would have large wardrobes, but they would not have many choices. Their dresses would be older or newer, or plainer or fancier, or made for summer or winter, but they would all be dresses — a woman could not decide among a skirt or pants or shorts. This was flood-tide ante-bellum America and young women would look very much like Scarlett O'Hara, lacking only Rhett Butler on the stairway. The dresses of the time were extraordinarily complicated and a stylish lady aspired to the shape of an elaborately-draped bell. Her outfit would be close-fitted down to the high waistline, then widen steadily to her toes over a skirt stiffened by several petticoats, one of which would have been a crinoline stiffened with horsehair, the whole decorated by flounces and ruffles to taste and worn over ruffled pantaloons and high stockings. Thus prepared, she would deflect any untoward meteorological effects with a shawl as wide as she could reach and a bonnet.

The workload of such an outfit would be considerable, but fashions of the late twentieth century are so distant from those days that an exact appreciation is difficult. So, in the interests of White Mountain studies, I brought illustrations from the 1855 section of a fashion encyclopedia to a dressmaker of my acquaintance for a comparison in real-world terms. She said that a woman of today who went out wearing a blouse and a comfortable skirt would be carrying between a yard and a half and two yards of material. Then, using a bridal gown she'd just made for dimensions, the dressmaker studied the 1855 illustrations and calculated that a stylish young woman ascending the heights in that year would be wearing at least 45 yards of material. Depending on the fabric, this could weigh as much as a well-provided overnight pack of our times, and the amount of moisture it would absorb on a wet day could make it a truly significant factor on a hike. But it would preserve a lady's modesty from throat to toes and, not incidentally, make anything unladylike not just unthinkable but practically impossible.

• LIZZIE BOURNE •
SEPTEMBER 1855

$\mathscr{O}$n the morning of September 13, 1855, Lizzie Bourne bowled a string of tenpins at the Glen House. The other guests were impressed. In those years a young woman was expected to be, at the most, demure. Here was a game girl, and the guests remarked on her vigor and vivacity.

Lizzie was the daughter of the Honorable Edward Emerson Bourne, judge of probate for York County, Maine, which included the large mercantile city of Portland. She was twenty years old in the summer of 1855 and she'd always wanted to spend a night in the hotel on top of Mount Washington. Her uncle George was a principal in the shipbuilding firm of Bourne & Kingsbury in Kennebunk, and he agreed to go with her on such a trip, then his daughter Lucy persuaded him that she could come, too.

Those three, together with George's wife and another couple, arrived at the Glen House on September 12, a day of damp and glowering weather in the valleys surrounding the Presidential Range. The next morning brought steady rain and no promise of better skies, so they engaged horses for a ride up the mountain the next day. Then shortly before noon the sky showed promise of clearing and while the 1:00 P.M. dinner was being served, Lizzie launched a campaign to walk for a way up the road on foot that afternoon. In fact, she and her cousin wanted to go to the summit and spend that very night, which would surprise the party they'd left behind. She prevailed, and George Bourne and his daughter and niece stepped off the veranda of the Glen House at 2:00. Lizzie waved goodbye to those who remained behind and she kept turning to wave until she was lost from sight. In the words of another guest, "Sunshine was around their steps as they walked cheerfully up this new road."

Lucy and Lizzie Bourne were very excited at the prospects of a night in the summit hotel and even more so when they crossed the

Peabody River bridge in the meadow fronting the hotel and met Mr. Myers, a particularly courteous gentleman who was supervising construction higher up on the mountain road. George Bourne glanced at his watch just then, and it showed 2:15 P.M.

Mr. Myers was going up the road himself, and he walked along with the Bournes for about two and a half miles, pointing out notable views and other objects of interest as they went along and describing the difficulties of building a carriage road under the unfavorable circumstances found on Mount Washington. At some point Mr. Myers was detained by his duties and the Bournes went on alone.

Only the first four miles of carriage road were built at that time, half of the eventual route, and the Bournes paused at the end of the prepared track. They'd risen 2,437 feet above the valley and there were 2,288 ahead of them.

The way ahead, however, bore no resemblance to what they'd just passed over. The first four miles led by steady but moderate grades through a mixed forest of hardwoods and evergreens and the shelter was about the same as they'd find in any forest lane at home. At the farthest advance of the carriage road there was a building known as Camp House, mainly used by guides on the bridle path and workers on the carriage road. The bridle path led on from here and soon rose above the tree line, and from there to the summit the Bournes would face a wasteland of jumbled broken rocks, sharp-edged, rough-faced, and often in precarious balance underfoot. Worse than that, they'd find no shelter at all from the violent weather that threatens at every season of the year: gale-force winds, rain and snow, and impenetrable cloud banks clinging to the ground.

In the summer of Lizzie's climb, many visitors would engage a guide to ensure their way to the summit. Mr. Bourne knew this but he decided that he did not need a guide; the carriage road was unmistakable and he knew that the bridle path was easy to follow, too. When the three Bournes reached the end of the road they met a construction crew and asked about conditions up ahead. The men replied that the path was clear and the weather seemed favorable, and the family started on to the summit. George was a meticulous person and he again glanced at his watch; it was exactly 4:00 P.M.

They made the short steep climb to the crest of a prominent ledge above the tree line — in the manner of the day, Mr. Bourne described this ledge as "a mountain." When they topped the crest they were immediately struck by a much stronger wind than they expected, so strong that the ladies had to sit down until there was a lull that let them start moving again. They were not dismayed; in fact, they seemed to relish the blast and Mr. Bourne thought that the ladies went on with renewed vigor.

They found another "mountain" up ahead, then another. They pushed on to the top of each one, every time expecting it to be the last. They were going more slowly now, because the ladies had to sit down frequently to catch their breath. Then they climbed what they expected was the last mountain and walked out onto the conspicuous flats of the Cow Pasture. There in the west was the setting sun that, as George Bourne wrote later, "enrobed in his mantle of gold and crimson, bade us adieu."

The three Bournes sat there for a few minutes, admiring the grand spectacle of the departing day. They got up to climb onward and suddenly the clouds dropped onto them. Two members of the Spaulding family emerged from the gloom; they were keepers of the hotel on the summit and they thought these late-afternoon climbers were in good spirits.

George Bourne, however, thought that Lizzie seemed to be tired—she needed to be helped over the rougher steps. They thought the next pitch was the last mountain they'd have to climb, so they gathered their strength and, as George wrote, "We at last reached the Summit. It was now late in the twilight and the shadows of night were fast creeping upon us; but to our sorrow another mountain stood before us, whose summit was far above the clouds."

The Bournes kept going as long as they could see well enough to find the bridle path, but Lizzie was weakening and they had to stop often so she could rest. Finally they could see no longer and they stopped. In George's words, "It was very cold and the wind blowing a

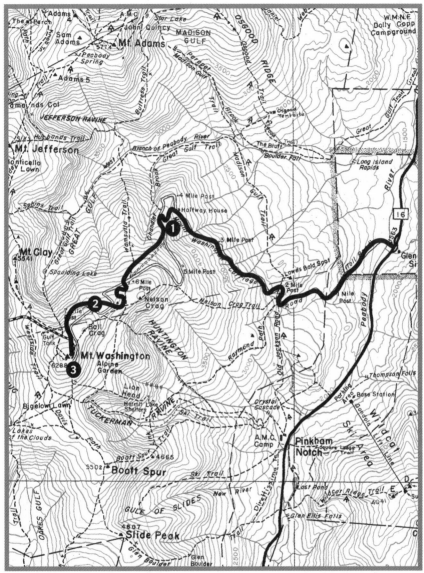

AMC map, circa 1992, by Louis F. Cutter

1 First hit severe weather at the Ledge
2 Admired sunset from Cow Pasture
3 Sought shelter just short of summit

gale, the night dark and fearful, and we were upon the bleak mountain without a shrub, rock or tree under which to find shelter. What was to be done? To lie down and commit our souls to the keeping of a merciful Father, probably to sleep that sleep that knows no waking?"

George Bourne decided not to sleep that sleep. He was very tired himself, but he realized that something had to be done and he was the only one to do it. Each of the ladies had a shawl, but Lizzie had lost her bonnet in the wind. They were still on the path, so the ladies lay down in the treadway and George went to work gathering stones and building up a wall to protect them from the wind. This was difficult work. It was full dark now, the wind was blowing a gale, the clouds were right down on the ground, and he had no light and no clear idea of what was around him. He'd work until he was tired, then he'd lie down next to the ladies to rest himself and give them a little warmth and a bit more protection against the terrible blast.

George Bourne made a routine of this: he'd gather stones, lie down, get up and, as he put it, "thrash around" to warm himself, gather more stones and for his windbreak, and lie down to warm the ladies again. This worked rather well. They seemed comfortable and George believed they'd survive the night. At 10:00 P.M. he finished a stint of thrashing and wall-building and lay down to warm the ladies again. He took Lizzie's hand to encourage her and found that it was cold: "Her spirit had winged its way to that better land where the black mountain chill could not reach her. She was dead — had uttered no complaint, expressed no regret or fear, but passed silently away."

Now there was only Lucy to keep warm, so George kept up the thrashing for himself and the warming for his daughter, "And thus passed the long, long weary night. Oh, how anxiously did we watch for the first gleam of morning." At that first light, the two of them got up, walked a few steps, and saw the Tip-Top House right in front of them.

George knocked on the door and, as he said, "aroused the inmates," who were keeper Spaulding and his family. They knew that the temperature had dropped below freezing during the night, so two ladies and two gentlemen left straightway and soon returned with Lizzie's body. A boy was sent to run down the mountain with word of the trouble while the others tried to help Lizzie. "Hoping against hope, for four hours they labored with hot rocks, hot baths, and used every exertion to call back her spirit, but all in vain."

Mr. Joseph Hall was stopping at the Glen House, a right-hand man for the Crawfords in their trail-building and a guide of deep experience in these mountains. He'd started up the carriage road that morning and had passed Mr. Myers' Camp House, then he met the boy near the Ledge. He returned to Camp House and directed the workers to make a long shallow box while he cut a stout pole in the woods. Then he took some straps from a horse's pack saddle and he and another man went on to the summit.

The Spaulding women prepared Lizzie's body and placed it in Mr. Hall's box and packed it carefully with bed linen. Then Mr. Hall used the pack saddle straps to hang the box from the pole he'd cut, and he and Mr. Davis and another man shouldered the load, tallest man in front, and they started down the road. It took them three hours to reach the Glen House. The news had preceded them and George Bourne's wife met them crying, "Oh! Lizzie — Lizzie!" The Bournes and their friends returned with her to Portland, "And," wrote her uncle, "though the angel of death had set his seal upon her brow, yet a sweet smile still lingered and she seemed as one lying in angelic slumber."

A little later, Mr. Hall received a letter from Judge Bourne. "Moses was taken up from Mount Pisgah, Aaron from Mount Hor, and Lizzie, frail child of earth, to heaven from Mount Washington. Knowing her as I did, I am sure she would have chosen Mount Washington as the place to pass from earth to heaven."

AFTERMATH

*F*riends said that the Bourne family never recovered from the loss of their beloved Lizzie. Curiously, though, several newspaper accounts and the marker on Mount Washington and her elaborate tombstone in the family burying ground give her age as twenty-three, not twenty. George Bourne wrote several sharp notes to local newspapers correcting the error, but the memorials were not changed.

Mr. Hall returned to the summit and built a tall pile of stones on the place where Lizzie died, and when he was done he topped it with a block of rose quartz. After his long life in service of the mountains, he never went back.

CHAPTER THREE

THE MAN WHO COLLECTED VIEWS

*P*oor judgment tends to multiply, once an outing begins to go wrong, the participants make one mistake after another in a sort of fatal contagion. One exception came the month after Lizzie Bourne's death. Against advice and with his eyes wide open, Dr. Benjamin Lincoln Ball walked straight into a lethal situation, but that was the last mistake he made.

Not only did the weather turn violently against Dr. Ball on the high slopes of Mount Washington, but he had no map because the mountains had not yet been mapped, he had no trail guide because no trails had yet been made north of the summit, he'd never been in the White Mountains before, and he had no idea at all of either the large or the small features of the terrain around him because the clouds were right down on the ground until his last day.

Dr. Ball's story looms large in the annals of these mountains and his name remains on Ball Crag, just below the summit of Mount Washington. Part of this fame was certainly due to his association with Lizzie Bourne, who died on the mountain a month earlier, and it was amplified by the book he wrote the next year: "Three Days on The White Mountains, being The Perilous Adventure of Dr. B. L. Ball On Mount Washington. Written by Himself."

The doctor was almost continuously mystified by his surroundings, but he was a precise chronicler of his attempt to negotiate them and his perilous adventure can be followed almost step by step.

• DR. BENJAMIN LINCOLN BALL •
OCTOBER 1855

*D*r. Ball was serious about views, he collected views the way other connoisseurs collect paintings. He graduated from the Harvard Medical School in 1844, but if he ever did practice, his infirmary days must have been short indeed, fitted into the space between extended trips to the Alps, to Java, to the Philippines, and through Asia.

In the summer of 1855, Dr. Ball was in Boston attending to the publication of his book *Rambles in East Asia* and thinking he ought to make a trip to the White Mountains of New Hampshire, a place that was so close he'd never been there. He was thirty-five years old and he thought it was time to make up that deficit, but preparing the text of his book took more time than he anticipated and it was October before he was finished. It was too late, he thought, to travel to the northern mountains.

One day he met Starr King, who was working on *The White Hills*, his monumental account of rambles in the White Mountains. Starr King was to writing what Albert Bierstadt was to painting, he was the prose laureate of the sublime acclivity and the dreadful abyss, the man who found forty-three adjectives to describe Mt. Chocorua, and he told Dr. Ball that he hadn't seen anything until he'd seen the views from Mount Washington. In fact, he'd always wanted to make a late-season trip himself, he'd never been there after the leaves had fallen and, no, October wasn't too late.

So Dr. Ball turned his face northward from Boston. He arrived in Gorham on the morning of Wednesday, October 25, and was dismayed to find that it was raining and no mountains could be seen. He engaged a horse at the local livery and rode nine miles to the Glen House, protected only by his umbrella. It was raining at the Glen House, too, and he could see nothing but clouds. Dr. Ball was determined to see what he described as The Mountain, to compare the sight with famous views he'd found around the world, so he took counsel with Mr. Thompson, the keeper of the Glen House.

Hotel keepers were an essential part of the White Mountain economy of the day. They not only provided food and shelter, they explored the hinterlands, they built trails, provided advice, guided visitors, and searched for lost trampers who had not partaken of their services. Mr. Thompson told his visitor that he might walk a way up the new road on Mount Washington and see what he could see.

This came as news to Dr. Ball — he hadn't heard of such an innovation. Mr. Thompson told him that four miles of the road were passable ending at the Camp House, a place just below timberline where workers were sheltered, though work had been suspended and only a few men would be there. Mr. Thompson said it was not a difficult walk that far, but above the Camp House the weather would be worse and the exposed terrain much more difficult, and it would not be wise to go up there on a day like this.

Dr. Ball decided to start up the road straightway, so he exchanged his hat for a cap he saw hanging on a rack in the hotel lobby, opened his umbrella, and set out in a chilly drizzle.

Dr. Ball reached the Camp House in two hours, sooner than he expected. The weather had not grown worse, in fact, he could manage without his umbrella and he thought of leaving it behind, but didn't. He could see a promontory called the Ledge above the Camp House and reasoned that the view might be better up there. "Casting my eyes to the top of the Ledge, and reflecting a few moments, I concluded, as it was not very high, that I should not be violating very much the advice of Mr. Thompson if I went to the top."

Soon Dr. Ball was above the trees and a freezing rain was crusting his clothes and his umbrella and the foot-deep snow. He kept going until he realized that darkness was falling, then he turned back but it was a near thing, he could find his way only by feeling for his ascending footprints. He found the Camp House with three men resident, they made him coffee and supper and he spent Wednesday night there, but he did not sleep.

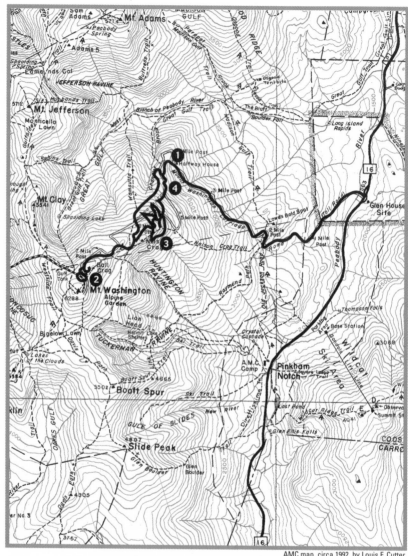

AMC map, circa 1992, by Louis F. Cutter

1 First sleepless night at Camp House, "Halfway House"
2 Looked for summit hotel on flats near Ball Crag
3 Umbrella Camp was just above Cragway Turn
4 Basin Rock

Mr. Myers was the foreman at the Camp House, the same man who had accompanied Lizzie Bourne on the start of her trip, and he cautioned Dr. Ball not to tempt the fate that befell the young lady who went by the Camp House last month. He told her party that it was too late in the day to continue, but they disregarded his advice. Dr. Ball borrowed Mr. Myers' boots and accepted the gift of his walking stick and set out, but not before being warned about bears. The boots were much too big for him, but that couldn't be helped. He followed the tracks he made above the Ledge on the previous day and saw bear tracks covering his own. At least Mr. Myers was right about that.

Dr. Ball climbed up the bridle path until the snow became too deep and he lost the track, but he kept going; he'd been told there would be four Mountains on the ridge, the last being Mount Washington, and he was sure he could find his way. At this point, the sleet and freezing drizzle had turned entirely to snow and he folded his umbrella. Conditions were not improving, but he hadn't yet taken a view, so he decided to keep going, he could always follow his footprints back. As a precaution against deeper snow, he made small cairns on prominent rocks to lead him down.

The footing and the terrain got more difficult as he climbed the ridge and several times Dr. Ball thought of turning back, but each time he remembered the many times he'd pressed on against both weather and advice only to be richly rewarded. Twice in Switzerland, he ignored the advice of guides and made his own way to majestic views. In Java, the natives told him that not even birds could survive the ascent to the top of the smoking mountain, but he pressed on and found "the grandest specimen of volcanic scenes." Besides, he'd been assured that snug lodgings awaited him in the Summit House on Mount Washington, provided with the makings of fire and light, with food and drink, and beds and bedclothes.

The storm grew severe, the worst he'd ever encountered in all his travels; he ached with cold and he fell more and more often. He lost his way completely and was just taking whatever upward direction that seemed to offer good footing. Toiling on, he felt an unusual pain in his face; putting up his hand, he found that it was completely encased in ice:

cap, beard, even eyelashes, were all ice. "I considered the aspect of affairs to be somewhat desperate, and looked back. But no, thought I, the summit must be near, and, after so long a time and so much labor, I will not turn yet. At the Summit House I can make myself comfortable; and the storm is too violent to continue long, especially so early in the season as October. Thoughts of this nature passed through my mind, and, holding to my resolve, I said to myself — I will still try for the Summit House!"

Finally, after a terrible battering, Dr. Ball reached a flat place he believed to be the summit, but he could not find the Summit House. "The storm pours down as if I was the only object of its wrath, as if avenging itself for some unknown offence. Blasts of the confused elements grapple each other, in rapid succession, and envelop me in commingled sheets of impenetrable snow. The wind, encircling me with its powerful folds, presses the cold to my very vitals, colder than the coldest robe of ice. Now it wrests me from my feet; again, it carries me furiously before it, and I sink down in fear that it will hurl me over an unseen precipice. For a few moments I remain to breathe and to rest. Shall I retreat, or shall I persevere? For I am freezing." He persevered. He persuaded himself that he lost count, that he'd climbed only three Mountains, not four. Then, seeing his situation more clearly, he realized that he must go down.

Again the plunging and falling, again the battering wind and his freezing hands and feet. Then Dr. Ball found a line of stakes, which he supposed were survey markers for the road builders. He followed these downslope, but with increasing difficulty. Then he lost the line altogether and he suddenly realized that the light was failing. "'My God!' exclaimed I, 'am I to pass the night here?' Much exhausted in strength, my whole body was trembling with cold. Darkness was closing in. A snowy bed, unsheltered from the piercing blasts, my only couch, awaited me. Is it possible to survive this?"

Dr. Ball found a flat rock and a patch of scrub spruce, with a little space in between. He'd saved a piece of string from some small duty the day before, so he used this to anchor his umbrella in a root, then he pulled up scrub growth and broke out slabs of snow and cut the twisted limbs around him with his penknife and piled them all around his umbrella, making himself a fortress against the coming ordeal. He worked himself to a frenzy here, "with the view to quicken the circulation of the blood and restore warmth to my body. But the cold, by the force of the wind, penetrated like water, and conducted off the heat as rapidly as it was generated." His small shelter perfected, he tried to light a fire; he burned almost all his matches, almost all his papers, even his money, but it was no use. "Here, shivering and chattering, I went to my dreary covert, not to sleep, not to rest, but to await in suspense the coming of another day.

"Sleep! Ah, that which now is most desirous of all, and which forces itself upon me with such power, must be averted. I know too well its fatal consequences. A few minutes' indulgence, and I never should awake, except in another world. But can I prevent it? Food I require, and thirst presses me hard. These I can endure. I can, at least, palliate their gnawings by the snow around me. But can I prevent this sleep? Have I sufficient vital force left to resist its influences? There I do not know myself. The ordeal I have never experienced. But it will be put to the test, and I can but try."

First, Dr. Ball avoided comfort. He twisted himself into one painful position after another, he invented difficulties every way he could, anything to avoid comfort. He thought of all the people he knew that were more comfortable than he was, all his friends, all his family. Then he thought of what few there could be who were in worse circumstances: soldiers dying in the Crimea, and an explorer he knew facing his ordeal in the polar sea.

Joseph Hall, the same guide who had been active in the unfortunate Bourne episode in September, was again stopping at the Glen House on Thursday evening. Given his reputation, word came to him that that a gentleman had stayed with Mr. Myers at Camp House the night before and it was assumed that he'd return to the Glen House sometime Thursday, but he had not appeared. This did not seem alarming; people in the Glen could see that the weather was very bad on the heights and they assumed that he was staying with Mr. Myers for another night. This seemed prudent; Mr. Myers was as familiar as anyone with the mountain, and he'd see to it that the visitor came to no harm.

In fact, Dr. Ball had not returned to Camp House to spend a second night with Mr. Myers, he spent the night in his umbrella camp. Day did come to his wretched shelter, and with it clearer air but no less wind. Dr. Ball was above the trees but he had no idea at all of where he was, there was only rock and snow and off to his right a sharp peak towering above everything. He assumed this to be Mount Washington, but he'd lost all his desire to go to the top and take the views and compare them to all other views he had known. Staying alive would now be sufficient reward.

He had no idea which way to go. "All was alike to me; there was no reason why I should go one way rather than another; and I could have no prejudices to bias me in favor for or against any particular way. If one thing, however, in my dilemma, seemed to be worse than the others, it was that there did not appear to be anything from which to form an opinion."

Lacking any hint or guidance, he decided to circle the summit cone of the mountain. This way, he'd be sure to cross the line of stakes or his track from the day before, or at the very least he'd see the Camp House or the Glen House far below and be able to chart a course.

Down at the Glen House, Mr. Thompson was told that a man had departed from the Camp House on the morning of the previous day and had not been seen since, so he sent Francis Smith and another man up the bridle path to look for him at the Summit House.

While those two were making their way directly up the mountain, Dr. Bell was struggling across the open slope of the mountain, heading for a promontory which he thought would have a path, or at least an orienting outlook. It took four times longer than he thought to cover the distance, and when he got there he could see only a long ridge dropping out of the clouds above and plunging into a vast chasm below, a place he thought was called the Gulf of Mexico (an old name for Great Gulf.) All he could do was retrace his steps.

When he was almost back to the place he'd spent the night, the clouds thinned and he could see the valley, but there was nothing there, no road, no clearing, no twist of smoke, only the endless forest, and he realized that he could not possibly push his way through the dense interlaced growth below him. Then he heard a sound, as of steel upon stone. Turning that way, he saw two men on the bluff a little way off. The sound continued and he thought they must be workmen on the new road and he called to them over and over, but they took no notice. He decided they must be stones, and turned again to retracing his steps.

Now he realized that the light was fading again, he'd spent the whole day on that traverse. "I sat down to rest and to reflect. What can I do? What is best to be done? What ought I to do? for I am yet free to move and act. There is no reason why I should act impulsively or without thought, but rather from sober judgement. What is the best course under the circumstances? Shall I push ahead with all my strength around the mountain, taking the course opposite that of today? Or shall I risk my chance in recklessly plunging through the brush among the rocks, precipices, or anything that presents down the mountain side?"

Snow was in the air again and the wind had not slackened, and he was wracked with intolerable thirst. He collected slabs of ice and crusted snow but the scrub growth was too thick to walk through, so he tried to crawl under the tearing branches, pushing his ice and snow toward the place he spent the night. With a heavy heart he again rigged his umbrella and piled on scrub branches and slabs of snow and ice, and he tried to smooth out the place where he lay inside and put some spruce branches on it for a bed, but it didn't help much.

Late that evening, Mr. Smith and the other man reached the Glen House with news that the visitor had not been seen at the Summit House, and that they'd seen his tracks at several places along the bridle path. They hadn't see any trace of the man, though, and Mr. Smith thought that he'd either perished on the heights or found his way down into the woods.

Dr. Ball was neither dead on the heights nor safe in the woods, he was settling himself for another night in his umbrella camp and he turned again to thought. This time he composed his own ironic epitaph. "How singular, that so immediately after the publishing of *Rambles in Eastern Asia*, this last and shortest of all my rambles, and within my own country, should be the winding up! — the thread caught and broken on Mount Washington, almost in sight of my own home. Terminated in such a manner, no one could know the circumstances. Different reports, if any, would be circulated. Some, perhaps, would have it that I was insane; others that I wished to commit suicide; and the most charitable might allow that I was lost in the fog. Of course there would be no one to say to the contrary of any of them."

The weather was, if anything, worse. The wind howled and the snow blew in through the front of Dr. Ball's shelter and the ice-laden blast threatened to tear his umbrella to shreds. This was his third night without sleep and he shook uncontrollably all through the dark hours. He was tormented by thirst and he sucked his ice supply, but his mouth was so cold the ice would not melt. In the midst of it all, he formulated a plan. If his umbrella is torn away, he'll head downhill, whichever way that might be. He'll keep going as long as he can, and when he reaches the end of his endurance he'll fasten his handkerchief in some conspicuous place and write an account of his perils on his remaining scraps of paper for the satisfaction of anyone who might remember him.

Then, a doctor again, he noticed that his lungs were not working properly, it seemed he could only half inflate them, and he studied this effect and formulated an explanation. He considered the condition of his heart and, as during the night before, he took his pulse often. Now, though, he could not feel it with his fingers, so he used the palm of his hand. The heart rate was accelerated, but reduced in force by about a third, and somewhat irregular. Dr. Ball concluded that he would live through the night, if only he could stay awake. Indeed, his assessment led him to the thought that, if need be, he could stay out like this for a third night, his fourth without sleep, "And I was glad I could think so, for I much preferred to have my hopes leading ahead of my actual powers, than to have them following behind short of reality."

Now Dr. Ball turned again to the only part of his situation he could control. He took refuge in his thoughts, he followed every thought to its end, and he chose successions of topics as different from each other as he could devise. He thought of the people he had known around the world, and as the hours passed it seemed to him that he reviewed every acquaintance he'd ever had. Then he wondered if the people he met in Gorham and the Glen House and the Camp House will ever think of him again. They probably won't, except for the liveryman in Gorham who will wonder why his horse is away so long. He thought of his umbrella, and how he would not have brought it if not for the sprinkle as he started up the road, and how he would surely have died during the first night without it, and how he'd almost set it aside when the rain eased soon after he'd started up the road, and how many times the first day he'd been tempted to throw it away as a nuisance and an impedance.

This night Dr. Ball never tried to stay awake simply by trying to stay awake, for he knew if he did that he would quickly fall asleep and that would be the end of him. Still, though, he was not sure his thoughts would last the night, he was not sure if he had enough of them. So he placed one elbow on a pointed stone and rested his head on the palm of that hand. This way, if he fell asleep the pain would waken him. Lacking that, his head would fall off his hand, it would, as he wrote, "recall the notice of my mind." Then he surrendered himself to that saving mind and let whatever impressions it might have come flooding in upon him.

It didn't work, no thoughts came. "The sensation of cold was succeeded by a kind of soothing glow stealing along through every nerve and fiber, filling the whole system as if with an invisible ethereal fluid. My body soon seemed like a mass of cold clay, over which I had no control, and in which my own self was dwelling as a mere tenant, and from which I was about to escape, leaving it behind me. My mind became perfectly composed and quiet, as if absorbing some balmy and mysterious influence that floated gently over and around me. I did not wish to move or make the least effort. I felt resigned and reconciled to whatever situation I might be in. The world seemed nothing to me, and life not worth living for. What tie could the world possess against the fascinating spell which was now riveting its bonds upon me! I would willingly and gladly give up all for a half hour of this delightful indulgence. I would not if I could stay its procedure. It comes — I am happy — and let it continue, was the thought or the sum of my sensations; and I believe I was fast sinking, as in a charmed and unresisting state, into the soft folds of that insidious enemy — SLEEP!"

Dr. Ball let himself drift thus for, he thought, ten minutes. Then he began to reflect on this sensation, he concentrated on it, he made it into an experiment. He realized that he was not directing the experiment, and this was not sound scientific practice. So, as a good clinician, he decided to pursue the course he would take if he was not subject to such languid temptations, to regain the control which he always brought to laboratories and to emergencies. So he woke up.

His third day on the mountain dawned and, looking out of his shelter, Dr. Ball saw a house far below him and a peak above it domed with white. He was profoundly puzzled by this. He thought the snow-capped mountain must be Mount Washington and the buildings the Glen House, but how can that be? He is on Mount Washington. Or is Mount Washington that pyramid across the Gulf of Mexico? He could go straight toward it, straight down the slope, but this would soon bring him to the impenetrable forest and he did not think he had the strength to push through its tangles and hazards. So, still hoping to find the bridle path or the line of stakes or his own track, he resolved to circle the mountain in the opposite direction than the one he took the previous day.

The men down there in the valley were thinking that the visitor had very little chance now. Even if he was alive at the beginning of this day, he'd certainly be dead by the time they could reach him. Nevertheless, they made an early start up the mountain to see what they could find. Mr. Hall was thinking that if they found their man at all, they'd find him "in the cold embrace of death," and the kit they brought was not chosen to help an invalid, but to carry down a dead man.

Mr. Hall, J. J. Davis, and Francis Smith started up the carriage road and they recruited another man at Camp House. When they had almost reached the summit they found footprints they assumed were made by the visitor and they crossed the bridle path from east to west, heading for the top of Great Gulf. They followed the track without much difficulty and before long it lost its heading and wandered for a while, then the maker turned toward the northeast with apparent resolution, a line that seemed to follow the surveyed route of the carriage road that Mr. Myers was building up from Camp House. They followed this track down the ridge for about half a mile and it crossed the old bridle path heading almost directly east toward the Glen House in the Valley.

At about this point they met the Culhane brothers, Patrick and Thomas, and the six of them pushed on along the easterly track. If they continued on this heading for very much longer, they'd come to the edge of the great ravine on the opposite side of the ridge from the Gulf of Mexico. The men were able to stay on this track for a mile and its purposive nature raised hopes in Mr. Hall, he thought the man might reach the woods after all and they'd find him alive. Unfortunately, they came to a thick patch of stunted spruce where new snow had drifted in, and they lost the track.

With renewed hope, the men stopped to consider their situation. Then Mr. Hall divided his group and spread three to the left, three to the right. They'd make a close search for signs of a camp or any other sign of survival they could find, and they worked their way almost to the end of this large growth of stunted spruce.

Dr. Ball was very weak now. He was no longer hungry and thought he would not eat if food was put before him, but his thirst was terrible. He could not hold both the cane and his umbrella, so he hooked the handle of his umbrella into his jacket against future need. He could move only in a stooped posture, supporting himself with his cane on one side and leaning against the uphill rocks. He pressed on, now resolving to circle the mountain a hundred feet higher to be able to see into the valley over the bulge of the terrain.

At about noon, as he counted the hours, he looked up and saw a line of men approaching. "They had long sticks or poles, and were advancing in a line a little distance from each other. They appeared to be looking around on the ground, as if for some object in the snow. With not the shadow of a thought that I could be the object they were in quest of, I cried out to them in a loud voice. All stopped short, and looked at me with a steady gaze. Why do they stare at me so? I wondered. They seem astonished and amazed. Perhaps they are surprised in meeting with any one on this side of the Mountain. But I am most happy to fall in with them. I shall soon know whether I am on the right course or not."

One of the searchers walked straight up to the haggard wanderer and said, "Is this Dr. Ball?" Dr. Ball said that he was that very person.

Joseph Hall said, "Are you the person who left the Glen House Wednesday afternoon to walk up on the new road?" Dr. Ball assured his interlocutor that he was still on the right track.

Joseph Hall said, "And you have been out on the Mountain since that time?" Dr. Ball replied that this was indeed the case.

Then Joseph Hall said, "It is indeed wonderful! How could you preserve yourself all this time? You had nothing to eat, nothing to drink! And you can still stand?" Dr. Ball asked for something to drink. They had nothing to drink, but they gave him a piece of gingerbread. He could not eat it.

The men said that they were searching yesterday as well. They said they'd gone to the summit and they were the people he saw making the metallic sound. Mr. Hall saw that Dr. Ball was in good spirits, but his hands were very much swollen and he seemed hardly able to stand on his legs. By now, Dr. Ball had again reverted to his professional training and he noticed that he felt less strong than before he was discovered, so he put his arms around the necks of two of the men and they started back along the way he had just come. "And I shall not forget the thrills of emotion I experienced, from their hearty good-will, readiness, and earnestness, in affording me their assistance, each anxious to render me some aid. But I could not but notice, from the implements they brought, that the party had no expectation of finding me alive."

He was perplexed by their course toward Mount Washington up ahead; shouldn't they be going away from it? They told him his idea of the mountain was turned around, that the peak was Mt. Jefferson, the place he thought was the Gulf of Mexico was Huntington Ravine. They might also have told him that the domed summit looming above the hotel was Carter Dome rising above the Glen House.

Dr. Ball was still wracked by a thirst no handful of snow could slake and soon they came upon a rock standing up out of the snow as if put there by Providence. There was a large bowl cut into one side, "Which," Mr. Hall thought, "like the rock that Moses smote, and water gushed out to slake the thirst of the children of Isreal, afforded the greatest luxury that could be administered." After his saviors had broken away the lid of ice, Dr. Ball finally drank his fill.

Thus refreshed, Dr. Ball regained the shelter of the Camp House, where Mr. Myers told of his own vigil on the Ledge that first night, how he stayed there so long his heels froze, how he couldn't sleep for worrying about what had become of the doctor. The rescue party warmed Dr. Ball and gave him warm tea, which he could not hold down. Then they gave him ice water, which he could. They found his feet were frozen, so they put them in cold water to draw the frost. Then they wrapped him up and put him astride a horse belonging to the bridle path company. The animal was named Tom and he was accustomed to carrying rather inert riders, so he went gently and without guidance down the carriage road. As they began to descend from the Camp House, snow began falling again on the heights behind them, so heavy that it quickly obscured all signs of human passage on the mountain.

Before long they met Mr. Thompson from the Glen House, upward bound with a horse and carriage. He'd arranged for the searchers to alert him with signal flags when they found Dr. Ball's body, and he was watching with a telescope as they made their way across the flank of the mountain toward the place they found Dr. Ball.

By now the rain had started again and the rescuers put Dr. Ball in the wagon and covered him with blankets, and as one of the men steadied his head, he descended comfortably enough. They arrived at the Glen House amidst cries of astonishment and joy; Dr. Ball was taken inside, warmed up, and asked what he would like first. He said he'd like a hot toddy, which agreed very well. Then, mindful that a starving man should not eat too much, he took part of a cup of gruel with warm milk. He took a little more gruel each hour, along with cups of water. His feet were blackened and without feeling, "like masses of cold clay attached to the extremities, with heavy dragging sensations." He feared for their vitality and also for his hands, which were numb and useless.

Dr. Ball thought that a poultice of flaxseed meal mixed with oil and charcoal would be the best restorative for his frozen limbs, but he gave way to the suggestion of a Mr. Hall, who seemed to have long experience with these conditions. So they made a poultice of charred hickory leaves, pulverized and simmered in fresh lard. This was applied to his hands and feet and wrapped in cloths and he gratefully took to a warm soft bed. He'd been out in the arctic storm for sixty hours, and without sleep for eighty.

"Toward nine o'clock in the evening I began to experience for the first time since my return, a strong desire to sleep. In this I was very soon able to indulge, happy with the thought that there was now no fear — that I might give myself up entirely to rest with no anxiety for the morrow." Mr. Hall stayed in the room with him and awakened him at intervals, lest he sleep too deeply.

Difficult times followed. "Slight chills, commencing at my feet, frequently ran though my body, causing the whole nervous system to vibrate. My feet, as if dead, were without feeling or sensation, distorted by swelling, and covered with water-blisters. About the ankles, and above the injuries, the pain was severe, with piercing and racking sensations, as if pointed sticks and nails were thrust into the flesh, and wrenched back and forth among the bones, tendons, and nerves; and, when cramp set in, the pain for a few minutes was excruciating. My hands ached and burned day and night, quite as if freshly immersed in scalding water; but, with no other frozen parts, I only experienced a general soreness and tenderness, and I thought my self under the circumstances comfortably well off."

Dr. Ball stayed at the Glen House for a week, then returned to Boston, where his brother and two other men, doctors all, supervised his recovery. He continued to study his situation, a habit that had already been his salvation. During the winter he read of a more recent climb to the summit of Mount Washington and realized that three climbs were made in successive months: Miss Bourne died in September, he nearly perished in October, and the climb made latest in the season was the only one that succeeded. He concluded that his own misfortunes were not the result of bad judgment, only of bad luck.

Four months later, Dr. Ball wrote a letter of advice for others who might want to try the hazards of Mount Washington. He urged the employment of a guide, or going with others, "It is true many prefer to go alone and independently, to the risk of an uncompanionable and unintelligent associate; but safety here demands more than the gratification of minor wishes."

He expanded on the matter of clothing. "I was informed at the Glen House that in the majority of cases it is very difficult to convince visitors that they will absolutely require warmer garments at the summit than at the base of the Mountain. When the weather below is very warm, they expect to find the same above; but in reality there is a difference of several degrees. In July and August the thermometer shows frequently a sinking to below the freezing-point; and in general overcoats and shawls are necessary for comfort, even in the warmest part of the day.

"Visitors arrive at the summit in a considerable glow and perspiration; they remain looking at the Mountain, absorbed with the beauty of the prospect, and forget the cold wind which is blowing upon them. Too late they think of their shawls or cloaks, that they might have brought with them, which would have obviated all difficulties. The result frequently is a cold and cough; perspiration has received a sudden check; pains in the chest, irritation or inflammation of the lungs follow, and ill health is often a consequence."

AFTERMATH

$\mathcal{D}$r. Ball's aggressive self-promotion leaves few mysteries and his route can be followed easily on a trail map of today. He followed the bridle path to the Camp House just as the Bourne party did a month earlier. The completed carriage road reached the summit in eight miles, so this name was changed to the Halfway House and all that remains of the historic building is a large clearing on the right side of the auto road just short of 4-Mile. The road goes straight past this site to make the sharp left turn around Cape Horn, but the bridle path turned left at the Camp House and climbed the amphitheater of loose rock directly across the road. Dr. Ball scrambled up the steep bridle path here and then on to the mass of rock just above timberline that he called the Ledge. This is still the most conspicuous feature of the area; it's the pivot of the large U-turn the auto road makes just above 4-Mile. There's a parking space at this point and the remains of an army Signal Corps installation built during the 1950s.

The carriage road company had just gone bankrupt when Dr. Ball made his climb and their work ended at the Camp House, though the route had been staked out for some distance above the Ledge. Dr. Ball knew this but he lost the track almost immediately. Accustomed as he was to trackless wastes, he pushed on. He knew there were four "Mountains" on the ridge, so he apparently kept to the highest ground he could find and this led him up the ridge on about the line taken by the present-day Nelson Crag Trail. His high point was almost certainly the flat area just below the summit now marked by the foundations of test facilities built in the 1950s.

Dr. Ball turned back there and the place where he made his camp can be located from the evidence he provides. When the weather cleared he was at the top edge of a thick patch of dwarf spruce, he saw an unbroken forest below him, a conspicuous pointed peak off to his left, and the Glen House in the distant valley, but he cannot see the Camp House. Only one place on the ridge matches all five of these conditions.

"Cragway Turn" is a sharp bend in the auto road where the Nelson Crag Trail meets the road and departs again at the apex of the turn. Above the turn the road enters a large patch of dwarf spruce and it was this barrier which stopped Dr. Ball as he tried to find his way down. The Nelson Crag trail ascends along one side of this patch and the site of his umbrella camp can be found by climbing a short way up the trail and then turning at the upper edge of the spruce patch. From this point he made his embattled way back and forth across the broad shoulder of Chandler Ridge, coming almost to the edge of Huntington Ravine to the south and back toward Great Gulf at the other limit of his swing.

All this is obvious from his chronicle and only one landmark remained to be found in the soft summer days I spent retracing his steps. This last one was the basin-shaped rock where he finally drank his fill of water and this detail seemed improbable — the rock on this part of the mountain is harsh and jagged and does not lend itself to basin shapes. Nevertheless, I found the traces of the old bridle path and started down the slope.

The footing was mild and the August day was sweet, and it was easy to let Dr. Ball's fierce ordeal drift out of mind. Then the corner of my eye caught a section of ledge rising about four feet above the grade. As the ice of the Laurentide glacier was melting, a stone got caught in an eddy of meltwater at just this place and began to spin on the bedrock. This tiny scrubbing went on for centuries, for a whole geologic age, until the ice drew back from our part of the continent. And there it was in front of me, the basin-shaped rock just as the glacial melt and Dr. Ball had left it.

Our monuments usually remind us of death. Lizzie Bourne is remembered by a conspicuous marker next to the railway tracks and just below the large bay window in the tourists' building on the summit, and thousands of people see it every summer season. Dr. Ball's persistent defense of life goes unmarked except at the hidden place where that ancient spinning stone cut a basin to catch a saving drink for him.

That is the only souvenir of his passing. Dr. Ball never found his view from Mount Washington and four years later he died in some unknown place and clime, still adding new prospects to his collection.

CHAPTER FOUR

CALAMITY IN THE UNROOFED TEMPLE

*E*ver since I can remember, a remote closet in our house has held essential things that have outlived their need. There's an ornate sword in there, the one great-grandfather Jenckes wore while parading with the Providence First Light Infantry. There's also a complex device made of tin; it has a small tank with a filler and three lamp wicks, each of which can be adjusted with a knurled brass wheel smaller than a dime. It's the power supply for what my grandfather's generation called a magic lantern, a kerosene-burning slide projector. Camera lenses of the day sometimes made an image that was brighter at the center than at the edges, so the three wicks would be adjusted to burn at different intensities and the magic lantern projected an evenly-illuminated image against a bed sheet stretched across the living room wall. If the room was large enough, the guests were in front of the sheet and the magic lantern behind it; this was called a shadow play.

Those generations did not require the elaborate distractions that fill our late twentieth-century days, there was not as much noise then, and one or two magic lantern shows in the course of a summer would be remembered all winter long. The outdoor equivalent of a magic lantern show was a hike up to the snow arch in Tuckerman Ravine.

For a geologist, Tuckerman Ravine is easy to describe: it's a cirque cut by a local glacier that remained after the continental ice sheet melted. It was more than that for Starr King. He published The White Hills in 1859, and tells us that when he saw Tuckerman Ravine, "One might easily fancy it the Stonehenge of a Preadamitic race, the unroofed ruins of a temple reared by ancient Anaks long before the birth of man, for which the dome of Mount Washington was piled as the western tower." The public preferred Starr King's version.

The ridges on three sides of the unroofed temple act as snow fences and break the force of the winter winds. As with snow fences of every kind, the snow falls to the ground on the downwind side; in this case, into the ravine. The snow piles in from October until May, not just the ravine's own allotment but also the accumulation that's swept from the treeless uplands on three sides. By the middle of spring the drift piled against the headwall of the ravine may be more than 100 feet deep and compacted to the consistency of glacial ice. There comes a time in early summer when that headwall snowbank is all that's left. Now meltwater from higher up cascades down behind it and tunnels through the icy mass, and the snow arch is formed.

Ethan Allan Crawford discovered the arch in the summer of 1829 and he was deeply impressed: "Such was the size of this empty space that a coach with six horses attached, might be driven into it. It was a very hot day, and not far from this place, the little delicate mountain flowers were in bloom. There seemed to be a contrast — snow in great quantities and flowers just by — which wonderfully displays the presence and powers of an all-seeing and overruling God, who takes care of these little plants and causes them to put forth in good season."

Major Curtis Raymond was also impressed. He spent his summers at the Glen House and he thought there should be a way to hike from the Glen up to the ravine to view the snow arch. In 1863, Mr. Raymond began to build a trail extending 3.3 miles from the carriage road to the snow arch and he maintained it until his death in 1893. By that time, the snow arch was drawing admirers from near and far; there was something about the dreadful grandeur of Tuckerman Ravine and the graceful relic of winter still there in mid-summer that people found irresistible. By that time, the snow arch had killed Sewall Faunce.

• SEWALL FAUNCE •
JULY 1886

C.E. Philbrook kept lodgings in Shelburne, New Hampshire. His place was called Grove Cottage, and on the morning of July 24, 1886, a group of eleven guests climbed aboard his mountain wagon and rode to Osgood's Castle, a picturesque creation built in Pinkham Notch where the Cutler River crossed the road. This was the start of the trail up to Tuckerman Ravine, where Mr. Philbrook's guests would view the snow arch. It was a bright and lovely day and they reached the ravine at two o'clock. Edwin Horne was the most experienced hiker in the party and he was accompanied by his wife, three other men, five other ladies, and young Sewall Faunce. The boy had just turned fifteen and his parents back at Grove Cottage had entrusted him to the care of Mr. Horne.

The hikers were in high spirits when they reached the snow arch and the weather, always uncertain on Mount Washington, was so fine that Mr. Horne decided to climb on up to the summit of the mountain and walk down by the carriage road. When his party reached the ravine they saw the snow arch at the right side and he knew the trail led up the headwall still farther to the right. Apparently not fatigued at all by the climb up from the valley, Mr. Horne quickly scrambled up the trail above the rest of his party.

Everyone in the group knew that the snow arch melted gradually until the span could not sustain its own weight, then it would fall and drop tons of ice on anyone underneath it. Accordingly, they did not climb up on top of the snow mass, but they did scamper into that space which Ethan Allen Crawford thought might hold a coach and six. Even the most hesitant visitors are tempted to do this; there's the deep cavern, the dashing water, and the twin contrasts between the cathedral darkness inside and the high blue sky at their backs, and between the frigid air in the cavern and the heat of the day outside. Returning to that new summer, the group found convenient rocks to sit upon while they contemplated the majesties on every hand.

Meanwhile, R. J. Beach and F. D. Peletier were just leaving Hermit Lake, the glacial tarn half a mile back along the trail. They were both from Hartford, Connecticut, and Mr. Beach was a cadet at West Point. They'd arrived by the Raymond Path, eaten their lunch at Hermit Lake, and started on up to the floor of the ravine. They planned to view the snow arch, then climb to the summit of the mountain.

Mr. Lathrop, one of the single men, was standing next to Miss Pierce, one of the single women. Sewall Faunce was standing farther away in front of them. Mr. Lathrop said a few words to Sewall and a moment later he found himself thrown forward as if by the hand of an unseen giant and someone cried out, *"We are killed! We are killed!"* The snow arch had not collapsed, it had not fallen down into the cavern; it had tipped over frontwards, toward the hikers Mr. Horne had brought to the ravine.

Mr. Horne was about 400 feet up the trail on the headwall when he heard the crash and looked down into a cloud of snow and flying ice. At that moment, as one of the men later put it, "We looked around us to see who were lost and who were saved." Mr. Horne rushed back to his friends and found Miss Pierce trapped by several blocks of ice and he heard his wife cry out, "Where's Sewall?" Mr. Horne answered, "My god! Think of his father and mother!" One of the other men remembered, "We did not dare to think, we must *do!*"

Miss Pierce was upright, but buried to her waist in ice and snow and unable to move. The men extricated her without much difficulty, but she was shaken and in pain and they laid her out on a nearby rock. Then they turned back to the enormous pile of snow and broken ice, tons and tons of it, and began picking and prying at it with their walking sticks, trying to find Sewall. They could make no headway at all, so after a brief discussion Mr. Horne decided to try to find help on the summit.

R. J. Beach and F. D. Peletier were just topping the rise above Hermit Lake known as the Little Headwall. They were hurrying to reach

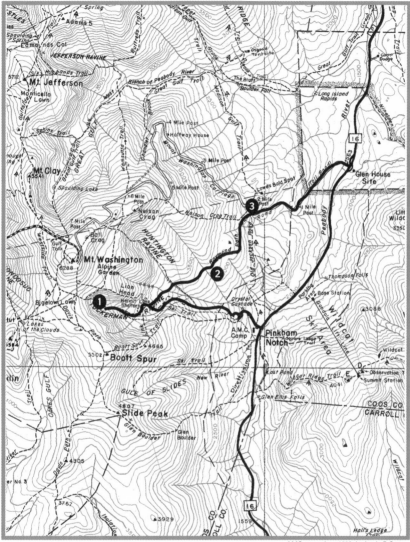

AMC map, circa 1992, by Louis F. Cutter

1 Snow arch is at base of ravine headwall
2 Miss Pierce carried out by way of Raymond Path
3 Met wagon at 2-Mile on Carriage Road

the summit but they were not sure of the way, so they were glad when they met several ladies coming down and asked them about the trail. The ladies, however, were not much help. They seemed distracted, they said they had to get to the bottom of the mountain as fast as they could and they said something about an accident. The two young men hurried up to the huddle of people at the snowbank and quickly added their efforts to those helping Miss Pierce.

Mr. Beach, the West Point cadet, asked her if she was hurt and she said she was; he asked her to describe the pain and she said it was in her back and she could not walk. Satisfied that her arms and legs were not injured, the two young men took off their belts and looped one under her arms and the other around her legs and, hoisting her with this crude sling, they started for the valley.

Mr. Horne reached the summit in forty-five minutes, about half the time usually needed for the steep rough hike. The summertime population of the top of Mount Washington was considerable. The U.S. Army Signal Service acted as the national weather bureau in those days and their observers occupied one summit building. The Summit House was a full-service hotel with a large roster of guests and help, some of whom stayed in the original Tip-Top House. The cog railway and the carriage road kept employees on the summit, and another building was occupied by the publisher, editor, reporters, and pressmen of *Among the Clouds*, the twice-daily newspaper published up there during the summer season.

Mr. Horne went straight to the Summit House with his terrible news and, as a guest said later, "It needed but the intimation of human suffering and death to start a sympathetic and willing company to the rescue." The signal service men, employees of the hotel, the railway and the road, and the entire staff of the newspaper all turned out and started down the mountain with axes, shovels, blankets, and "restoratives," which in the language of the day usually meant brandy.

The rescue party from the summit reached the trouble at 4:00 P.M., just as four other men were leaving with Miss Pierce. Hope for Sewall's life still ruled and the summit group began chopping and digging above the point where they were told he was entombed, but it quickly became obvious that their tools and forces were inadequate. Someone suggested a tunnel and in about four minutes one of the men uncovered Sewall's head, pressed against a rock. As they continued to dig they realized that he'd been standing on top of a rock and was still in the same position, but jammed hard against another rock. There was, as one of the men put it, no breath in his body.

Seven men started back up the headwall with the body, but the going was so difficult that one of them soon hurried on to the summit to find a stretcher and recruit three more men. They rejoined the others just above the headwall of the ravine and regained the summit at 6:15. A doctor staying at Horace Fabyan's hotel had taken the late cog train to the summit and he was puzzled to find scarcely a sign of injury anywhere on the boy's body, though the sole of one shoe was partly torn off.

The women who started for the valley immediately after the accident brought the alarm to the Glen House and Mr. Milliken, the keeper, organized a six-horse mountain wagon with fourteen men and a doctor who would go two miles up the carriage road to the point where the Raymond Path departed for the ravine.

Meanwhile, the West Point cadet, his hiking partner, and two other men were making their way down with Miss Pierce, but they found the carry exceedingly difficult. It could be worse, she reminded them, and pointed out that she weighed only 112 pounds. Thus encouraged, they struggled on down the Little Headwall with the belt arrangement, but this proved so awkward for them and, they feared, so painful for the plucky Miss Pierce, that they decided they could get only as far as Hermit Lake by nightfall. Three of them would stay there and one would go to the valley and return with provisions for the night, then they'd start out again in the morning.

To their surprise, a relief party from the valley met them at Hermit Lake. There was a new telegraph connection from the summit to the Glen House and word of the accident reached the valley immediately after Mr. Horne reached the summit, a factorial advance in the speed of communications. Now they determined to improve the carry and press on through the evening. Having no axe, they hacked down two birch trees with a shovel and improvised a litter with their raincoats, their belts, and what the West Point cadet gallantly described as "the lady's gossamers." These would have been her stockings, though no gentleman would use that word lest he reveal too great a familiarity with a lady's legs.

Major Raymond's path left the carriage road at the two-mile mark and gained 1,900 feet in 2.7 miles to reach the ravine, a rather moderate grade by local standards. The way was complicated, however, by four stream crossings, two of them twenty feet wide and all filled to the top of their banks this evening with the runoff of waning snows higher up. The rescue party's birch poles cracked twice and they stopped to cut new ones.

A giant of a man joined them and he held back branches and lifted blow-down trees out of the way that four other men together couldn't move. A large stone rolled onto the foot of one of the crew and he was lost to the carry, but after three hours on the Raymond Path, R. J. Beach heard a shout from somewhere in the darkness ahead of them.

"Come and give us a lift," he called, and the answer came back, "I will if you'll hold my horse." It was the Glen House crew with the mountain wagon on the carriage road and in a few more minutes they had Miss Pierce eased onto a mattress in the wagon and they reached the Glen House at 9:15 P.M., just seven hours after the accident.

Two hours later, the body of Sewall Faunce arrived at the Glen House; it had been brought down the carriage road by mountain wagon. The next day, the grieving party gathered once more at Grove Cottage and composed a formal resolution of thanks to the many people who had helped them. Then they passed it by unanimous vote.

CHAPTER FIVE

A PRESIDENTIAL BRAIN TRUST

*T*he Canadian Grand Trunk Railroad ran past the north end of the Presidential Range and on July 1, 1900, their engineers undertook an experiment to see if an electric light would be more effective than a kerosene lamp to illuminate the track ahead of their locomotives. That same day, more than seventy-five members of the Appalachian Mountain Club gathered at the hotel on the summit of Mount Washington for their thirty-fifth field meeting.

The principal impetus for the AMC came from the faculty at the Massachusetts Institute of Technology in Cambridge, Massachusetts. That was in 1876, but the heart of the club was already deeply rooted in New England sensibilities.

Inside every Massachusetts Bay Puritan there was a Calvinist trying to get out, a person devoted to the sturdy conviction that the virtue of any undertaking is directly proportional to its difficulty. This tenet did the heavy lifting, it cut down the forests and pried the boulders out of the fields and built all those hundreds of miles of stone walls.

By the middle of the nineteenth-century, the calluses had gone west and a new salvation took hold on the roads between Cambridge and

Concord. The first generation of priests were the Transcendentalists; for them, landscape was a moral category, they spelled nature with a capital N and they believed that there were lessons to be learned in the wilderness that would make us better. Starr King found their gospel in the White Mountains: "Nature is hieroglyphic," he wrote. "Each prominent fact in it is like a type; it's final use is to set up one letter of the infinite alphabet, and help us, by its connections, to read some statement or statute applicable to the conscious world."

The members of the AMC were drawn by their own nature and by New England geography to the White Mountains and they got to work quickly. In 1877, Jonathan Davis laid out an AMC path from the town of Jackson, New Hampshire, north to Carter Notch. Beginning in 1879, the AMC maintained the Crystal Cascades Trail from the Pinkham Notch road up toward Tuckerman Ravine. The club built the Hermit Lake shelter at the entrance to the ravine in the early 1880s, they built the Imp Shelter on the mountain range across Pinkham Notch from Mount Washington in 1885, and the first high-altitude hut at Madison Springs on the Presidential Range in 1888.

At intervals the club would hold a field meeting in some suitably rusticated upland site where they would discuss club business, listen to papers read by their peers, and stride vigorously into the landscape. These meetings were not easy, as witnessed by an address by AMC president Charles Fay. He took his text from Mind, a quarterly review of psychology and philosophy, and the article he chose was titled "The Aesthetic Evolution of Man." "We must never forget," he began, "that the taste for scenery on a large scale is confined to comparatively few races and comparatively few persons among them. Thus the Chinese, according to Captain Gill, in spite of their high artistic skill, 'the beauties of nature have no charm, and in the most lovely scenery the houses are so placed that no enjoyment can be derived from it.' The Hindus, 'though devoted to art, care but little, if at all, for landscape or natural beauty.' The Russians 'run through Europe with their carriage windows shut.' Even the Americans in many cases seem to care little for wild or beautiful scenery. They are more attracted by smiling landscape gardening, and, it seems to us, flat or dull civilization. I have heard an American just arrived in Europe go into unfeigned ecstasies over the fields and hedges in the flattest parts of the Midlands." This opening is extended through twelve pages of rumination. That is to say, the field meetings of the AMC had elevation, and they also had loft.

By the closing years of the nineteenth century, the really important values in the academic community of Boston had to be faced. The Harvard-Yale game loomed on the fall horizon of 1897, a situation that called for the best the temples of fortitude could muster, so Harvard planned to send its team up to the Presidential Range for a pre-season hike. The Harvard *Crimson* student newspaper did not fail to note the gravity of the situation and its proper response: "We know little of football, but we have great faith in White Mountain air and exercise to make hardy and resolute men."

William Curtis was the referee for thirteen Harvard-Yale games, he was himself a celebrated athlete and the very image of a hardy and resolute man, but in July of 1900, he and his friend Allan Ormsbee lost their game in the White Mountain air.

•WILLIAM CURTIS AND ALLAN ORMSBEE •
JULY 1900

$\mathcal{T}$he thirty-fifth field meeting of the Appalachian Mountain Club was announced for the summit of Mount Washington and more than seventy-five members gathered there on Saturday, June 30, 1900. By this time, the summit had achieved a very considerable degree of civilization. There was the Summit House hotel, a large observation tower, the old Tip-Top House hotel, the editorial and printing office of *Among the Clouds*, the office of the carriage road, the observatory of the U.S. Army Signal Service, the engine house of the railway, a garage for the carriage road, and two stables.

Reverend Harry Nichols did not favor such latter-day novelties. He and his sixteen-year-old son Donaldson planned to approach the summit by way of an overnight hike up the Davis Path on Montalban Ridge. William Curtis and Allan Ormsbee were of a similar mind, they'd make the meeting the last stop on a lengthy tour of the White Mountains.

William Curtis lived in New York and he was noted for his physical prowess. He was affectionately called "Father Bill" in recognition of his leading role in the establishment of the Amateur Athletic Club and the Fresh Air Club in New York, he was an admired writer for *The Spirit of the Times*, and he was nothing short of a sporting prodigy. In 1868 he set the record for harness lift at 3,230 pounds, and he set records in the 60- and 100-yard dashes, the hammer, shot put, and tug-of-war. He set rowing records in single, double, and four-man sculls, and he won in the 100-yard hurdles, 200-yard and quarter-mile runs, the mile walk, the high jump, swimming, skating, and gymnastics. He was sixty-three years old in 1900 and described as a splendid figure of a man, deep-chested and vigorous, a man who did not wear an overcoat even in the harshest winter weather. He often led hikes and his circulars of notification were apt to include notes such as, "This outing will not be can-

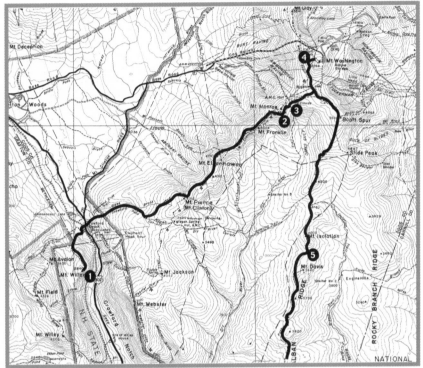

AMC map, circa 1992, by Louis F. Cutter

1 Climbed Mt. Willard in the morning

2 Took shelter in stunted spruce

3 Curtis died on Bigelow Lawn

4 Ormsbee died just below summit

5 Reverend Nichols and party came up Davis Path and spent their first night near Mt. Isolation, a trip made longer by bushwhacking up Razor Brook from Bartlett celled or postponed due to inclement weather." His friend Allan Ormsbee was thirty years old and he too was from New York, a trained athlete and a man of notable physical prowess.

The two friends had come north a week before the AMC meeting and climbed Mts. Lafayette, Whiteface, Passaconaway, and Sandwich Dome with another friend, Fred Ilgen. The three of them spent Friday night at the Pleasant View Cottage in Twin Mountain, the first town north of Crawford Notch, and they separated on Saturday morning. Mr. Ilgen wanted to climb Twin Mountain, then he'd take the train to Fabyans and go to the summit on the cog railway. Messrs. Curtis and Ormsbee had a slightly odd day in view: they'd take the train to the head of Crawford Notch and climb Mt. Willard, then come down and climb the Crawford Path up the Southern Peaks to the meeting on the summit.

Reverend Nichols took the longest and most difficult approach to the meeting. In the large topographical view, the Presidential Range is more than Mount Washington joining the Northern and Southern Peaks; the lower but longer Montalban Ridge lies just east of the Southern Peaks, and the long and largely untracked Rocky Branch Ridge is still farther to the east. The Davis Bridle Path up the Montalban Ridge bumped along in the woods for an interminable twelve miles before it broke into the open on the shoulder of Mount Washington and this dreary prospect found no favor among the stylish gentry who did their mountain climbing on horseback. Mr. Davis lost his shirt, his trail was abandoned in 1854, and when Reverend Nichols started up to join the 1900 field meeting, no less an authority than Professor Frederick Tuckerman had long since declared that the Davis Path was "in a state of innocuous desuetude."

Reverend Nichols was not deterred. He'd made the same trip six years earlier and this time he added several miles by bushwhacking up Razor Brook from the town of Bartlett, at the south end of Crawford Notch. The reverend and his son were accompanied by Walter Parker and Charles Allen, two experienced woodsmen from Bartlett hired to serve as guides, packers, and aides-de-camp. It did turn out to be tough going, but it was a fine summer day and the four of them reached Mt. Isolation, about two-thirds of the way along their route. They built a lean-to shelter here, had a good supper, and lay down to sleep on beds of fresh balsam boughs.

A sharp thunderstorm broke over them in the middle of the night and a strong north wind pushed it on past them, then Saturday dawned with dark skies and heavy gusts of drizzle blowing through the woods. The next four miles were a struggle through the undergrowth of the abandoned trail and seemingly endless blowdowns; later Reverend Nichols wrote, "By eleven o'clock, after a final hour of toilsome crawling under, over, and through gnarled and unyielding and water-soaked scrub, we stepped out, presumably on Boott Spur, into the full fury of the storm." The fog was so dense they could hardly see each other at shouting distance, the mist soon turned to sleet, and the ferocious wind knocked them down again and again.

At about that time, a driver was approaching the Cow Pasture on the carriage road, a place two miles straight across the Alpine Garden from the crest on Boott Spur that the Nichols party had reached. This was Nathan Larabee and he'd started his four-horse mountain wagon up from the Glen in bright sunshine, then he hit rain at the Halfway House and at 6-Mile he came to ice and such a strong north wind that he had to pile heavy rocks in the windward side of his wagon to keep it from tipping over.

Reverend Nichols was familiar with the terrain and the hazards of the weather, and he realized that the wisest course was to get down to the valley by the shortest route available. But, as he wrote later, "Who would have done so on such an expedition — what climber, what explorer? You say, "Keep straight up — on and up steadily, resolvedly, bucking the wind.'"

So the Nichols party plunged on across the long and completely exposed crest of Boott Spur. There were places where the trail was almost lost in the ice and the abyss of Tuckerman Ravine was at their elbows, but they kept on and up, steadily, resolvedly. Soon they could make their way only in short rushing bursts, crouching behind rocks when a gust hit, then rushing again, sometimes falling flat if no large rock was nearby to shelter them. "It seemed," said Mr. Allen, "as if the hail would take the hide off."

In normal weather, this part of the trail is a pleasant stroll, the terrain is virtually flat and the footing is no more difficult than a garden walk. The Nichols party required two hours to make a mile of this walk against the fierce barrier of storm. As agreed, their guides left them where the Davis Path joined the Crawford Path and those two men found their own way down the Southern Peaks with the camping gear. Reverend Nichols and Donaldson pushed on toward the summit cone. The reverend tied blankets around his son's head and around his own, partly for warmth, partly as helmets to ward off the rocks when they fell, and so they kept on, the blankets blowing wildly in the gale.

The reverend's diary recounted the harrowing trip: "Suddenly I stumbled on a cairn, a stoneman one and one-half feet high, with another just beyond in sight even through that driven rime; they were cairns built the day before by the Lowes for the Appalachian Meet. I knew at once that we were safe. We had only to follow those cairns to the summit. I bade my son crouch behind me, await a lull in the wind at each cairn, then make a rush on hands and knees for the next — making least resistance, yielding full subservience, to the storm's blast. And so we made port, reaching the summit about two-thirty P.M."

Among the Clouds reported, "The thermometer had fallen from 48 on Friday evening to 25 on Saturday morning, and so rapid had been the formation of the ice, and so fierce the velocity of the wind, that even small particles, driven like from a gun, broke dozens of panes of glass on the Summit House." Inside, bellboys hastened to each new break and replaced the broken glass with wooden panels while the Appalachians had lunch and began their scheduled events with the reading of papers and following discussion. Reverend Nichols and Donaldson joined them and, as the minister wrote later, "Along toward supper-time the chairman remarked, "It surely is time for our two friends to come in.' 'What friends?' said I. The chairman replied, 'Two of our party, Mr. Curtis and Mr. Ormsbee, who kept around by the Crawford House to walk up the trail.'"

At this time, William Curtis and Allan Ormsbee were some four miles away down the Southern Peaks, pressing on toward the AMC meeting. Father Bill was familiar with the area and when he was on top of Mt. Willard he could have looked up the range and seen the heavy cloud cover on Mount Washington. He could also have stopped in at the Crawford House earlier in the day and inquired about conditions on Mount Washington; the Crawford family was connected to the summit by telephone and they were in the habit of warning hikers of threatening conditions. Instead, Father Bill and his friend descended from Willard, crossed the road to the beginning of the Crawford Path without talking to anyone inside the lodgings, and started right up toward the summit of Mount Washington more than eight miles away.

They reached timberline on Clinton and turned south, against their line of travel, to sign the weatherproof register the AMC kept at the top of that mountain. Turning north again, they reached Pleasant Dome and, rather than take the level bypass trail that avoided the climb up the dome, they took the higher trail. Two workmen were cutting overgrown brush on the bypass at about 1:30 P.M. and, since there was already a high wind and blowing sleet, they tried to overtake the two hikers and warn them not to go on. Failing that, they called after them but could not get a response.

By 3:00, the trail workers decided that the storm was rising past endurance, so they packed up their tools. The Bartlett guides appeared just then and reported that they'd passed two hikers, headed uphill and into the storm. Guide Charles Allen said that he'd greeted the younger hiker but got only a grunt in reply. Mr. Allen told him that it was very bad up ahead, so bad that they'd had difficulty getting down and out of it themselves and it was unlikely that anyone could climb upward against such a storm. This caution drew no response, and the two parties continued on their opposite courses.

In the interval between passing the workmen and passing the guides, Father Bill and Mr. Ormsbee had climbed Pleasant Dome and again left their names in the AMC weatherproof register. They added, "Rain clouds and wind sixty miles — Cold."

By this time, most of the AMC members had reached the summit by way of the cog railway. As they neared the summit they admired the delicate tracery of rime ice collecting on every surface and they were inconvenienced by the wind as they hurried from the cog trains across the platform into the hotel, but this was, after all, Mount Washington — vigorous conditions were the reason they'd chosen the summit for their meeting. They settled themselves, had dinner, and then gathered to hear the schedule for the coming week. The AMC had written a full menu of activities and this introductory evening began with remarks by John Ritchie. He was one of the two secretaries of the club and he took as his theme, "Simple Rules Which Will Insure Safety to all on Any Mountain Walk."

"A high mountain range," he began, "introduces into a country certain elements of uncertainty so far as the weather is concerned." He went on to urge the members to make a good hiking plan and keep to it, to stay close together, to wear strong clothing, to avoid high-spirited shouting which might be interpreted as a distress call, to avoid the temptation to roll rocks down steep slopes, and to avoid touching the streamside plant known as hellebore. As Mr. Ritchie spoke, the most dangerous summer storm in living memory was still gaining strength on the other side of the walls.

The Appalachians were expecting Messrs. Curtis and Ormsbee. Fred Ilgen came up on the cog train that afternoon and he put word around that his two companions would be along presently, but when they did not appear a telephone call was made to the Crawford House. The people there said they had not seen anyone meeting that description and as far as they knew no hikers had started up the Crawford Path that day.

The Appalachian Mountain Club had gathered a notable group on the summit. J. Rayner Edmands was there, the greatest trailbuilder in the history of the Presidential Range, the man who built the Gulfside Trail, the Randolph Path, the Link, the Israel Ridge Path, and the Edmands Path, to name but a few. Louis Fayerweather Cutter was there, the man who drew the definitive White Mountain maps for fifty years. Vyron and Thaddeus Lowe were there, the renowned trailbuilders and guides from Randolph, as strong, as experienced, and as reliable mountain men as any in the region. It was little short of a Presidential brain trust, and now the chairman of the AMC program took counsel with the Lowes and they were uneasy; there were summit loops and bypasses on two of the Southern Peaks, and if Father Bill and Allan Ormsbee were living up to their reputation for vigor and determination, they might well have taken a summit loop while the two Bartlett guides were on the more prudent bypass.

Accordingly, the two Lowes lit their lanterns and started out the door to see what they could find on the Crawford Path. They'd barely stepped onto the platform when their lanterns blew out. More ominously, the platform was heavy with ice and it wasn't the light and crumbly rime that often comes with an off-season storm, it was clear solid ice. The Lowes had all they could do to get back to the door of the hotel.

Inside, however, fears were being allayed. Reverend Nichols told of the severe weather his group met and how their two guides had turned back at the Davis Path junction and gone down the Crawford Path. Surely they'd meet Father Bill and Allan Ormsbee and tell them not to go any farther up the ridge, to come down to the valley with them. Surely Messrs. Curtis and Ormsbee were safely down in some valley lodgings by this time in the evening, and they'd join the Appalachians' field meeting as soon as the weather cleared.

Father Bill and Allan Ormsbee were not safely lodged in the valley. They passed the Bartlett guides and the trail workers between two and three o'clock, then they pushed on up the rising and entirely exposed trail over the crests of Franklin and Monroe. This section of the Crawford Path is about a mile long and the terrain is very similar to the ridge of Boott Spur, where Reverend Nichols and Donaldson were taking two hours to cover the same distance that storm-lashed afternoon. Those two were able to reach the safety of the summit hotel before Saturday nightfall. Father Bill Curtis and Allan Ormsbee were not.

Sunday was impossible for any outdoor purposes on the AMC schedule, but there was inside work to do, there were papers to read and proposals to be heard. One proposal asked if the Appalachian Mountain Club would accept the gift of a house and land on Three-Mile Island in Lake Winnipesaukee and, if so, would it also buy the rest of the land on the island for a club reservation? Both proposals were approved.

Outside, the wind remained at gale force and the temperatures dropped into the 20-degree range, but, curiously, the precipitation did not turn to sleet or snow, it was rain and it froze on every surface as solid ice. Frank Burt, publisher of *Among the Clouds*, wrote, "At the end of the turntable lever, whose dimensions are three by four inches, there projected on Sunday morning a solid block of ice in the teeth of the wind a foot and a half in length."

The storm blew itself out on Monday morning, the summer sun warmed the ice-clad summit buildings, and soon whole walls of ice were falling to the ground. Several parties of Appalachians set out to make up the planned hikes they'd lost to the storm on Sunday while others remaining on the summit looked out for the arrival of Father Bill and Allan Ormsbee.

Mapmaker Louis F. Cutter started down the Crawford Path to meet the missing hikers or, failing that, to see if he could find any trace of them. He reached the bottom of the cone and started toward the twin peaks of Monroe about three-quarters of a mile away across Bigelow Lawn. This is a remnant of the ancient upland peneplane; the summit cones of the peaks rise above it, the ravines cut into its sides, and the ice sheet scrubbed its surface to leave a gently rolling place of ledge, tundra-like grass, and broken rock. Mr. Cutter stayed on the Crawford Path until the trail up Monroe was only 300 yards ahead and the Lakes of the Clouds were just to the west; then he came to a place where the path ran between two sections of ledge. The floor of this slot was barely wide enough for the path and there, face down with his head resting on a rock, lay Father Bill Curtis. He was wearing strong hiking boots, a medium-weight woolen coat, a shirt made of shoddy, and long pants; a light cap was near his head.

Mr. Cutter determined that he was dead, then he went looking for Allan Ormsbee. A few hundred paces south on the Crawford Path, not far beyond the beginning of the trail up to the summit ridge of Monroe, he found a camera and a milk bottle lying in the Crawford Path. Just downslope on the left, there was a patch of dense scrub that seemed to have been modified in a curious fashion; it seemed like a sort of shelter, but a quick glance revealed no trace of Allan Ormsbee. Mr. Cutter continued down the Crawford Path almost as far as Pleasant Dome, where he met a group of upward-bound hikers. They said they hadn't seen anyone else on the trail, so he turned back toward Mount Washington.

At the junction of the Davis Path he met three Appalachians who were starting for Boott Spur; these were Messrs. Coffin, Parker, and Weed. Mr. Cutter told them of his discoveries and went on up to the summit where he alerted several more Appalachians. Two members of that cadre started down the Tuckerman Ravine Trail to intercept a group of clubmen returning from a hike to the edge of the celebrated chasm and they were added to the work force.

While these excursions were afoot, the Coffin, Parker, Weed group went on toward Monroe to make a more thorough study of the shelter in the scrub patch that had caught Louis Cutter's eye. These patches are impenetrably dense on top, but there is often some space among the lower stems and it looked as if someone had cut away several pieces of the tangled mass and used them to close up an opening on the exposed north side and at the same time make more room inside. Crawling into the opening, they found three slices of bread wrapped in waxed paper with one of them partly eaten, and, in the deepest and most protected corner of the shelter, they found another camera. Mr. Parker knew Allan Ormsbee and he recognized the camera in the path as belonging to him. It seemed reasonable to assume that the camera inside the shelter belonged to Father Bill. This precipitated a close search of the area in hopes of finding Mr. Ormsbee, but there were no further traces.

Now the three men returned to thought. They reasoned that Allan Ormsbee was less than half the age of Father Bill and, since both were heading for the summit and seemed determined to get there through Saturday's storm, the younger man would probably have gone farther. And, since Father Bill was found lying right in the Crawford Path, it seemed likely that they were trying to stay on the trail come what may. They would be crossing the same terrain that the Nichols group had needed two hours to negotiate a little earlier on the same day and, calculating the daylight available, the searchers decided that if Allan Ormsbee survived a reasonable length of time, he would have made his way some considerable distance up the cone of Mount Washington. Offsetting this calculation, they realized that the moss inside the shelter was noticeably worn down. How long had the men stayed there? Had they both stayed the same length of time, or had the younger and presumably stronger Allan Ormsbee gone ahead for help? Had Father Bill rested in the shelter and started out again Saturday afternoon, or had he stayed in the shelter and then started up on Sunday when his companion did not return? Had one or the other of the men left the camera and the milk bottle in the path to serve as a signal?

Bearing these imponderables in mind, Messrs. Coffin, Porter, and Weed divided their three-man force; one stayed on the Crawford Path while the other two moved out on either side, Mr. Weed on the right, Mr. Coffin in the center, and Mr. Parker on the left. Thus arrayed, they went along the Crawford Path to the Davis Path junction and then followed the Davis Path out toward Boott Spur for a distance before deciding that such a divergence was unlikely. Returning to the Crawford Path, they paused again to think.

Mr. Parker was the only one among the Appalachians who knew Allan Ormsbee personally. He made the point that his friend was a strong and resourceful man who favored a direct approach to problems. Given this nature, Mr. Parker suggested that he might have left the wandering Crawford Path and taken a direct line to the summit, which would have the added advantage of moving him somewhat toward the lee side of the cone. Accordingly, the three men altered their course and made straight for the summit while keeping their spread pattern for greater efficiency.

Their progress was slow and difficult because their new route was almost entirely over the large, angular, and unstable rocks that make up most of the cone, and this day they were further slowed by the ice remaining from the storm. Pausing to rest, they decided that if they were having so much trouble, Allan Ormsbee must have had a great deal more. Taking this into account, they changed their route to the staggering zig-zag pattern they thought a man *in extremis* would have taken. Mr. Weed, farthest to the right, passed the pile of stones marking the place where Harry Hunter gave up the ghost twenty-six years earlier. Mr. Parker was farthest to the left and at 4:30 in the afternoon he found the body of his friend Allan Ormsbee. He was about fifteen paces west of the Crawford path and within sight of the back wall of the signal station on the summit.

Mr. Parker could see some ladies of the Appalachian group near the signal station and he called to them, they passed the word to the AMC men, and a group quickly formed to carry Mr. Ormsbee's body the little way remaining to the mountain-top settlement. The other body lay a mile and a half distant, so a stretcher was improvised and a group set out at 6:00 P.M., then when more Appalachians returned to the summit from their days' excursions they went down the Crawford Path as reinforcements. This made twenty carriers in all, and even with this considerable strength the remains of William Curtis did not reach the summit until the middle of the evening. Colonel O. G. Barron, keeper of the Fabyan House, made the necessary arrangements in the valley; he called on two undertakers in Littleton, brought them to the base station of the cog in his carriage, and ordered two caskets to be sent up by a special train. Another special train brought the bodies down that evening and Fred Ilgen accompanied them to New York the next day.

That was the end of the sad affair for Father Bill Curtis and Allan Ormsbee, but not for the Appalachian Mountain Club. Given the strength of their numbers on the scene, the concern any deaths on the Presidential Range would cause, and the many prominent members of the club who were present, the accident that opened their field meeting had several consequences.

The cause of the deaths was the first matter to be settled. Dr. George Gove of Whitefield was the medical examiner and he made the rulings. Mr. Curtis was discovered with his head resting on a stone and Dr. Gove found a large bruise at that point on his forehead. The depth of the bruise indicated that Mr. Curtis was rendered unconscious by the blow, the position of his head on the rock proved that he did not regain consciousness, and the maturity of the bruise showed that he did not die for several hours after he fell.

Allan Ormsbee's body was covered with bruises and lacerations that testified to the battering he sustained as he tried to reach the summit. If a strong hiker such as Reverend Nichols could not stay on his feet in daylight, much earlier in the storm, and with far less ice to contend with, it was obvious that Allan Ormsbee's night must have been terrible indeed, and that he gave everything he had to give in his effort to find help for his friend before he himself died at the place of his last fall.

This episode involved many prominent people in the Boston community and, needless to say, the press was not slow to react. As so often happens at times like this, the more distant the reporter, the more lurid the report. Thus the Wednesday edition of *The Boston Globe* included the news that during the course of his ordeal Allan Ormsbee broke his leg and tore loose the branch of a tree to make a splint. Dr. Gove did not agree.

More substantial studies were undertaken by the Appalachian Mountain Club. During the week of the field meeting they agreed that Mr. Ormsbee would not have left Mr. Curtis unless the older man could not go on. Following on this, three theories emerged. One was that the two men reached Mt. Monroe and improvised the shelter in the scrub, Mr. Curtis remained there while Mr. Ormsbee went for help after leaving his camera and the milk bottle as a sign, then Mr. Curtis revived himself and pushed on alone. The second theory was that both men rested in the shelter and then went on together, but became separated and were not able to find each other in the storm. The third theory was that they rested in the shelter and went on together until Mr. Curtis fell, then Mr. Ormsbee went on alone.

As reported in *Among the Clouds*, "Those who advocated the first theory are divided as to whether Curtis followed Ormsbee on Saturday night or on Sunday morning. Against the Saturday night theory it is argued that he would be more likely to stay overnight in comparative shelter than to set out in darkness, which must have come on soon after Ormsbee left. Against the Sunday theory it is argued that he possibly could not have lived through the night, and if he had, why was the bread left uneaten? As to the theory of their both leaving the shelter together, it is asked why did they leave their cameras behind?" The editor of the paper further wondered about the milk bottle: If the men understood the seriousness of their situation, why didn't they leave a note in the bottle?

By Thursday, another theory had emerged. T. O. Fuller was a member of the Appalachian gathering and he had gone down to the cleft ledge where Father Bill died. The exact situation was well known by this time, and as Mr. Fuller was studying the place he found a deep hole among the rocks. He saw something down there that caught the light and, reaching in, he pulled out a pair of gold-rimmed bifocal spectacles.

Mr. Fuller and two others studied the rock upon which Mr. Curtis was reported to have hit his head and they decided that this rock and two others had been placed there recently. Father Bill, they decided, had not fallen and hit his head, he fell and then those three rocks were put there so he could rest his head. Furthermore, Mr. Fuller's group thought, the ground where he lay had been newly formed into a slight hollow. His spectacles, presumably, fell off as he rested there and they dropped down into the hole.

All this suggested that the two men rested together in the scrub shelter and then went on together to try for the summit. There was a large rock in the trail near the spot where Father Bill was found, and Mr. Fuller's theory was that he had tripped on this rock and fallen. Then, this theory held, the two men decided that in light of Father Bill's weakened condition he should stay in the shelter provided by the trough of ledge while Allan Ormsbee went for help. The younger man improved the hollow and made the rough rock pillow to ease Father Bill's suffering, then set out for the summit.

Before the field meeting was over, a committee was appointed to study the deaths and write a report to settle the matter: Albion Perry, John Ritchie Jr, and J. Rayner Edmands. They reviewed and considered the experience of Reverend Nichols and Donaldson, their two guides, the trail workers, and Messrs. Ormsbee and Curtis, and they reconstructed the distance and timing of those four parties, and the progression of the storm.

The study committee decided that the bread, the cameras, and the milk bottle were moot points, they were silent witnesses and nothing important could be learned from them. The committee deputized Mr. C. F. Mathewson to study the place where Mr. Curtis was found and he concluded that the body fell where it was found and the weight was too great for Allan Ormsbee to move it very far, if any distance at all. The study group also concluded that Mr. Curtis had not fallen at some other place, then gotten up and walked to the place where he was found. They discounted the report that Mr. Curtis had experienced some slight heart problem a few years earlier and had now suffered a major attack. Dr. Gove certified that death did not occur for some time after the fall and the accumulation of blood in the bruise indicated that Mr. Curtis' circulation was not impaired. The committee approved Professor Parker's written report that Mr. Curtis fell from exhaustion and that the position of the head did not lead to any helpful conclusion.

The committee considered the layout of the Crawford Path, noting that the air-line distance from the fatal site to the summit was about a mile, but the wandering route of the bridle path covered a mile and a half. Since Mr. Ormsbee had never been to the area before, it was not likely that he was able to follow the path. Rather, he had gone straight for the summit and had fallen repeatedly in the chaos of broken rock.

Here they cited Reverend Nichols' written report: "The wind increased in force. It blew us over on the sharp rocks. It blew the breath out of our bodies. Our progress was by a series of dashes — a few rods, then a rest, then a dash again for shelter. The rest must be but for a moment, lest the fatal chilliness come on. I could feel it creeping over me, I could see it in my boy's chattering teeth. The fog had become sleet, cutting like a knife, it gathered on the rocks, every step meant danger of a slip, a fall, a jagged cut. Whether the wind, or the sleet, or the ice under foot, were the greatest element of danger is hard to say. I lost my hat, though it was tied down; my alert boy found it, he shouted its safety to me from three feet away, but I heard nothing save the howling wind." The committee pointed out that the ordeal of the Nichols party probably fell short of the conditions Mr. Ormsbee faced, that the effect of higher wind and the onset of darkness could be judged by at least fifty severe bruises and lacerations on his body.

The makeshift shelter was puzzling. The men were probably in good shape when they came over the low crest of Franklin; they were in good physical condition when they started and, although there had been warnings, the severe conditions were still up ahead. So why had they taken the time to make the shelter and, once made, why had they left it before conditions moderated? Was it made because one of them was already exhausted or injured, or was it abandoned because one of them was in need of attention, or because the conditions were already so difficult at the shelter that they decided they might as well push on? Was Mr. Curtis already in such bad condition that they couldn't descend to the greater safety of the woods so Mr. Curtis could rest while his companion went down to the valley for help?

If the shelter was not vitally needed, there must have been some vitally important reason for the two men to separate farther on. The committee decided that if for some reason the two men could not go back, they both should have gone down to the woods rather than one or both going on toward the summit. They urged any readers of the report to remember this point, but at the same time they recognized that most people would try to keep going onward toward their original destination and, in this case, the safety and comforts of the summit hotel.

The committee again cited Reverend Nichols' writing on this point: "Coming out from the scrub into the wind, just one step back means safety; that is surely the step to take, though the way down by ravines and brook beds be long and tedious. All pushing on makes return less possible and develops new elements of danger. The only safety on finding such a wind above tree level is to turn back at once. There is always protection under the trees and a chance to work one's way out, however toilsome." On this point, however, the reverend did not follow his own advice.

The committee continued to ask questions. Did Mr. Curtis push on alone after he was left at the shelter? Did Mr. Ormsbee go on alone after being with the older man when he fell? Did he know that his companion had fallen? These and many other conjectures occupied the select committee for eleven published pages, but they had no further evidence beyond the injuries and the artifacts and they reached no conclusion.

At the end, they returned to the manuscript of Reverend Nichols: "The one essential is to retain hope. To have missed the line of cairns across the Lawn, to have got out of the trail, to have left the old corral of the Bridle Path just on one side, or not to have known that it was but a short distance from the Summit House — for one moment not to have known where we were, would have meant discouragement, despair, exhaustion, death."

AFTERMATH

$\mathcal{T}$he Curtis-Ormsbee accident precipitated well-organized searches and engaged several elements of the valley population, it was intimately studied and widely debated, and it was the object of a scholarly report. As such, it can stand as the beginning of the modern age of misadventure on the Presidential Range.

More concretely, it resulted in immediate planning for a refuge shelter on Bigelow Lawn, the saddle connecting Monroe and Mount Washington. This was in service by the next year, 1901, a minimalist structure accommodating six or eight hikers in distinctly minimal comfort. (The AMC guidebook warned, "It is far too uncomfortable to attract campers.") It seemed obvious that a similar provision on the Northern Peaks would make sense, and in 1901 Guy Shorey and Burge Bickford spent two nights at Madison Hut while scouting for a refuge location along the Gulfside Trail. That shelter would not be built until 1958, in Edmands Col, but both of the men would go on to wider and more immediate fame, Guy as one of the greatest of all White Mountain photographers and an indefatigable North Country promoter, Burge as the most famous of the guides working from Gorham. The presence of the Bigelow Lawn refuge shelter provided a strong impetus to the construction of the nearby Lakes of the Clouds Hut in 1915 and, by extension, the rest of the AMC hut system.

The landmarks of this episode can still be found 100 years later. The Camel Trail starts at the three-way junction with the Crawford Path and Tuckerman Crossover, just a few minutes' walk above the Lakes of the Clouds Hut. Near the height-of-land on the Camel Trail, two iron bolts rise from the ledge a few paces south of the trail, and the stubs of two more bolts are broken off level with the rock. These bolts anchored the refuge hut. The old Crawford Bridle Path can be found here, too; its visible relics are a narrow but distinct depression in the ground, thin grass cover or none at all, and rocks that have been moved to make easier footing for the horses.

Unlike most modern trails, this trace does not run straight at all, it turns and meanders as a horse would prefer to go. Heading south, the Lakes of the Clouds and the hut can be seen on the right and before long the old bridle path passes between two slabs of ledge rising opposite one another to make a narrow trough. This is the place where William Curtis died, and the hole where the gold-rimmed glasses were found is still there. The bridle path meandered on toward Monroe, and numerous traces of the old location can be seen as the Crawford Path climbs the summit cone of Mount Washington; they're easily recognized by the hollow made by the horses' hooves among the rocks and grasses and by the large shifting of rocks to make the horses' way easier. The place where Allan Ormsbee died is on the Crawford Path just below the summit and twenty yards off the trail to the west, marked by a plain wooden cross.

It is probable that the clump of scrub spruce that so vexed the AMC study group still exists. This scrub is found all along the range at timberline; in fact, it *is* the timberline. The spruce trees of the valley diminish in stature as they gain in altitude until they form very dense clumps that may be only a foot or so high, full-grown trees that never grew up, nature's own bonsai.

Nature's metabolism in the subarctic conditions at timberline is very slow, and it's likely that the scrub patches have not changed very much since William Curtis and Allan Ormsbee passed by. The scrub cave they fashioned was on the eastern side of Monroe and described as close to the Crawford Path in a place with a short downward slope.

The scrub on the eastern side of Monroe shows two patterns. Heading north from Franklin, as they did, a hiker first finds a wide and unbroken mass of scrub that is continuous from above the trail all the way down to the full-grown trees on the floor of Oakes Gulf. This does not meet the "scrub patch" definition from 1900 and it is unlikely that it ever did.

That continuous mass of scrub ends about halfway along the flank of Monroe. From this point on, the surface is either the grasses typical of Bigelow Lawn or scattered patches of scrub. There is only one patch that's on a short slope below the trail, and this is also the largest in both area and height. It is L-shaped and there's enough room for several adults to crawl in among the stems under the greenery; in fact, the presence of old tin can fragments shows that others have had the same idea. There is one thin place in this patch of scrub, it's at the inside angle of the L and it faces north; this matches the Curtis-Ormsbee effort to cut branches and put them in the north-facing opening of their shelter. This patch is 400 paces south of the place where the body of Father Bill Curtis was found lying in the old bridle path.

CHAPTER SIX

THE GRAND SCHEME

*L*ife was good in 1912. There had been no European wars since 1871, it was la belle epoque, *and the last generation had brought a dizzying profusion of wonders: electricity, telephones, automobiles, airplanes, moving pictures, pneumatic tires, phonographs, diesel engines, and Woolworth 5 & 10 Cent stores. The germ theory of disease, chromosomes, and X-rays were discovered, and the Hague Conventions were established to replace war with arbitration. The North and South Poles were reached, the oceans were being joined in Panama, and Chester Beach invented the first electric motor for use in home appliances. On top of all that, there was a plan to build a new railway to the summit of Mount Washington.*

The famous cog railway had been finished in 1869, but by 1912 the pages of Among the Clouds *announced that "it is safe to say that the little engines and closed cars are becoming insufficient to handle the growing traffic." Further increases in that traffic could be expected because of developments in hotel accommodation on the summit. The great fire of 1908 had destroyed everything but the old Tip-Top House, and the business boom and buoyant optimism of the day made it obvious that a new hotel would be built, grander and more modern than anything previously known or even imagined.*

The hotel would be three stories high, it would be star-shaped and made of stone and steel and plate glass, there would be 100 guest rooms and many would have private baths, and there would be a dining room seating 400. There would be a wine cellar, a barbershop, a billiard room, a grand lobby, and a rotunda 150 feet in diameter. There would be an observatory with a circular walkway on the roof, and above that there would be a searchlight so powerful that it could be seen from the ocean. Most remarkable of all, the summit of Mount Washington itself would rise up through the floor of the grand lobby so guests could climb to the top of the mountain without first climbing almost to the top of the mountain.

All of this, however, seemed modest when compared with the new railway that would bring up the guests. The cog railway ran three and a half miles straight up a west ridge of the mountain, but it was small and noisy, it shook in every joint, and it trailed clouds of smoke. Work had started before the Civil War and the train looked old-fashioned even when it was new; now it seemed faintly silly. Clearly, it was time for a conveyance befitting the new century and the new age.

Mr. Charles S. Mellen was ready. La belle epoque was an age of unrestrained commercial expansion and Mr. Mellen began his climb by taking over the New York, New Haven & Hartford Railroad. He found a willing ally in J. P. Morgan and expanded his influence throughout southern New England, then gained control of the Boston & Maine Railroad and, through that, of the cog railway. Now Mr. Mellen had just the ticket for the new age: he would build an electric trolley line to the summit of Mount Washington.

The power would be carried on overhead wires suspended from poles set in pairs about every 100 feet along the track and the traction drive meant that the gradient could not exceed six percent, so several routes were considered. The most dramatic climbed the walls of Great Gulf from Pinkham Notch, but on reflection this seemed to promise more drama than most passengers could probably endure.

The terrain on the west side of the mountain was more suitable, and it was also available. This area was largely owned by timber companies in Berlin and Conway, New Hampshire, and, since they both depended on the Boston & Maine to move their lumber, they would not be likely to oppose Mr. Mellen's plan.

The land rose 4,200 feet from the Boston & Maine connection in Fabyans to the summit; given the limits of gradient, this dictated a rail line of 19.8 miles. It would follow the Ammonoosuc River up to the base station of the cog railroad, then swing left up the flank of Jefferson Notch to cross the lower slope of the Ridge of the Caps and rise across the western slope of Mt. Jefferson toward Castellated Ridge. The railroad would tunnel under the ridge, swing back and pass over itself below the lowest Castle, then climb the side of Jefferson again to a switchback, upward to a higher point on Castellated Ridge and another switchback, then across the flank of Jefferson for a fourth time. It crossed Mt. Clay below its summit ridge, then circled the summit cone of Mount Washington two and a half times to end at the door of the new hotel. It was an audacious plan, even fantastic, but it suited the age and survey work began, fittingly, on the Fourth of July, 1911. "Soon," the planners said, "Mount Washington will have an electric necklace and a crown of cement."

• JOHN KEENAN •
SEPTEMBER 1912

$\mathscr{I}$n 1912, John Keenan was preparing to make his way in the world. He finished high school in Charlestown, Massachusetts, and secured a position as an elevator operator. Then, in the third week of September, he went north to take a job with the survey crew on the Mount Washington trolley job.

John was an unlikely candidate for such heroic enterprise; he was afraid of darkness and easily frightened by animals and other woodland hazards, and he reported for his first day of work on Mount Washington wearing fashionable street shoes and a pink-and-white striped shirt better suited to a lawn party. That was Friday, September 13, and he was assigned to odd jobs around the base of the cog track. The next Wednesday he was sent up the mountain with the surveyors.

Mr. H. S. Jewell was in charge of twenty-one men, and it was a rough and ready crew. They lived at the base and after dinner they played poker with such passion that Mr. Jewell often had to step in and restore a measure of order by redistributing lopsided pots. The men carried guns all the time and shot at almost anything that moved. One got a huge deer, but, as a thankless beneficiary put it, "You might just as well try to eat your shoes." If live game was not in sight, they'd shoot at improvised targets and bet on their hits. They found the slide boards the cog railway company had confiscated a generation earlier and survived every ride down the mountain on them, and they found a huge but rickety Winton automobile that was rigged with railroad wheels and for a nightcap they'd get this started and drive seventy miles an hour down the Boston & Maine track, no lights. The fresh-faced elevator operator from Boston didn't fit in, and they teased him about his fears.

The valleys around Mount Washington had been unusually warm for September and on the day John went up for his first day of work it touched 81° in the valley, the leading edge of a cell of hot air that would push temperatures into the 90s later in the week. At times like this, the prevailing westerlies drive warm damp air up the windward flank of the Presidential Range, orographic cooling condenses the moisture, and clouds as dense as milk can envelop the rocks with startling speed.

John was to serve as the back-flag man, the one who stands at the last point fixed by the transit party to give them the base for the next angle. The crew was working on the south side of the summit cone and not far from the summit; the place where William Ormsbee died was just below them and the place where Harry Hunter died in 1874 was further down the cone and a bit to the east. Lifting their eyes, they could see the broad and lovely expanse of Bigelow Lawn and the place where Father Bill Curtis died.

John Keenan's first day on the heights was not pleasant. The wind on the summit was blowing more than 50 miles an hour, the sky was overcast, and the temperature was about 40°. This was not uncommon for September and the survey crew went to work, first warning their new man that the clouds could close in very quickly and if this happened he should stay where he was and they'd come to get him. By midmorning the transit crew was near the Ormsbee marker and facing the Lakes of the Clouds, and John had the back flag about 100 feet away. At ten o'clock a sudden cloud enveloped them and he disappeared.

The crew waited half an hour for the cloud to lift. It didn't lift, it grew thicker. The crew yelled for John to come in, but he didn't. One of the men went to the place where they'd left him and he wasn't there. They all fired their guns, still with no result. Then one of them went to the summit and telephoned the base. "Jewell," he said, "that new fellow you sent up here, we lost him." Mr. Jewell said, "Well, stay up there until you find him."

The survey crew searched the area until nightfall and found no trace of him. There was a large bell on the summit and that was rung steadily all night, there was a steam plant at the base station of the cog railway and Mr. Jewell arranged to have a whistle blast sounded every minute all night long, and the base crew strung lanterns all around their dormitory by the river in case young Keenan used his head and followed the Ammonoosuc

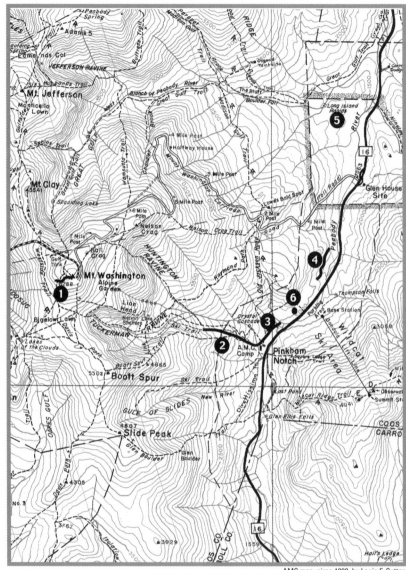

AMC map, circa 1992, by Louis F. Cutter

1 His only known time on Mount Washington was here
2 Probably reached road by lower Cutler River
3 & 4 Seen twice on road
5 Milliken's Pond drained
6 The Darby Field

stream down. Mr. Jewell sent a telegram to the B&M headquarters in Boston and the reply came back, "Spare no expense. Find the boy."

That evening calls went out to the principal hotels in Fabyans, Randolph, Gorham, and Bretton Woods, the four tourist centers around the Presidential Range. A strong wind continued to blow all night on the heights, but by the next morning the air was almost calm, with the same chill.

High-elevation weather continued bad on Thursday, but Mr. Jewell lead a search party of survey workers, cog railway crews, and the staff of *Among the Clouds*. They spent the whole day groping through the dense clouds above timberline and found no sign of their back-flag man. The weather turned sharply colder on Friday and the enveloping fog was glazing the rocks with ice. Search parties widened their scope and still found nothing. Mr. Jewell called Burge Bickford, the famous one-armed guide in Gorham, and asked him to gather a crew of all the woodsmen he could find and head for the Glen House. Mr. Jewell said, "I saw fifty men go into the woods and I saw fifty come out." Burge Bickford's men had searched far and wide and had no words of hope.

Friday was marked by one of the weather contrasts which so often complicate hiking on the Presidential Range; the surrounding valleys enjoyed what residents thought was one of the finest days of the season, with bright sun and sweet warm airs, while fog and ice beset the searchers on the heights.

At about 11:00 that morning, Fire Warden Briggs was making a tour of some of the skid roads left by the many logging operations that had been pursued in the White Mountains. This one led to the Pinkham Notch road near the Darby Field, a clearing around a lodging house two miles south of the Glen House. Warden Briggs heard a noise in a thicket of spruce slash and stopped to listen. Then he saw a man and they both said hello. The stranger climbed up to Warden Briggs and asked what day it was. Learning that it was Friday, he said that he'd been out for two days, that he was lost, and that he was looking for the Keenan farm.

Then he said that he'd been working for a survey party on Mount Washington and his boss was Mr. Jewell and he had fallen down a ravine thirty feet deep, but he did not say that he was hungry, he just asked for a piece of spearmint gum. Warden Briggs thought it was an unsatisfactory exchange; the man's talk was rambling and incoherent, the clearest part having to do with his search for the Keenan farm. Warden Briggs had further doubts. For one thing, the man was wearing a fancy pink-and-white striped shirt. Beyond that, the warden did not believe the account of Mr. Jewell's survey party because he knew that Mr. Jewell ran a livery stable in Gorham. He thought the stranger could not be a surveyor or have any other kind of work on the mountain because no person would go to the heights wearing the clothes this fellow had on.

Warden Briggs knew the territory as well as anyone could and he knew that there was no family named Keenan anywhere in the Glen, so he decided that the stranger was sound of limb, but failing in his mind. Warden Briggs brought him out to the road and directed him to the Glen House two miles north along the road, then he went to his own camp half a mile away in the opposite direction to attend to other duties. The incident was certainly unusual, but Warden Briggs was a man of experience and he took unusual incidents in stride.

That day, Honorable George Turner and Dr. Gile were driving the roads around the Presidential Range. Mr. Turner was familiar with the area; he lived in Bethlehem, just west of Mount Washington. Now he was a representative to the state government in Concord and a member of the Governor's Council. Dr. Gile was a representative from Hanover, and on Friday he and Mr. Turner were inspecting the state roads in the north country, roads which at this time were little more than one-lane rocky tracks.

Shortly before noon, they were on the Pinkham Notch road and they passed a young man who made an odd impression on them. They were driving slowly in their open car, but he did not call out to them; he seemed to have a vacant expression on his face and he waved his arms and pointed up at Mount Washington looming above them. The two inspectors did not know that a man was missing, so they continued their drive along the road.

There was a second car in the inspection party that day. It was driven by a Bethlehem chauffeur named Howard Lightfoot, who had been engaged to carry the luggage of Honorable Turner and Dr. Gile. Mr. Lightfoot had fallen some ways behind them, and later in the day he reported that about noon he was flagged down by a young man who asked for a ride. This was on Darby Field hill, a little less than two miles south of the Glen House, but the story was soon contradicted by men in more authority than the chauffeur.

The inspectors were lodging at Fabyans, fifty miles away on the opposite side of the mountain, and when they arrived that evening they learned that a man was lost and that his description matched the apparition they'd seen in Pinkham Notch. Honorable Turner called the base station of the cog railway with the news.

This was the day of heavy clouds and ice on the upper elevations and the search party was going to spend the night in one of the summit buildings. Word was passed along that they should go down to the Glen House early the next morning, Saturday, and join Mr. Bickford's men.

Reporters from the Boston newspapers had gotten wind of the story and soon they were everywhere. There was no news to report, so they began making up their own. One of them offered Mr. Jewell a large sum of money to go off for a week so he could write that even Mr. Jewell had gotten lost and came struggling out of the wilderness a week later. One of them made himself the hero of his own news story, saying he'd joined the search party and been attacked by a wildcat.

Saturday was a day of mixed weather in the Glen, by turns sunny and gray with temperatures in the 70s and afternoon showers. The newly formed search party at the Glen House soon found Warden Briggs. The searchers told him that a man was missing from the heights; they described John Keenan, and asked the warden if he'd seen anything out of the ordinary.

He had indeed. Warden Briggs said that the previous morning he'd met a crazy man coming down the old logging road at the Darby Field, very near the place on the state road where the inspectors had seen a person of the same description, and Mr. Briggs provided so many details that the searchers knew it was John Keenan. Now they knew that John had been started along the road toward the Glen House the previous morning and that Warden Briggs thought he was in good physical condition, so they decided that he must have gotten most of the way to the hotel before nightfall. On the basis of these assumptions, they spent all of Saturday searching the area between the Glen House and the Darby Field, but they found no sign of hope.

This day, Lawrence Keenan took the train north from Charlestown to attend the search for his son. He went to the base station of the cog railway and spent the night at the surveyors' camp, then on Sunday morning he took the train to the summit and rode down the carriage road to the Glen House and joined the search party there.

This was September 22, and the first stretch of tolerable weather since John disappeared four days earlier; it was almost 20° warmer, but steady rain began in the afternoon. By now, more than 100 searchers had gathered at the Glen House, including photographer Guy Shorey. They made a detailed search of the land between there and the Darby Field, they pushed into the woods for a mile on either side of the road, they waded through the Peabody River running beside the road, and they even drained Milliken's Pond, still without effect.

Mr. Keenan pronounced himself satisfied with the effort and that night he went back to Charlestown, stating that he had given up all hope of seeing his son again. The next day the search party was disbanded, though a small group of guides and surveyors continued to look for difficult places they might have missed.

Later that week, Howard Lightfoot returned to the Glen and pressed his story on whoever would listen. He said that on Friday he was driving through Pinkham Notch with the inspectors' luggage and about noontime he was half a mile from the Glen House and he came upon a man waving his arms wildly, as if to stop the car. Then the man got in with the chauffeur.

Mr. Lightfoot said that his passenger was about twenty years old and was wearing a pink-and-white shirt with attached cuffs from which the cuff links had been lost. He said that he remembered this in particular because it was not something he'd expect to see on a tramp or a mountain boy, and because the fellow was not wearing a coat or an undershirt despite the inclement weather.

The chauffeur carried this strange person about two miles along the road and when they reached the old lumber camps near the Darby Field the stranger said, "I think I want to get out here. Yes, this is the place I want to get out." Then he asked where the Keenan farm was and how far it was to Charlestown and how far it was to Franklin. Learning that it was more than 150 miles to Charlestown, he said, "Yes, I guess it is quite a ways." Mr. Lightfoot was struck by his rambling talk and how he didn't seem to be much bothered by his situation even though it was cold and raining hard. But time was wasting and Mr. Lightfoot was anxious to catch up with the inspectors, so he drove away down the road without even looking to see where the fellow went.

In fact, Mr. Lightfoot already knew that a man was missing from a survey crew on Mount Washington, but he did not believe he'd met that person because, as he put it, "I would have looked for a bright-looking fellow dressed as you might have expected a surveyor would. This fellow was not bright looking. He had a slightly receding chin and, if I remember right, his nose was a little larger than the average man. He drooled at the mouth, which might have been due to his being cold and wet, although he was apparently suffering from neither cold nor hunger."

When the chauffeur got home the next day he was shown a copy of *The Boston Post* with a picture of the lost man, but it did not seem to be the person he'd met on the road. Then he was shown a picture in *The Boston Herald*, and he decided at once that it was Keenan who had been his passenger.

This new account reached the Glen House after the 100-man search party had been disbanded, but it was quickly understood that at the time of the great effort on Sunday none of the searchers knew that John Keenan had been taken two miles back to the Darby Field, so their search had not covered some likely terrain. Another group was organized to cover the territory around the Darby Field and the old logging camps, but they found nothing.

A week after the disappearance on Mount Washington, strange nighttime noises were heard near the Glen House, it was as if someone was shouting or crying out. A new search was organized the next morning and concluded before dark. The same week, Mrs. Keenan came up from Boston and visited the spot where her son was last seen, then she went home. A call came to the Glen House one night that week to say that John had been found, but the source of the call was never learned, nor the place of the sighting. Another sighting was reported in Woodstock, nearly 100 miles away at the south end of Franconia Notch, but nothing came of that report, either.

Ten days after the cloud settled over John, his mother had new word for a reporter with *The Boston Journal*: "My son is alive," she said, "and confined in a hospital alongside a river in the west." Pressed for an explanation, Mrs. Keenan said that he'd been picked up by an automobile driver and taken there. Then she began to sob and said, "The lad is in an unconscious condition, and if I only knew the hospital where he is located I would go there immediately." The reporter could not learn where she'd gotten this news, but she said that her in-laws had gotten the same report. Some said that the source was a clairvoyant. By this time, skeptics were denying that John had been seen by anyone at all since he disappeared in the fog.

Two weeks after the disappearance, *The Littleton Courier*, published twenty miles west of Mount Washington, had more plausible news. According to the *Courier*, Mr. O. A. Wood, a guest at Pleasant View Cottage in Twin Mountain, had found a water dipper and a knapsack while hiking on Mount Washington, and it was presumed that John was carrying just such items as these when he disappeared. Closer study showed that it was not a knapsack but a particular type of double-closure bag used only by surveyors, but Mr. Jewell's men said that John did not have one of these on his first day of work. John was wearing a coat and a hat and carrying his back-flag staff when he disappeared, but the man seen by Honorable Turner and Dr. Gile, by Warden Briggs, and by Howard Lightfoot did not have any of these things and none of them was ever found.

The Keenan family had not entirely given up. They'd been writing to hospitals in the United States and Canada, and on November 26 *The Boston Post* carried a story that a person answering John's description had been found in the hospital of St. Jean de Dieu in Montreal, an asylum for the insane. George Villeneuve was the superintendent at St.

Jean and he'd written to the Keenans: "In answer to your letter of November 23 I beg to inform you that the person answering the description you give in this letter has been admitted into this hospital since September. All those admitted since that date are known."

Hope surged, and the Boston & Maine Railroad sent Mr. Jewell to investigate. He was met in Montreal by a driver in a handsome sleigh with a luxurious robe, but he found no basis for the report. Then it was discovered that one word in the letter had been miscopied by the doctor's secretary. "I beg to inform you that the person answering the description you give..." should have read, "I beg to inform you that *no* person answering the description you give..."

That was the last entry in the story of young John Keenan, but the mystery continued to occupy the citizens of the North Country. Many of them were guides or hunters, or they worked on the carriage road or on the cog railway, and they knew how frightening and disorienting the sudden cloudbank whiteouts can be even for someone perfectly familiar with the trails and the lay of the land above timberline.

John Keenan knew nothing at all of that world, he was in his first hours on Mount Washington, and he was not on a trail when the cloud covered him. Indeed, he might not even have known that the piled-up rocks marked a trail, and the white paint marks along the trail might have looked like the lichens that grew everywhere above timberline.

That day, rain was being driven by a cold wind at a steady 50 miles an hour from the west, and those familiar with such situations knew that there's an almost irresistible impulse to walk downwind: it avoids a cold face, it takes less effort, and there seems to be a subtle prompting from nature itself that this is the right direction to go.

That wind would have pushed John eastward around the summit cone and toward the terrain funnel leading into Tuckerman Ravine, but the precipices ahead of him would have been intimidating. The ridges of Lion Head and Boott Spur on his left and right would have been easier going, but he might not have been able to see them in the fog and they would have kept him in the wind for much longer, so the chances were good that John had scrambled down through the ravine. He could have picked up the trail on the floor of the ravine or he could have followed the watercourse of the Cutler River which drains the ravine; in either case he would have come out on the Pinkham Notch road in the near vicinity of the place Warden Briggs had seen the demented stranger.

As it happened, he'd been seen by Warden Briggs at about 11:00 A.M., by the road inspectors between 11:30 and noon, and by Howard Lightfoot perhaps fifteen minutes after noon. Warden Briggs was in the best position to help him, but his doubts about the story were confirmed when he heard that the survey party was led by Mr. Jewell. He knew that Mr. Jewell was not a surveyor, he kept a livery stable in Gorham. Warden Briggs did not know that there were two men named Jewell: H. S. led the survey party, W. W. kept the livery stable.

In addition to these many missed connections, there was the condition of John Keenan. By the time he met Warden Briggs he was already in such a distressed state that he did not recognize help when it appeared, nor perhaps even his own need for help. Instead, he tried again and again to make his way back into the perils that had already cost him so much. No trace of John was ever found and no cause of death ever assigned, but a coroner's jury might rule that he died of complications attending the sudden onset of dread.

AFTERMATH

There is no marker anywhere to remember the death of John Keenan, and even the tokens of his difficulties are almost gone. There is no water today that could be Milliken's Pond and the name does not register in local memory. Mr. C. R. Milliken built and managed the second edition of the Glen House, 1887–1903, so the pond must have been in the near vicinity of the Glen House and it must have been large enough and deep enough that draining was both necessary and possible. The Peabody River is not a large stream here and its bed near the Glen House does show the footings of an old dam about 100 yards upstream from the crossing of the Mount Washington auto road. But the channel is very narrow and, given the terrain, any ponded water would have been so shallow as to be transparent to the bottom, not anything that would require draining.

This puzzled me. Then, while looking through an old family trunk for a mid-nineteenth century property deed, I found a panoramic photograph I'd never seen before. Given family habits, it must have been taken by my grandfather in about 1910, and the view was straight up Great Gulf, with Mount Washington on the left, the Northern Peaks on the right, and a lake in the foreground. An hour of bushwhacking established the place where grandfather must have stood, then I walked straight into the picture.

The terrain drops to Route 16 and runs level for about seventy yards beyond the road, then there's a steep drop twenty feet down to a broad flat swale which, by the evidence, is a favorite with moose. Then there's the Peabody River. Not far downstream the stubs of heavy planking rise up through the shallow water and for another 100 feet the rocky bottom is laced from shore to shore with immense square-cut timbers fastened with wrought-iron spikes, all bracing the planks against the pressures of long-gone freshets. This was the dam which formed Milliken's Pond, with a spillway for draining.

Then, in one of the converging surprises that can accompany even the most obscure studies, I came across a framed picture in our house which I'd been looking at for many years without ever really seeing. The back shows that it came from the Cummings & Son art shop in Oberlin, Ohio, and it shows the long prospect up Great Gulf from a point somewhat south of the panorama. There's quiet water in the foreground, it's only a few inches deep and it reflects the tree-framed mountains. This can only be the far upstream end of Milliken's Pond, there's no other flat water in the Peabody River until several miles farther along toward Gorham.

My aunt Harriet was born in 1900, and her first job after college was in Oberlin. So Milliken's Pond provided no help in the search for John Keenan and its very existence was ephemeral, but it gained a much longer life as foreground for our family pictures. My grandfather probably took this one on the same day as the panorama and when aunt Harriet set out to make a career far from home she put the picture in her suitcase; when she reached Oberlin she went to Cummings & Son and had it framed to remind her of the mountains she loved so much.

There's another landmark in the Keenan story. The search parties kept passing what they called The Darby Field and contemporary texts suggest that they did well not to stop there: it was a large but ramshackle hostelry serving hunters, fishermen, and other travelers and run by "Hod" Reed, a man well known for his close association with Demon Rum. This, the old accounts say, was just past The Darby Field hill. Now the Wildcat Ski Area is at the crest of a long hill and a little farther along is the state road camp, the place where snowplows and sand are kept waiting for winter storms. Mr. Reed's establishment stood on this spot in the days before snowplows and even before most automobiles, excepting the small caravan of road agents who narrowly missed saving John Keenan. Today, a metal sign stands across the road from the state camp announcing that it was near this spot that Mr. Darby Field began his historic first ascent of Mount Washington in 1642. Denizens of the notch must have chuckled at the tidy little play on words that let them call this mountain pasture The Darby Field.

The many missed connections in this episode contrast with a step into the future that had been made at Madison Hut, less than six miles across the Northern Peaks from the place where John Keenan disappeared. The Ravine House was a large hotel and highly favored by the hiking community that animated the town of Randolph. That summer the hotel contracted with the Coos County Telephone Company and a telephone line was strung 3.7 miles from the Ravine House up the Valley Way trail to Madison Hut above timberline. This was for the convenience of hikers who might want to send messages in either direction and it earned $7.60 in tolls the first summer and $13.00 the next year. It was disconnected soon after that, but some of the white china insulators that carried the wire can still be seen screwed into the trees along the Valley Way.

Mr. Mellen's enterprise fared no better than John Keenan. The Boston & Maine Railroad collapsed under his management, and although he spoke vaguely of reorganization, the lumber companies had other straws in the wind. The Weeks Act had just passed and the national forest was being established. Perhaps sensing that the United States was a more substantial partner than Charles Mellen and his amazing schemes, the lumbermen sold their land and the trolley's right of way to the government.

Still, though, it seemed that the survey marks left by Mr. Jewell's rowdy crew must still be in the rocks — it is in their nature to endure. The crew used a 3/8-inch drill to make some 6,300 holes about half an inch deep in the rock; they ran along the center line of the right of way the crew pushed through the woods of the lower elevations, through the almost impenetrable thickets approaching timberline, and across the rocks and ledges of the alpine zone.

The trolley plan called for a double row of utility poles to carry the many miles of electric lines, but the organizers didn't say how and for how long they thought these would withstand the violent weather on the heights of the Presidential Range. Now, eighty-six years and perhaps 20,000 cycles of melt and freeze have passed and even the drill holes seem to have been smudged beyond discovery.

The work of many patient summer days, however, found three sets of marks that do not match the scallop-shaped weathering on the mica schist rocks above timberline on the range. The first to catch my eye was below the point where the Caps Ridge Trail crosses the Cornice Trail on Mt. Jefferson; they're aligned in the right direction and they're at the right elevation for the trolley route between its upper switchback at Castellated Ridge and its passage along the col between Mts. Jefferson and Clay. But they weren't neat 3/8-inch drill holes half an inch deep, they were rounded squares half an inch deep and I regarded them with caution. I found a pair of similar marks just above the location of the old Gulfside tank beside the cog railway track on the side toward the Great Gulf headwall and these, too, were aligned as logic and terrain suggests they would be. But they still didn't look like the holes I was expecting, two holes do not a survey make, and I rejected them for lack of confirming evidence.

Then I found a contemporary citation indicating an exact spot the trolley would pass on the lower of its two circuits around the summit cone, so I bore down on this area, I studied it on my hands and knees. An alpine meadow starts here and it rises with a moderate grade, just the sort of natural aid a prudent survey crew would favor.

As on the Northern Peaks, the rock of the Mount Washington summit cone is a grainy mica schist and the surface weathers into myriad small dishes overlapping each other on every upturned side. At a point near a corner of the meadow I found a change in the pattern; instead of another scallop, there was a rounded hole half an inch deep and about the size of a small postage stamp, and very much like the holes on Jefferson and on the north side of the summit cone. I'd been looking for 3/8-inch holes for six days, but I found none. So perhaps the work of those 20,000 cycles of melt and freeze did not leave the rock untouched, perhaps the grainy schist flaked away around the small round drill hole and left this larger rounded shape as its descendant.

Seventy rising paces across the meadow there's another one of these marks, and seventy rising paces farther along there's another one. That convinced me. These must be all that's left of the electric necklace that lifted those boardroom hearts at the floodtide of *la belle epoque*. Now they reward the attentive eye with a tiny variant in the patterns of ancient weathered rock, and Sylvester Marsh's cog trains still pant and chuff up the western flank of the mountain, neither train nor terrain substantially changed since 1869.

CHAPTER SEVEN

THE MAYOR OF PORKY GULCH TAKES OFFICE

*T*he shape of the Presidential Range is very largely the work of the Laurentide ice sheet which arrived in 23,000 B.C. The character of the Presidential Range is very largely the work of Joe Dodge, who arrived in 1922 A.D.

The Dodge family arrived on the American shore in 1638, they settled in Salem, Massachusetts, and in the next 260 years they moved only a few miles north to Manchester-by-the-Sea, where they pursued the woodcrafter's trades. Joseph Brooks Dodge made his first appearance on December 26, 1898; as he liked to put it, "I was a great Christmas present." When Joe was a boy the family was still engaged in the furniture business; his own interests, however, had already turned elsewhere.

A strong nor'easter blew up the New England coast a month before he was born and the City of Portland sank with all hands off Provincetown, Massachusetts. Disasters always make good story-telling, Joe heard this account over and over again, and it pulled his young attentions toward the sea and also toward the weather. Joe wanted to be a locomotive engineer when he grew up, an urge that is widespread in young boys. He also wanted to go to sea, an urge that is widespread in shore-dwellers.

This second calling was more easily tested, and the summer Joe was twelve he managed to secure an entry-level position on a fishing smack and went as far as the Grand Banks before he was required to resume his career in grammar school. All was not lost, though. There was a great fire in Salem when he was fifteen, and, noting that one of the firemen had not come to work, Joe alertly stepped forward and filled in for him stoking Manchester's steam-powered fire engine. This did not lead to a job driving locomotives, so Joe turned to another chance at the future.

One of the central events in every imagination was the loss of the Titanic in 1912. Joe had become interested in radio two years earlier and now he was absorbed by the stories of the radio messages that might have averted the disaster, but did not. The first transmissions from the doomed ship had been picked up by a teenager on a rooftop in New York and Joe learned that there was a Marconi wireless station in Wellfleet, out on Cape Cod, so he built a small radio and taught himself Morse code by listening to the Wellfleet traffic.

The first adventure in radio was played out in the Dodges' kitchen. Early radios looked complex, even mysterious, and Joe strung the antenna wires across the ceiling, which was not what most people expected. The very idea of radio was new to most people, and one winter day a relative came to visit and quickly inquired about the unusual utensils in there with the pots and pans. Joe provided a first lesson in the propagation of radio waves and said that the wires would intercept the waves when they came in. The relative, not fully in touch with the new world of electronics, said, "You'll freeze us out when you open the window to let in the waves."

Joe moved on to more powerful radio sets and news of this novelty did not escape wider notice. The Manchester Cricket sent a reporter to inquire and his story ran in the next issue: "Joseph Dodge, who has one of the most complete amateur radio outfits in the country, has achieved some wonderful results of late, and one evening this week gave a startling demonstration in reproducing the voice of a lady as she sang 'solos' in Chicago. The fact of her voice coming from a distance of nearly a thousand miles without the aid of wires and heard perfectly, is almost beyond comprehension. The sound is caught from an antenna and amplified by means of a gramophone horn."

The relative's fears about snowstorms coming through the open window with the radio waves proved unfounded and Joe kept moving. He got his first commercial license when he was sixteen and quickly gained employment on the SS Bay State for the Boston-Portland run, a position that required him to wear his first long pants. Joe telephoned his father to tell of his advancing station in life and was told to come home at once. He didn't. He went on board and told the captain that he was a radio operator. The captain cast off and two days later tied up again at the Portland dock. The senior Dodge met the ship, asked Joe how he'd liked it, and took him home. Nothing more was ever said.

Two years later the United States was being drawn into the World War; Joe quit high school the day war was declared and joined the navy on February 14, 1917. He was assigned as instructor in the radio service at Harvard, then in January of 1918 he was reassigned to the Western Electric laboratories in New York to learn radio telephone and this led to the navy base in New London, where he set up a radio telephone school and research laboratory. One day he was put aboard a submarine for a training mission and, once at sea, the vessel sank. No one on board could find a way to bring it back to the surface and the situation looked grave indeed; then the young radioman stepped forward and, with only a pair of pliers, he found the trouble and effected the repair. The engines were restarted and the ballast blown, and the submarine was soon back on the surface.

Joe mustered out of the navy in 1920 with the rating of Chief Electrician (Radio) and quickly joined the merchant marine. He signed onto the J. M. Danziger, an oil tanker under Mexican flag, and made port in Tampico just as Alvaro Obregon's revolution was breaking out. The rebels attacked the ship with machine guns and Joe returned fire by throwing rocks at them. That proved sufficient and the Danziger eventually headed into harbor in Newport, Rhode Island. The captain had not picked up a pilot, though, and first they hit a sewer line and then they took thirty feet off the end of the dock. The skipper leaned over the rail of the bridge, spit a cud of tobacco past Joe's ear, and said, "Well, Sparks, I guess we made a grandstand finish."

Thus ended Joe's ocean-going career, but another stone had already been cast. In 1909, he and his father headed north toward the mountains. They followed the usual route of the day: a steamer from Boston to Portland, Maine, a train from Portland to Glen, New Hampshire, and a buckboard from there up the narrow rocky road through Pinkham Notch to take lodgings in the Glen House, the famous hotel at the foot of the carriage road that led to the summit of Mount Washington.

The senior and junior Dodges did not take a carriage. They hiked up the road to 2-Mile, then turned off on the Raymond Path that led to the floor of Tuckerman Ravine. They climbed up through the ravine and spent the night in the old Tip-Top House, hiked down the Southern Peaks on the Crawford Path, found the station in Fabyans and took the train back to Portland, thence home by steamer.

In those days young men were expected to take their place in the family business, and when Joe left the good ship Danziger he made a try at the furniture trades, but it didn't work out. He odd-jobbed his way around Maine for a year or so, then in 1922 he learned that an organization called the Appalachian Mountain Club had a small encampment in Pinkham Notch, at the foot of Mount Washington. He remembered that the hiking trip he'd taken with his father had gone right past that place, so he made inquiries. The club had one employee at their office in Boston and he offered Joe a bunk at Pinkham Notch.

That was June 9, 1922, there were two log cabins and several army surplus pyramid tents at Pinkham, and Joe went to work. His first job was to fasten a roof over the outdoor washstand, the better to shelter guests against inclement weather.

Other visitors were both better adapted to the elements and more frequent in their visits: porcupines. These natives were so numerous, and so attentive to the buildings and supplies, that Joe and his partner would kill as many as a dozen in one night. The state game wardens paid a bounty on porcupines, so the noses would be taken to Gorham and redeemed at the rate of twenty-five cents per. Then the hutmen would redeem the coins for strawberries and cream, which they'd take back to the notch and make what they called porcupine shortcake. The recipe for that staple is lost to history, but the name that summer inspired is not — Joe called his new lodgings Porky Gulch.

Bears were also frequent visitors and they, too, were convertible assets. The Cutler River flows out of Tuckerman Ravine and eventually drops into Crystal Cascade just above the AMC settlement beside the Pinkham Notch road. There's a deep pool below the cascade and one day

Joe found a dead bear in the water there; as he told a visitor, "Committed suicide, I guess." The late bear was many days gone and quite smelly, and Joe thought that no game warden would want to give him even temporary accommodations, so he took the bear around the circuit of game wardens and collected the five-dollar bounty in four different towns.

The AMC camp in Pinkham Notch was open for summer use only and Joe kept coming back. In 1925 and 1926 he was chief carpenter in building the "portables," which were bunkhouses to extend the lodging capacity. As the summer of 1926 drew to a close he proposed a plan that would keep him at the AMC settlement over the winter: he'd care for the cabins there, attend to the needs of what few climbers as might come by, and make occasional trips to the huts at Lakes of the Clouds, Carter Notch, and Madison Springs to see that they were holding out the elements and other intruders who might have designs on them. Joe did not have to wait long for the first real test in the thirty-six years he would spend in Porky Gulch.

· MAX ENGELHART ·
OCTOBER 1926

*N*o warm season ever matched 1926 for cold. The snow arch in Tuckerman Ravine did not fall until September 3, the last snow in the ravine disappeared on September 23, and five inches of new snow fell the next day. The last of the old winter's snow melted on October 4; then on the evening of Friday, October 9, a great storm broke over New England and by morning ten inches of snow had fallen on the AMC encampment in Pinkham Notch and it was still coming down hard. After breakfast the temperature suddenly dropped and a strong wind began to drift the snow. By noon, it was worse.

Joe Dodge was not yet fully rigged for winter and Pinkham froze up. The storm continued; indeed, it seemed to intensify. The AMC had a Model T Ford truck called Ringtail and Saturday afternoon Joe drove fifteen miles down the notch road to Intervale to meet the train. On the way back he rescued a dozen vehicles on the steep northbound grade of Spruce Hill, which had not yet reached the standards of a gravel road; in fact, it wasn't much more than a rocky one-lane track. By Sunday afternoon the weather had broken in the valleys, but Joe could see the cloud base racing across the ridges above Pinkham and he knew that was a sure sign of desperate conditions on the heights.

On Monday afternoon, Joe drove ten miles north to Gorham to borrow blowtorches so he could thaw the water pipes of Porky Gulch. On the way back, he stopped at the Glen House to get some milk and they told him that Max Engelhart was missing.

The two hotels on the summit of Mount Washington had closed in the third week of September, but there were still hikers on the range and if they wanted shelter and found a closed building, they tended to break in. The auto road company had a small building on the summit known as the stage office, so the plan was to keep it open until October 15 in hopes of deflecting people who might otherwise break into the Summit House and the Tip-Top House.

Max Engelhart had been the cookee at the Glen House, the second cook, and he'd been sent up to the stage office. Max was to provide sandwiches and small provisions as needed for hikers or others who might come up by the road. He was supplied with food, water, and firewood, and he was there at the onset of the great storm on Thursday evening.

Two hikers had taken lodgings at the Glen House in hopes of climbing to the summit. They'd arrived with the storm and waited four days for the weather to moderate, then on Monday they started up the auto road. They'd been told that Max Engelhart was living in the stage office and they should tell him to come down with them.

This sentiment was widespread. Dennis Pelquark worked for the summit road company and he wrote, "Much concern had been held out for the man, cast alone on the wind- and storm-swept mountain for two days. The gist of the talk in mountain camps, hotels and the countryside was about the keeper's danger." The wind was still strong, but the two Glen House guests pushed through the drifts and blowing snow and reached the summit, then they went to the stage office for shelter and found a room full of snow. Max Engelhart was not there.

The hikers brought this news down to the Glen House and Joe stopped by on his way back from Gorham with the blowtorches. The clerk asked Joe if there was a stranger with him at the AMC camp. There wasn't, but Joe knew Max was an old woodsman and trapper from Quebec and his friendly salute was more direct than the road worker's elevated words. Max was, Joe said, "A goddam wild Frenchman."

He also knew that Max was fifty-eight years old and although he was very much at home in the woods, he was not accustomed to the rigors of life above timberline on Mount Washington, much less was he equipped for surviving an assault such as the storm just ending. Joe also knew that Max was smart. If life in the stage office became too difficult,

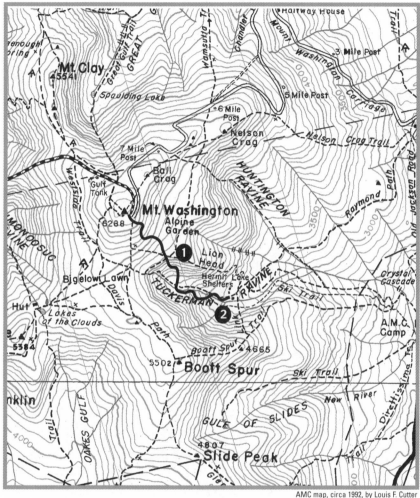

AMC map, circa 1992, by Louis F. Cutter

1 Probably went down Right Gulley in Tuckerman Ravine
2 Found in brook near base of Little Headwall

Max would surely move a few yards to Camden Cottage, a sturdier building and a well-known fortress against the wintry blast.

The two climbers brought down a note from the stage office: "Laf at 12 for Tocmans Arien — no wood." The Glen House crew thought it might be some kind of code. Joe asked to talk to the climbers and they said there wasn't any firewood in the stage office and there was a six-foot drift of snow that blew in through the cracks. They also reported footprints in the hard packed snow of the auto road about a half-mile above the Halfway House, as the old "Camp House" was now called. They said the track led downhill and they thought it was made by Max, nearing the safety of the woods.

No one could make much sense of this — if Max had gotten that far, why hadn't he come the last, easy sheltered miles? Plans were made to send a search party up the road early the next day. Joe said, "You can count on two of us in the morning." He meant himself and Arthur Whitehead, his partner at the AMC camp, and always called Whitey. The two of them talked it over and, as Dennis Pelquark put it, "they, being of the character of real mountaineers, God-fearing and healthy strong youths, brought to light all their theories."

Other theories were brought to light during Monday evening at the Glen House. Someone remembered that a carpenter named Paul LeClair had been working on the summit the previous week and he came down a few hours before the storm started on the ninth. His boots had probably cut into old snow and the prints were bared by the wind after the four-day snowfall just ended. That would account for the tracks the climbers saw. The puzzling note from Max could be read: "Left at noon for Tuckerman Ravine."

Joe and Whitey returned to the Glen House the next morning with heavy clothing, a hatchet, a hunting knife, a long coil of rope, a flashlight, food, hot coffee in Thermos bottles, and binoculars. They were joined by five men from the Glen House: Fred Pike, Elliott Libby, Dennis Pelquark, and two others. The news of the missing man was already in the state and national press, but no men came from Gorham, as they had hoped, much less from farther away.

The rescue party started up the auto road in one of the vehicles that were used for the summer trade. These were monumental seven-passenger 1917 Pierce Arrow touring cars with the high sweeping lines of a steel-and-leather prairie schooner. The men put tire chains on the Pierce and got almost three miles up the road before it foundered in the new snow. They knew there was a crew closing up the Halfway House for the winter and they expected them to join the search effort, but those men declined the chance to help, which struck Joe and Whitey as rather callous.

The Halfway House was just below timberline, and a mile farther up the road the rescue party ran into the full force of the storm. They could see only about thirty feet and rime quickly built up on their clothes and hair as they pushed on to the summit through waist-deep drifts and stinging blowing ice. Joe and Whitey and Dennis realized they were stronger climbers than the other four and they went on ahead, taking care to look for places along the road where Max might have tried to find shelter. The stage office was, as Dennis wrote, "a grotto of frost, snow, and emptiness, the remaining coffee in the pot frozen solid, indicating very severe temperatures." Max was indeed missing.

The bed in the stage office was in good order and there was a considerable amount of food on the shelves, but as the men looked through the other effects they realized that there were heavy clothes hanging on the wall. One of the men thought he remembered another bed in the stage office and found its splintered remains in the large airtight stove, charred but not burned. They also noticed that there was no money in the box where Max kept the coins he collected for sandwiches and they knew that the keeper had not brought much of a wardrobe up to the summit, so they gathered from the missing money, the failed fire, and the clothes on the wall that Max had probably departed quickly, without intention of returning and without much thought of what lay ahead.

The slower members of the party appeared twenty minutes later and joined in a tour of the summit buildings. Nothing seemed amiss and Camden Cottage had not been used. Back in the stage office, Joe spotted what appeared to be writing on the wall, mostly covered with rime. He brushed it clear and found: "*Je pars, date Oct 11 1925. Poudre de*

neige; le vent souffle d'une force de 100 miles a l'heure; maisante, tempera-
ture tres mugir. Max" (Snowing, wind blows 100 miles an hour, temperature very low.) The caretaker had left the building two days ago.

Joe knew of several non-standard ways of getting into the Summit
House and the Tip-Top House, and, thinking that Max might know of
them too, he and Whitey looked into those possibilities and also into
Camden Cottage, but there was no sign of Max. They considered the
situation and reasoned that when Max left the summit there was a very
strong northwest wind blowing, so he would almost certainly have gone
downwind, to the southeast. Joe and Whitey decided to continue their
search and returned to the stage office to prepare their kit.

During these summit perambulations Joe had been kicking at the
frost feathers that formed during the storm, those friable horizontal ici-
cles which build out into the wind and give a sure index of its direction
and a good indication of its strength. One fell more heavily than Joe
thought it should, so he broke it apart and found a stone inside. Then
he knocked loose some of the frost coating the windward side of the
stage office and found many small rocks embedded there; the wind had
swept them up from the flat graveled area near the cog trestle and
hurled them into the ice accumulating on Max's fragile shelter. Now
someone remembered that a storm door had been hung on the outside
of the door frame and this was gone, evidently torn from its hinges and
blown to some distant place. The reasons for his hasty retreat were
becoming more clear.

It was now about eleven o'clock in the morning, no sign of Max
had been found in the valley, and all the evidence suggested a panicky
flight from the summit. Since bewildered hikers tend to go downwind,
Max would have gone down the steeper side of the summit cone toward
the greater hazards of Tuckerman Ravine. Joe took charge and said that
Whitey and Dennis Pelquark should come with him. The others, less
experienced, not so well equipped, and apparently more fatigued,
should stay in Camden Cottage.

Those four men argued that Joe, Whitey, and Dennis should not
continue; they said it was too dangerous to go out onto the unmarked
and wind-blasted slopes, and that if Max was still on the higher terrain

he was certainly dead. Joe said they were going to do it anyway, and the four announced that they would go back down the road to the valley.

The weather was still severe, with scudding clouds and a strong lashing wind, and Joe and Whitey realized that they were probably searching for a dead man. They stayed thirty or forty feet apart, which was as far as they could see, and as they made their way downslope one or another of them spotted what seemed to be tracks, but each time it turned out to be a trick of the wind-carved snow. They'd see what they thought was a body, but each time it was an oddly-shaped rock. At times they lost their footing and took battering slides down the slope; other times they sank armpit-deep between windbreak rocks.

They crawled on all fours to stay on top of the snow and eventually they reached the dwarf spruce near the tops of the ravines. They hoped to find a viewpoint down into Tuckerman Ravine but the going was all but impossible; there were windslab drifts covering the dense scrub growth and they could neither push through the snow nor stay on top of the limbs, so they huddled together for their first rest of the day and considered the situation.

It seemed likely that they'd moved too far to the south, so Joe decided to make a climbing traverse northward across the east side of the summit cone, above the Alpine Garden. It was terribly difficult going; this was the lee side of the mountain and heavily drifted, so again and again they'd break through the windslab surface and sink into shoulder-deep drifts and have to pull themselves out of their sudden prison. Still reasoning that Max would have kept the wind to his back, the three of them pushed on until they'd passed the point at which no downwind line could be drawn from the summit. It occurred to them that, since Max must have had some sense of the shape of the mountain, he might have continued along the lee slope to intercept the auto road above 6-Mile, but still there was no sign of him. They found shelter behind a rock here and took a few minutes for sandwiches, some still-warm coffee, and an eggnog that Joe favored. Then they climbed back to the stage office. It had taken four hours to equal the span of a pleasant summertime hour.

Still not satisfied with the job they'd done, Joe and the other two made another line of search, this time descending to the west of their first track. Max would probably know that there was shelter at the Lakes of the Clouds Hut about a mile away on this heading, and he might have tried for that.

Almost immediately, Dennis found a line of distinct footprints and they followed them with their highest hopes of the day, but the track soon disappeared in a tremendous drift of snow. They struggled back and forth and back and forth over this snowbank, but found no sign of Max. They also noticed that their own tracks, made only a few minutes before, were quickly obliterated by the wind. This meant that there was little chance of finding any tracks Max might have made two days earlier. Now the storm was picking up again, darkness was coming on, and, as Whitey put it later, "the cold came down with almost a crash."

Joe and his two mates hurried back up to the top, had a sip of chilly coffee from their Thermos, and started down the auto road. The wind had risen to such a blast that they had to hold onto each other and push ahead in a kind of stiff troika; they saw white spots on each other's faces where the flesh was freezing and they took off their mitts to wrap on silk handkerchiefs. They hoped to find relief at the Halfway House, and perhaps a little warmth, but when they got there no smoke was coming from chimney and the shutters were all nailed up. At last they found the normal warmth of October and went slipping and sliding in mud on the lower stretches of the auto road.

They had supper at the Glen House and returned to thought. Joe felt that there was no point in spending more time on the summit cone until the air cleared and the wind abated, but Max might have been able to get down into one of the ravines. They had no snowshoes, but if they could borrow some from the Glen House they'd go up and search Tuckerman and Huntington ravines and the adjacent ridges of Boott Spur and Lion Head. The others thought they were crazy, Max was surely dead by now, but Mr. Libby of the Glen House was persuaded to bring some snowshoes to the AMC camp in the morning, so Joe and Whitey drove Ringtail back home, hung their wet clothes out to dry in the cold kitchen, fed the cats, and went to bed. It had been a dispiriting day, nearly twenty-five miles of hard going to learn that they'd do it all again the next day.

Joe and Whitey were almost numb with fatigue, but their minds kept running away from sleep and they were not much rested when they got up on Wednesday. Mr. Libby did not arrive with the snowshoes until 11:30 that morning; he explained that he'd been on the telephone for several hours, talking to Boston newspapers.

This day's climbing was terribly difficult. The snow line was at Crystal Cascade, only a few minutes above the AMC camp, and they had to put on the snowshoes about a mile up the trail. The improved equipment was not a success. The webbing was good, but neither Joe nor Whitey could get their bindings tight enough and the snowshoes flopped about in the snow and snagged on every twig, so the men plunged this way and that trying to keep from falling. Whitey's binding soon broke, and they had to stop while he made a jury-rig from his moccasin laces.

The snow was drifted thigh-deep on the Tuckerman Ravine Trail but they reached Hermit Lake, two and a half miles above the valley, in a time most people couldn't match on a fine summer day. Now they were within the extended arms of the ravine and there was a Forest Service register at Hermit Lake, so while they were resting Joe improved the time by looking over the entries to see when the last hiker had come through.

It was at just this moment that they heard an unexpected sound. Perhaps not trusting their own ears, neither Joe nor Whitey said anything about it. Then they heard it again. Then they heard it a third time. Their first thought was that it came from a steam engine; the air was still, trains ran frequently through Gorham, and the sound of a whistle could certainly carry eleven miles up to Hermit Lake. It might also be a cry from some other search party; given the fair weather and the anxiety for Max's safety, another group might have started up the mountain without the AMC men knowing about it.

Realizing that they'd both heard the strange wail, Joe and Whitey yelled as loudly as they could. Several echoes come off the walls of the ravine here, but mixed in with their own resounding voices there seemed to be one that did not belong to them, one that sounded like a long tenuous... "Help!" Still not trusting their ears, neither Joe nor Whitey said anything hopeful. Instead, they yelled again. When the echoes died away, they still heard the other sound, weak, but unmistakable.

The sound seemed to come from Boott Spur, which forms the south wall of the ravine. Max could certainly be up there. Given the mindless, wind-driven track they imagined for him, he could certainly be up there on the wall of Boott Spur, but Joe and Whitey both privately hoped he wasn't; bringing him down from those steep and rocky heights would be difficult. By now they were rushing toward the sound as fast as they could on their flopping snowshoes and exchanging calls with the undiscovered voice and suddenly Whitey saw a head through the scrubby spruce and birch. It seemed to be disembodied, just a head low down on the snow. Joe said, "Do you see him?" And there he was.

This was just at the place where the Tuckerman Ravine Trail crosses the newborn Cutler River below the steep pitch known as the Little Headwall of the ravine. The stream had not frozen, so there was open water flowing past a large boulder between high banks of drifted new snow. Max was down on the edge of the channel, clinging to a sort of shelf he'd either made or found. It was 1:00 P.M. on Wednesday, October 14, and he had been out in the weather for seventy-three hours.

Max had no hat and what parts of his clothes that were not frozen solid were soaking wet. He was wild-eyed and his face was mottled with frostbite, his lips were black, his tongue was swollen, and his arms and legs were so stiff that Joe and Whitey could hardly bend them at all as they lifted and dragged him out of the Cutler River channel.

Max seemed almost incoherent, then he saw that Joe and Whitey were stripped down to their shirts and steaming with effort and he said, "Oh, my dears, put on some clothes before you freeze!" Joe and Whitey arranged their snowshoes to make a sort of bed for him and laid him down; they took off his wet clothes and wrapped him in their own spare clothes, and they gave him some food and coffee with brandy mixed in. These attentions revived Max somewhat and he told them to be careful of his jacket because he had the money from his trade at the stage office, it wasn't really his, and he didn't want it to be lost. Then Joe and Whitey lay down close beside him in hopes of giving him some of their body heat and Max did what he could to make them understand his two nights above timberline on the mountain, then a terrifying slide down Tuckerman Ravine and the twenty-four hours he'd been in the stream channel.

Suddenly the three of them were in shadow. The sun had dropped below the barrier of Boott Spur, the temperature dropped abruptly, and they realized they had to get a move on. They'd found Max about halfway out the long floor of the ravine where the terrain is thick with stunted birch and spruce. Joe tried to carry Max on his back while he pushed through the scrub to the trail on his snowshoes, but Max weighed fifty pounds more than Joe did, he was an awkward load, and the snowshoes still flopped uncontrollably. Joe fell almost immediately, then he fell again. This kind of carry was also very painful for Max and, to complicate matters, he couldn't keep anything on his stomach.

Joe and Whitey decided to try a litter carry, so they cut two birch poles and rigged a stretcher with their extra shirts and jackets, but their snowshoes kept jamming between boulders or snagging on the broken branches of the stunted trees and the two men couldn't keep in step with each other. Their progress was so slow and tormented that they gave it up after about three-hundred feet and decided to try a drag carry, what woodsmen call a travois.

They'd need to cut a pair of fir trees for this, so they went down the trail to where the growth was larger and Max became terribly agitated, he thought they were leaving him behind. So Joe and Whitey made as much noise as they could and talked loudly to cheer him up. They came back with two fir poles and this seemed to bring Max back to his old self and his better nature. He told them that in his days as a woodsman he'd always found that it helped to shave the bark off the lower ends of an improvised drag to reduce friction, and he showed them how to rig their ropes to best advantage.

Now they'd brought their tools and devices to as great a perfection as they thought possible and they pushed off again. The terrain here is flat, gravity was not helping at all, and it took almost three hours to go a third of a mile through the deep snow with one man between the poles pulling and the other in back pushing. There were places where they couldn't move the drag at all, so they changed Max's position, but that didn't help much. They plunged and staggered along on their snowshoes, then they lifted Max off the drag and helped him crawl along on all fours. This was more difficult and more time consuming than anything else they'd tried, so Max told them how to rig tump lines and hitch themselves in tandem like a yoke of oxen and they struggled on through the snow, lurching and falling every few steps.

By now they were on the summer trail. Or, more properly, over it. The trees grow very densely at this elevation and they could make out the route of the trail by following the hall-like opening through the trees, but they were past the flats now and the trail twisted and dipped and rose again as it followed the lay of the land. There were places where the turns were sharper than the length of their drag could negotiate and Max rolled off and crawled so they could move the poles around the corner. The snowshoes were a continual agony and Max joined in the volleys of curses directed at them, so they concluded that he was feeling better.

Darkness began to overtake the embattled trio by the time they'd made a half-mile to the good, and there was still a quarter-mile to go before they reached the upper crossing of the Cutler River. By this point the stream was no easy hop-across, it was a full mountain torrent and they'd been dreading the ordeal of crossing even as they tried to imagine a way they could do it. They also realized that their progress with the drag was becoming prohibitively slow, so they left it near the junction of the Raymond Path; one of the men carried all their equipment and the other slung Max over his shoulder and carried him, or half-pushed him and half-dragged him along on the ground.

The stream crossing was worse than they'd feared. They'd gotten across only with difficulty on their way up, and now the warmer weather of the day had added more meltwater to the stream and they faced a flood of freezing water and ice. The summer crossing is a matter of hopping from one rock to the next, but that was out of the question; the snow and ice made the footing far too uncertain and they were burdened with their awkward packs and with the almost helpless body of

Max. The only solution was also the most drastic: Joe and Whitey filled in the gaps as well as they could with blocks of ice, then they lay down in the rocks and rushing water and made a bridge of themselves that Max could crawl across.

It was full dark now and, with the crossing behind them and less snow to slow them, they turned on their flashlights and made good time. This also encouraged Max, and he told them his story.

He said that the carpenter Paul LeClair looked in on him just before the weather broke and then hurried on down the mountain. The force of the storm rose quickly and reached a pitch of fury Max had never imagined, and he feared that his shelter would break its bonds of chain and blow right off the mountain. His firewood was soon gone, so he tried to get to Camden Cottage but the storm blew him off his feet and he couldn't even crawl across against the wind, so he broke up what little furniture he had and burned that. By Sunday he was thinking that this must be the onset of winter and, fearing that he'd be marooned, he decided to make a break for the valley. So, taking only a handful of raisins, he started down at noon.

His hat blew off immediately, then he went slipping and floundering down the lee side of the summit cone until he found the edge of Tuckerman Ravine, but he couldn't find a way down that seemed safe enough to try. He dug a snow cave and let the blowing snow fill in on top of him, then on Monday he broke out and tried again to find a way down, again without success. By this time the uncertain shelter of the stage office seemed more desirable than a snow cave and he tried to climb back up to the summit, but with the storm and the slope against him it was beyond his strength. He hadn't had anything to eat since the raisins the previous afternoon and he believed that eating snow would kill a dying man, so hadn't had anything to drink, either. Thus reduced, he dug in for a second night of full storm above Tuckerman Ravine.

On Tuesday morning Max believed he was close to death, so anything else that happened would not be much lost. He found the edge of the ravine, pitched over into his final effort, and fell until he stopped sliding about seven-hundred feet down the precipitous slope. Finding himself battered but still alive, he set out to find water and reached the place in the brook bed where they found him after his third night in the open.

This halting account filled the time as Joe and Whitey half-carried him down the trail, still carrying their own packs which added eighty pounds to Max's very considerable heft. They'd turned on their flashlights and, stopping to rest at a spot called Windy Pitch, they saw the lights of a car at what they knew was the Darby Field. They signaled with their flashlights, but got no response.

The trail was steeper and rougher now, and they had to be careful not to hurt Max. To complicate matters, his mind was drifting; he thought they told him it was two miles to camp, but he was sure they'd gone sixteen, which meant they'd lost their way.

The last landmark was the lower bridge over the Cutler River, and as they grew near they finally indulged the luxury of planning ahead. Joe would hurry on from the bridge and start a fire in their cabin, then fill the radiator in Ringtail and let it warm up while he heated some broth to reinforce Max before the long jolting ride to the hospital. Accordingly, Joe took both their packs at the bridge and started running the last quarter-mile. He fell and broke his flashlight almost immediately and kept running without it.

The parking lot at the AMC cabins was a blaze of light, it was filled with the cars of reporters and curious citizens. Joe said he and Whitey had found Max Engelhart, and they wouldn't believe him. Then, persuaded, they asked what had taken them so long. Then they asked if Max was all right. Joe decided not to pursue this interrogatory any further.

He sent a reporter to the Glen House to call Dr. Bryant in Gorham, then he opened the cabin and began preparations for Max. The reporters kept asking questions and Joe did not fail to note than no one offered to go up and help Whitey. Soon his mate came in with Max slung over his shoulder and they noticed that it had taken seven and a half hours to bring him down from his small refuge in the bank of the stream.

Joe and Whitey got Max out of his frozen clothes, but he was very much concerned about the knife he'd lost during his ordeal. They found it in his boot, which helped. They put him into warm dry clothes, wrapped him in blankets, and got some hot broth into him before Dr. Bryant arrived and started Max on his way to the hospital.

Now, in the first time they'd had to themselves in three days, Joe and Whitey began wondering why no one had come up to help them; even the people parked at The Darby Field had known it was their flashlights moving so slowly on the trail and had not come to help. Not finding any answer, they fed the cats and made a sign saying "Don't bother us, we're asleep!" Then, too exhausted to eat, they went to bed.

They were also too exhausted to sleep. They rolled to and fro in their blankets, but they were still awake when the sky began to lighten so they made breakfast at 6:00 A.M., but they still couldn't eat. They cleaned up the cabin and as they worked they thought how nice it would be to have somebody else do the work. This idea took hold, so they put on their best clothes, fired up Ringtail, and drove twenty miles north to the Berlin YMCA. They took showers there and went on to the Ravine House in Randolph, where the faithful Mr. and Mrs. Bradstreet cooked steaks and vegetables and biscuits for them.

Joe and Whitey read the Boston papers and learned of their adventures and then they went upstairs for a long sleep in a proper room, stayed on for breakfast and noontime dinner, and stopped in Gorham to have supper with photographer Guy Shorey and the honored guide Burge Bickford to talk over the storm and its consequences. Then they went to Berlin to see how Max was getting along. The toes and heel of one foot had been amputated, and the toes on the other foot, but he wasn't much bothered by this. He told them many stories of the days just past, including how he'd discovered gold in the Cutler River while he huddled by the rock and how he was just about to make some snowshoes out of twigs and branches when they found him, and then he proposed that they come up to his place in Canada and go trapping with him.

Max was kept in the hospital for almost five months. He went home and there was no news of him for many years, then two young women stopped by the AMC cabins in Pinkham Notch. They found Joe and told him that they'd talked to an elderly man in Canada who said that if they ever met Joe Dodge they should tell him that Max Engelhart had a job cooking for the railroad. Nothing more was ever heard of him.

CHAPTER EIGHT

THE WRECK OF OLD NO. 1

*S*ylvester Marsh was born in 1803 in Campton, New Hampshire, at the southern end of Franconia Notch. He was the ninth of eleven children, a situation which latter-day psychologists say fosters a certain competitive push, and when he was nineteen years old he set out to make his fortune. He had three dollars and he headed for Boston, 150 miles away. It took young Sylvester three days to walk there and he found employment on a farm in Newton, west of the city. Soon he had a stall in the original Quincy Market in Boston and he was a passenger when the DeWitt Clinton pulled the first steam train on the Albany/ Schenectady run.

By 1833, he was in Chicago, a place of 300 souls that Sylvester thought had a bright future. Fortune seemed to hitch Sylvester to this star and the first railroad to operate out of Chicago ended just behind his property. He alertly went into the meat packing business and built a large plant to abut the railroad terminus. Then he developed a revolutionary method of preserving corn. All this earned a very considerable fortune, familiarity with the many uses of steam, and a fulsome salute from The

Chicago Press and Tribune: *This "enterprising, ingenious inventor will live in history as one of the benefactors of his species."*

Sylvester Marsh retired from his several businesses in the mid-1850s and moved to West Roxbury, Massachusetts. Inactivity did not suit him; in fact, it brought on a sinking spell that was diagnosed as dyspepsia. Seeking more salutary air, as the fashion of the day indicated, he returned to his old neighborhood in the White Mountains. Further obedient to the fashion of the day, he sought to climb Mount Washington by way of the Crawford's Bridle Path. The weather turned against him and he barely reached the Tip-Top House.

Characteristically, Sylvester resolved to improve the condition of suffering mankind, in this case, to find a better way to reach the heights. Three years later, he approached the New Hampshire state legislature with a model of a mountain-climbing railway. A charter was granted, sort of — one generous voice in the debate said that Sylvester Marsh could build his railway to the moon if he wanted to. The tone suggested skepticism.

Work began in 1866, the rail line was built up a western ridge of the mountain, and on the Fourth of July, 1869, word went forth that the railway to the moon had reached the top of Mount Washington. The train was driven by a rack and pinion system under the engine, which was itself one of the oldest designs in the whole inventory of steam power, a firebox with a vertical boiler on top of it and a smokestack on top of that. Engine No. 1 was officially named "Hero," but the look was familiar: people thought it resembled the bottle used for a popular condiment called pepper sauce. It didn't take long for the north-country tongue to sharpen the word and Engine No. 1 entered history as Peppersass.

This pilot model retired from active duty in 1878. It went west for display at the World's Columbian Exposition of 1893, more widely known as the Chicago World's Fair, then it was at Chicago's Museum of Natural History, and in 1904 it went to the Louisiana Purchase Exposition, popularly known as the St. Louis World's Fair. Then it disappeared.

Reverend Guy Roberts lived in Whitefield, New Hampshire, at the northwestern edge of the great mountain ranges, and he developed a consuming interest in finding the well-loved Mount Washington native. He followed the engine's trail to Baltimore and through heroic personal efforts he managed to have it returned to the place of its first fame, where it was reconditioned and pronounced sound in June 1929. The annual Conference of New England Governors was scheduled for the Bretton Woods Hotel in July, the base station of the cog railway was just up the road, and it seemed like a fine thing to send the official parties up Mount Washington to see the ceremonial return of Old Peppersass.

• DANIEL ROSSITER •
JULY 1929

$\mathcal{E}$ven today, the base station of the Mount Washington cog railway is like any other train yard in the elder days of steam, only smaller; there are whistles tooting and cinders underfoot and smoke and steam swirling overhead. On the morning of July 20, 1929, however, the party clothes were out of the closet, there were grandstands and flags and banners and bunting and a grand patriotic display to greet the double holiday proclaimed for the arrival of the six New England governors and the return of Old Peppersass.

In the language of the cog railway, a train is one engine pushing one passenger car up the mountain. The engine is not connected to the car and there is no turnaround for the return trip: the engine backs down the track with the passenger car resting against it in front. The engine and the car both have primary brakes and back-up brakes and either unit can stop itself independent of the other.

The program for this festive day was elaborate. The governors and the other invited guests were served a grand breakfast at the very grand Bretton Woods Hotel, then the governors and Reverend Roberts climbed aboard an original and bunting-bedecked Concord stagecoach drawn by six prancing horses which took them to the Boston & Maine Railroad station. Two special trains, also draped in red, white, and blue for the day, took those distinguished gentlemen and more than 900 other guests the few miles to the base station of the cog railway. The two trains proved insufficient for the multitude, and those who had to wait for a second run were entertained with selections by a brass band and a splendid tenor soloist.

Once everyone was at the base station of the cog and seated for the ceremonies, the president of the Baltimore & Ohio Railroad officially returned ownership of Old Peppersass to the president of the

Boston & Maine, who in turn presented the relic to the governor of New Hampshire. Then the governors, their entourages, and other invited guests boarded six cog trains that would take them to the top of the mountain, trailing yet more bunting and flags as they climbed.

After those trains were well-started up the track, Old Peppersass began a ceremonial final climb up to the trestle called Jacob's Ladder, two-thirds of the way to the summit and the steepest, highest, and most spectacular section of the whole route. This would prove that even after seventy years, the old campaigner still had what it takes to climb Mount Washington. The program called for the erstwhile Engine No. 1 to descend for the last time and, filled with honors and achievement, go to an honored retirement and permanent display in the valley.

When the presentation ceremonies were over, fireman William Newsham topped off the firebox, engineer Edward Frost opened the valves, and Peppersass headed up the mountain. The antique climbed slowly but it climbed well, and when it reached Jacob's Ladder the fine performance and the spirit of the day inspired the crew to change the original plan and keep going to the summit, so they kept going. Then they changed their plan again. Peppersass moved so slowly that a complete climb would delay the six trains on top beyond the departure time needed to get them all back to the base at a prudent hour. Engineer Frost engaged the reverse gear and began to back the engine down the track. Then he heard a sort of snap; it seemed to come from the front of the engine. A tooth in the cog driving wheel had broken.

Almost every steam engine in the history of railroading towed its fuel tender as a separate element. Peppersass did not. The boiler and the tender were on a single frame and the engineer and fireman stood out in the weather as they did their work. This day three extra people started up the mountain on Peppersass, riding on the fuel bunker any way they could. One was the engineer's sixteen-year-old son Caleb; the two others were photographers Daniel Rossiter and Winston Pote.

Reverend Guy Roberts, the man who led the recovery of Old Peppersass, rode on the last of the six trains sent up ahead of the day's honoree. No cog train ever moved very fast, and the reverend stepped off the platform of his train just above Jacob's Ladder. He thought this was the right thing to do; he'd hike along beside Peppersass as it made its last climb. He stopped at Jacob's Ladder, the better to savor the noble sight as the engine climbed the trestle for this last time, the crown of his twenty-three year effort on behalf of history. Then he thought he'd walk beside the train, or perhaps catch a ride, all the way back down to its final rest at the bottom of the mountain.

The reverend was somewhat surprised to see the engine continue on above Jacob's Ladder and then out of sight over the skyline. He waited forty minutes before he heard a rumbling in the tracks that signaled the return of the train. Then, he wrote later, "Glancing up the track I saw steam or smoke as from her stack, the engine was being concealed by a brow of the mountain. But in an instant she was in sight and I thought, 'Here she comes.' Then I realized that her speed was very fast and the next instant I thought, 'Why, she is running away!' On she rushed, careening and tottering, when with a sudden lurch, off toppled her smokestack, crashing onto the rocks at my right. Then I noticed that a man was hanging to the flaring top of its tender, swaying as it careened! The terrible outfit flashed past, showering me with its cinders, as on it dashed in its mad rush to death down Jacob's Ladder, tearing and crashing. When but some fifteen feet beyond me the man dropped from his hold on the tender and was shot down some forty feet through space outside the upper side of Jacob's Ladder, where he crashed to death on the sharp jagged rocks and huge timbers at the foot of the trestle and about midway its length.

"Watching Old Peppersass as she shrieked out her swan song, she continued tearing down the Ladder until coming to the reverse curve at its foot. Being unable to make the curve she leaped from the rails into space over the brink of Burt's Ravine, where with a thunder-like report the boiler exploded amid a great puff of steam, landing her some thirty feet from the rack and with pieces of metal and debris flying in all directions, at last burying her shattered and scattered self amid the rotten wood, stunted spruce and birches that there were growing."

The engineer, the fireman, one photographer, and the boy all jumped clear of Peppersass while it was still going fairly slowly. They were all considerably battered and some were broken in minor ways, but

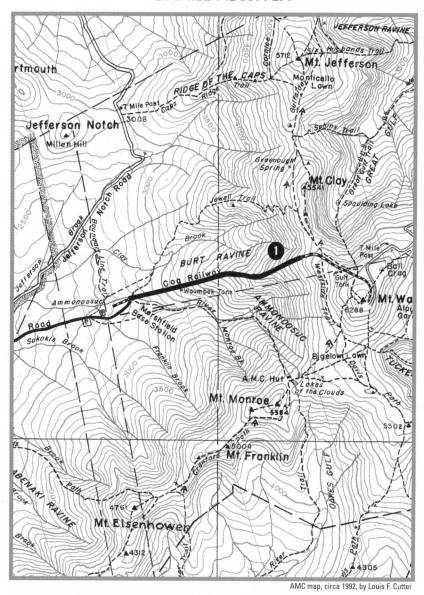

AMC map, circa 1992, by Louis F. Cutter

1 Peppersass crashed on cog railway

their lives were not threatened. Daniel Rossiter was the other photographer and he had the same chance to escape the mad plunge as the others did, but for some reason he hung on to the tender. Some say he seemed to be reaching for his camera, as if to save it from the wreck that must occur.

The enormous explosion of the boiler hurled fragments of the engine more than 900 feet down the mountain and Reverend Roberts hurried to the wreck, putting out small fires beside the trestle as he went. Just below Jacob's Ladder he found "the bruised and broken body of what proved to be that of my friend, Daniel Rossiter, lying on the jagged rocks below and in such a broken position as to not in the least resemble a man as seen from above." A caddy had hiked to a vantage point a little farther up the trestle and he ran to help Reverend Roberts. As the savior of Peppersass put it, "We lifted Dan and placed his head and shoulders in a less terrible position and thus was he found by those who removed his body."

The caddy slipped when he climbed down from the trestle and a large splinter was driven into his thigh, but after he'd helped the reverend with Mr. Rossiter's body, the caddy hobbled and ran all the way down to the place he called Kro Flite, the name applied to the settlement at the base of the cog railroad in 1925 and 1926. As a reporter wrote, "He gave the first news of the disaster, just before he fainted."

The situation was difficult. Old Peppersass was destroyed, five people were injured and one was dead, and, since a section of track on Jacob's Ladder had been damaged by the crash, six trainloads of guests were stranded at the top of the mountain. There was one spare engine at the base and a fire was lit under the boiler, but no engineer could be found. The first of the six trains had started down from the top with a full load of passengers, then it stopped when the first damage to Jacob's Ladder came into view.

Joe Dodge had been engaged as a guest lecturer for the ceremonies and he knew how to dress for celebrations like the return of Old Peppersass: he was wearing plus-four knickers from a golfer's outfit and a bright red Hudson Bay jacket. Joe was on the first train to start down from the summit, but it stopped some way above Jacob's Ladder and out of sight of the wreck. The train was also below the Gulfside Tank, the place where upward-bound engines took on water to finish the trip to the top. Joe knew this meant trouble for the guests; the train apparently could not go on down the mountain and, not having enough water to make sufficient steam, it could not get back to the top.

Soon the passengers knew there was trouble, too. Nightfall was approaching and they were stranded above timberline with no news of their future. As Joe remembered, "It was getting dark and sort of cool and I had about twenty-five men and women to look after, all of them complaining. One woman on the train got hysterical. Her husband wasn't much help, so I picked her up piggy-back, and I said to her, 'Come on, sis. You'll have to get going if you want to get down the mountain.' Well, sir, she clawed at me, she screamed, and she talked baby talk all the way down. It was rough going along those tracks, but I kept my footing. When we finally got to a path, I gave her a shove and said, 'Get going, sister.'"

The reserve engine at the base was kept hot while an engineer walked the three miles down from the summit, and as dusk was falling he started the engine back up to Jacob's Ladder pushing a flatcar loaded with timbers and tools and a work crew to study the damage.

The men were able to make the trestle marginally passable, and at 10:00 P.M. the work train returned with the engineer of Old Peppersass, his fireman, and the others injured in the crash. Before long, Joe's group reached the base station. He'd led them down in the dark and there were no injuries, but they noticed that someone had taken down all the flags and bunting from the morning's ceremonies.

Five trains and the guests riding on them remained on top long after nightfall; as one of the passengers said, it was like being shipwrecked at sea, families were separated and not to be rejoined until the small hours of Sunday morning. They were eventually taken down the mountain on the auto road and, true to the spirit of shipwreck, Governor Tobey of New Hampshire was the last to leave the summit. They all finally gathered at the Bretton Woods Hotel, the place they'd left with such fanfare less than twenty-four hours earlier. Colonel Barron owned the hotel, and he and Senator George Moses served sandwiches and coffee until Governor Tobey arrived at 4:15 A.M. with the last of the guests that were stranded on the summit.

Mr. Rossiter's camera was smashed beyond repair, but the first three pictures he took that day survived and they lived on for their posterity in the archival memory of Old Peppersass. His spectacles and his monogrammed gold watch, now dented and stopped at the moment of his death, were found near the trestle of Jacob's Ladder and returned to his family. More than anything else, the broken watch told of changing times. On Friday of that week, July 25, 1929, the White Mountains Air Line began daily service to Boston and New York from the new airport in the hometown of Reverend Guy Roberts, ten miles from the cog railway for which he'd worked so hard. The plane carried five passengers in addition to the pilot, and the cabin was enclosed for greater comfort.

CHAPTER NINE

SUMMER PEOPLE GO NORTH

amily stories made it seem as if my forebears had lived in Providence forever. There was no shortage of stories because, by an unlikely but verifiable coincidence, both of my parents' families arrived in the New World on the same boat, the good ship Mayflower. Life was not perfectly harmonious in the Plymouth Rock neighborhood and in 1630 family member Roger Williams left the Massachusetts Bay Colony and crossed Narragansett Bay to make a new start in a place he called Providence. By the 1870s, the family was headed by John Howe. He was an actor in a troupe led by Edwin Booth, and they were occasionally joined on stage by Mr. Booth's brother, John Wilkes Booth.

In 1872, the mail brought news from a forgotten past. It concerned the French Spoiliation Claims which, though obscure, would loom large in the future. The notice was addressed to Seth Russell & Son, forebears of John's wife, Louise Russell Howe, familiarly known as "Gubba." Her family had been in the shipping trades after the American Revolution, but those were unsettled times. The long run of royalty and absentee rule was destabilized by the American revolution against George III and then by the rising of the French proletariat against Louis XVI, and these shocks left things at loose ends on several fronts. One popular approach to knitting up loose ends is conflict and the War of 1812 was launched, a curious affair in which the most important battle was held three weeks after the war was over.

Then the several parties to the war gathered for the really useful part, the peace conference. This resulted in the Treaty of Ghent, written in the Belgian city of that name. The first job in any treaty gathering was a sort of bluffing game in which the diplomats put their claims on the table, so our man entered a claim asserting that American shipowners who had lost value to the British should be indemnified by the French.

This is known as spoiliation, and the improbable claim survived the scrutineering phase at Ghent and it was written into the treaty. The mills of the gods may grind slow, but the mills of the nations grind slower. Seth Russell & Son had owned a ship that was put at risk by British raiders after the Revolution, and somewhat more than 100 years later Gubba received a check for damages suffered by a long-forgotten ship named the Fox.

The family was already spending summers with Providence friends who had a place in Jackson, New Hampshire. Now Gubba applied the Fox money to the purchase of the old Moody property in Jackson so her family could have a summer place of their own. There was a farmhouse with a carriage shed and a large barn and several outbuildings, and it wasn't long before Gubba's family began inviting friends up for summer visits. These friends were from Providence at first, then they began coming from Boston and other outlying districts. This was very much in the summer fashion; for an urban world with no air conditioning in the houses and many horses in the streets, summer in the mountain breezes was irresistible.

The Jackson house was enlarged a bit, then the carriage shed was made livable, then the house was enlarged again. They called it "Overlook" and friends began bringing along their own friends, and the house grew larger. Gubba's older daughter was named Fannie, she was first in line as matriarch presumptive and her first child was born in 1887. This was my father, and before long he had a brother and two sisters, and by the time they were in school they began bringing up their friends. They'd pitch tents in the meadows, and then my uncle dragged some cots out into the field and built a sort of cabin over them for the boys to stay in. The girls soon asked him to exercise his teenage carpentry skills on their behalf, and then regular guests began asking for their own cabins.

By the time I was a child there were nine cabins ringing the property and the barn was partly converted for rudimentary summer living and the old farmhouse had a great many rooms. Once, in the grips of summer ennui, I took stock. There were forty-nine spaces I identified as rooms in the main house, but that included bathrooms. Even so, upwards of sixty people could be accommodated in the house and the cabins and the barn, and the stories of four generations of family, friends of family, and friends of friends had grown so numerous and so complexly entwined that I was never exactly sure who was kin and who was not. There was, for instance, a recurring class of guests who were called "loose connections," and to this day I don't know if they were relatives or not.

It didn't matter, because the elders and their heroics were recorded in a pile of black photograph albums in what we called The Big Living Room. The pictures showed gentlemen in suits and ladies in skirts that swept the ground and boys in white shirts and ties and girls in middy blouses and bloomers and black stockings, all of them up there on the mountain heights with blanket roles over their shoulders. Those of us in the rising generation would study those pictures through many a rainy afternoon, and we understood that, as it is said in Genesis, there were indeed giants in the earth in those days.

The Big Living Room had a large bay window that faced the north meadow. A sofa faced the window and that's where we sat to look at the photograph albums and when we looked up we saw Mount Washington rising at the end of the meadow, and even as children we knew that people died up there. We thought about them and we thought most about Lizzie Bourne; she reminded us of the ladies in the photograph albums as they went striding across the heights in skirts that swept the ground. Closer to the moment, we thought about Jessie Whitehead.

· JESSIE WHITEHEAD ·
JANUARY 1933

*J*essie Whitehead was a notable person. We knew that, because she was at the head of the list of notable persons who stayed at Overlook. Charles Evans Hughes stayed with us, he was Chief Justice of the Supreme Court; there were Rockefellers; there was Curt Chase, commanding general of the First Light Cavalry Division, and there was a large and energetic family from Boston named Kennedy whose father was the ambassador to the Court of Saint James. But my father always told us most particularly of Jessie Whitehead and her terrible fall in Huntington Ravine.

We knew Jessie because of her stutter. It wasn't that she had an occasional stammer, that she stumbled over a word now and then — Jessie could hardly talk at all. Father said she'd broken her neck in the fall, and that was why she stuttered. Grandmother Howe ran Overlook in the summer and she took it for granted that children should not be heard. She believed that we shouldn't be seen very often, either, and the children of my generation stayed in our various families' cottages at the perimeter of the property. This reduced our contact with the notable people to zero, but we did know one way we could see Jessie Whitehead.

Overlook had a back porch that had been made into a room. It was called the Trough, and this was where employees, disreputable relatives, and children of my generation were fed at a long trestle table. The Trough had windows on the outside wall and also the old windows on the inside wall. One day Jessie sat down for dinner at the end seat of the biggest of the dining room tables and we could see her through the inside windows of the Trough.

At the beginning of a meal the waitresses always went around their tables saying, "Tea, coffee, or milk?" and they'd take the orders on their fingers. They'd hold their hands behind them and count on one hand for tea and the other hand for coffee. Back in the kitchen, they'd subtract the total number of fingers from the total places at the table and the remainder would be milk.

We could see the waitress's fingers when she took Jessie's order, and as the choking, gasping sounds began to sound like "Tea," one finger began to record the message; then as the sounds veered away toward "Coffee," a finger on the other hand would move. We watched through the back windows and we were fascinated. We understood that Jessie's fall in Huntington Ravine must have been terrible indeed.

We knew about Huntington Ravine. When we looked out past our croquet lawn, Mount Washington rose directly in front of us: Tuckerman Ravine was hidden behind Boott Spur, but we could see straight into Huntington Ravine. There was a huge boulder at the corner of the croquet lawn that we called Mount Washington Rock. It had the same general shape we could see on the skyline and there was a deep cleft for Huntington Ravine. We'd look at that and think of Jessie Whitehead.

Jessie had a wider fame. She was the daughter of Alfred North Whitehead, a leading member of the last generation of great philosophers, the last generation of scholars whose ideas were on the front pages of newspapers. He was British by birth, but he made his career at Harvard and Jessie had an elevated childhood, she'd say, "I grew up in a cloud of Huxleys," meaning the most powerful family of intellectuals of the age.

Jessie lived in an apartment near Harvard Square and she almost always had one or two cockatiels with her. They're small parrots from Australia and during the harshest winter storms she'd be out there striding along the sidewalks of the Square and smoking a pipe, with her birds sitting on her shoulder and ruffled out to twice their normal size to hold off icy blasts their homeland never knew. She liked to take her meals at the popular and economical Hayes-Bickford restaurant on Harvard Square and the Bick did not allow animals to mingle with the diners, but Jessie was a person of character and of consequence, and the management of the Bick let her bring the birds to her regular place at one of their front window tables. Jessie was a scholar in ancient Arabic languages and she worked at Harvard's Widener Library in her academic specialty. One day the hushed precincts of Widener were suddenly rent by a great cry: "Oh God, if there is a God, what does it all *mean?*" It was Jessie, whose own long silences were occasionally broken by questions like that.

Perhaps it was those silences that had made Jessie a devoted hiker and a serious rock climber long before anyone thought such a calling would include women, and she was not afraid of anything. She and three men made the first ascent of the northeast ridge of the Pinnacle in Huntington Ravine, considered unclimbable until her group climbed it in October 1928. She was a relentless champion of what she called "manless climbing," and she and three other women spent the summer of 1931 on the major peaks of the Alps. Inevitably, they went to the Matterhorn. The weather was bad, but they reached the highest hut on the mountain and found it filled to the rafters with hikers from every point of the compass, an alpine Tower of Babel. Jessie couldn't make out any of the tongues, so she stood up and called for attention, then she addressed the multitude in Latin. Two climbers answered and those were her friends for the evening. The bad weather persisted and they were turned back from the top of the Matterhorn four times, so they went to Africa and took a fleet of camels into the desert.

Jessie was an early skier and a literate reporter of her outings. "In nothing is Katahdin more praiseworthy," she wrote, "than for the enjoyment it affords to bad skiers." She had a hike-to cabin on the slope of Mt. Chocorua and she was a year-round habitué of Pinkham Notch, where Joe Dodge regarded her with affection and respect. Jessie was thirty-eight years old in 1932 and she went to Pinkham to spend the Christmas season with Joe and his family.

Winter had not taken hold in Pinkham. There was only four inches of snow on the ground and it had been raining for several days, but on December 31 the temperature was dropping from 51° to 8°, the wind was gusting up to 40 miles an hour, and late in the afternoon the drizzly rain turned to snow flurries. Undaunted, Jessie left Pinkham by the trail called the Old Jackson Road, reached the Mount Washington auto road after two miles, hiked six more miles up the auto road to the summit, and spent the night in the frigid shelter of Camden Cottage.

During the night, the wind veered from the southeast into the northwest, the sky cleared, and the temperature dropped below zero. The next morning, New Year's Day, Jessie descended by way of Boott Spur to the AMC cabins in Pinkham Notch. Later she wrote, "Nowhere had I seen snow conditions that seemed to make solitary skiing a desirable proposition for the next day. I had worn crampons the whole time and did not feel that an elementary acquaintance with stem turns would avail me very much on the hard crust of the trails."

The AMC encampment included the house Joe built for his family in 1928 and the two log cabins that were not yet rearranged and joined to form the Trading Post of later years. Jessie had supper with Joe and his family, then she walked three miles down the road to the Glen House; the caretaker kept a few rooms open for winter hikers and she knew that a group from the Harvard Mountaineering Club was there. Jessie hoped to find some Harvards to accompany her up to Huntington Ravine the next day and have a look at the gullies, and Walter Sturges agreed to go with her. After breakfast the next morning they started up with crampons, ice axes, carabiners, two ice pitons, and 120 feet of rope. There are seven climbing gullies in the ravine: Escape, South, Odell, Pinnacle, Central, Yale, and Damnation. Jessie and Walter decided that Odell Gully offered, as she put it, "a tolerable problem."

The first winter ascent of the gully was less than four years past. It was led in March 1929 by Noel Odell of the Harvard Mountaineering Club, who had already earned his place in mountaineering history: he'd been on the epochal British Everest Expedition of 1924 in which Mallory and Irvine disappeared in the mists just below the summit and were never seen again. Odell Gully in Huntington Ravine had been the goal of AMC groups since 1929, and Jessie had been a member of two of them. All those trips had been in March or April, when there was better snow and more tolerant weather.

Odell Gully is on the left side of the ravine and the approach rises over a broad scree slope, then winter climbers find a steep narrow ascent with several frozen waterfalls. A three-man rope from Yale had climbed

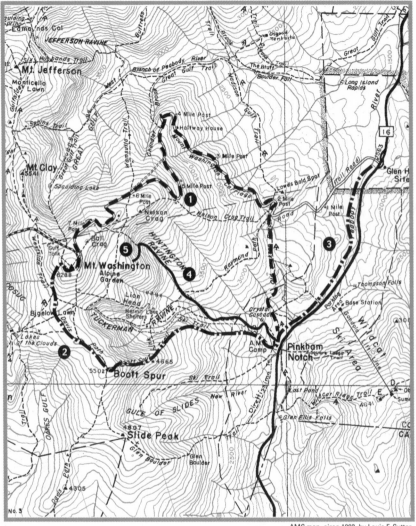

AMC map, circa 1992, by Louis F. Cutter

1 Climbed auto road first day (dash line)
2 Descended by Boott Spur second day (dash-dot-dash)
3 Walked to Glen House after supper (dash-dot-dash)
4 Up Huntington Ravine third day
5 Fell in Odell Gulley

here the day before and they did not like what they found; the ice was brittle and they thought the snow was dangerously unstable. Now Jessie and Walter agreed that they would not force the issue. This policy was further recommended by the fact that they had never climbed together and neither knew the habits or capacities of the other.

They climbed the snow-covered scree to a prominent rock just at the beginning of the serious terrain. They had lunch and then roped up. They decided that Jessie would select the route on the basis of her greater experience, and her first decision was that they should change leads often because the day was cold and a strong wind was blowing down the gully. Jessie knew from experience that a person standing on belay would get chilled quickly. She also felt that this would allow each of them to become familiar with the way the other one moved.

The first pitch resembled the frozen snowpack that Jessie had found in previous late-winter climbs up here. She thought she'd be all right on crampons, but approaching the first steep pitch she chopped a few steps as a test. Walter Sturges led up to the first frozen waterfall. He kicked steps to a rock at the extreme right side of the steep ice, then as he moved to his left Jessie drove her ice axe into the snow to see if there was underlying ice which might increase the danger of a slide.

Walter cut handholds and footholds across the ice, and when Jessie followed him she cut some of the holds deeper and was surprised to find hard water-ice. She set a piton here, then led over the next pitch of ice. This was hard work and complicated by a bitter wind sweeping down the gully, but she reached a sloping shelf of glare ice and stopped to consider their situation. She was a rather small woman, she didn't consider herself to be very strong, and she realized that she could not hold Walter from the stance she had, so she drove in a piton before he started up.

Odell Gully forks at this point, and they started up the right side on a rather easy ice slope to the second frozen waterfall. This was not as steep as the first one but it looked higher and more complicated. Jessie was surprised by this, too, she'd never seen ice here nor had she ever heard of any. Wisps of cloud were blowing down the gully and she wondered if she and Walter would be able to see each other if the clouds got much thicker. Nevertheless, she wanted to get to the second pitch of ice because she thought it might be wiser to move to the right at that point and go up the rocks, even though this route would not be much easier on the glaze that covered them.

While she was considering these factors and the time they had taken so far, she chopped a stance for Walter and called down to him to knock out their lower piton and bring it up. Still thinking of the difference in their size, she decided he should drive that piton at the stance she was cutting and she'd set the next one when she was out on the severe section of ice, or near the rocks if she decided to go up that way. Then, she thought, they'd be secure even if the clouds thickened and they lost sight of each other.

The lower piton was about halfway across the ice toward Jessie's stance and Walter reached to take it out. He hit it quite hard, and it came out easily. The disparity between his large effort and the piton's small resistance threw him off balance and he slipped out of his step and slid down the ice on his face. Up above, Jessie saw the rope begin to run out and she realized that something had happened at the other end.

She dropped her ice axe and lunged for the rope, hoping at the same time that he hadn't pulled out the lower piton. Walter felt a slight pop in the rope as Jessie took the strain. It seemed for a moment that his fall had stopped, then Jessie was torn off her stance. In the slow motion of a dream she felt herself sailing down the 50-degree face, never touching anything until she hit the lower pitch of ice about 140 feet below the shelf she'd been standing on. Jessie hit the ice upside down, taking the force of the blow on her head and shoulder.

Moments like this divide us into two camps. It's a matter of time: some will say later that everything seemed to happen at once, others find that time slowed down, everything appeared in bright detail and the mind provided extended observations. As Jessie hurtled headfirst down the gully, she thought, "This is grotesque, if true." Then she took inventory of her physical sensations and thought, "It probably is true." In fact, her neck and shoulder were broken, there were five fractures in her jaw, and severe lacerations in her neck and head.

Then Jessie concentrated on slowing down. She was falling headfirst and on her back and she found it difficult to get much traction with her elbows and crampons, but she tried. Then she was swept with anger and humiliation at the thought that she'd dropped her ice axe and could not remember where it was. As she wrote later, "I also knew that my subsequent moments of consciousness were to be quite limited. In fact, I rather hoped they were."

She thought of Walter and decided that he was dead, forgetting at the moment that he hadn't necessarily taken the same fall as she had. Then she thought that a body making such a strong pull on the rope could not be lifeless and she decided that he was alive and he probably had his ice axe, and if this was true, he could probably start slowing their fall when he got to the snow-covered scree slope. She wanted to tell Walter that the rest was up to him, though she wasn't sure if he could do anything to stop their fall. "Still, I longed to tell him that he could no longer count on any cooperation from me. I thought he ought to be told, I longed inexpressibly to tell him, but as I reached the fan I passed out." As Jessie feared, Walter did lose his ice axe and they both were finally stopped by the bushes at the bottom of the scree slope. They had fallen 800 feet.

At about eleven o'clock that morning "Stitch" Callender and John Howell had crossed the floor of Huntington Ravine, and as they put on their crampons near the lower edge of the fan they saw two other climbers coming into view behind them. Stitch and John were headed for Central Gully, and as they started their own climb they saw the other people putting on their crampons. Stitch and John spent two hours cutting steps up the ice in Central before they moved onto the milder slope above and headed toward the rocks on their right. It was just at that point, about one o'clock, that they heard someone calling for help.

Stitch called back, and although he could not see where the trouble was, he and John immediately started down. It took them about half an hour to reach the two people on the snow slope below Odell Gully.

Jessie slid 100 feet farther than her companion, but Walter was still conscious and he heard voices somewhere in the ravine. This was the moment when he shouted, then he began to move down toward Jessie. He could hear her moaning, but at first he didn't realize how badly either of them was hurt. Just as he reached her, two men appeared through the mist and Walter saw that it was his friend Stitch Callender with a companion. Stitch untangled their packs and rope and saw that Jessie was badly hurt. Stitch and John tried to make Jessie comfortable with their extra clothes, but they quickly realized that more help was needed than they could provide, so Stitch started down the ravine at a run, heading for the highway three miles away. Walter Sturges followed, making his way through the rocks on the floor of the ravine, moving very slowly.

The Huntington Ravine Trail soon crossed the Raymond Path and continued downslope until it met the Tuckerman Ravine Trail a mile and a quarter above the highway. These paths were narrow and they had all the humps and twists that the terrain dictated, but travel habits on Mount Washington had just been dramatically changed. The Forest Service had built a new trail from Hermit Lake down to the AMC camp at the highway. Work began in 1930 and now it was a smoothly-graded route, 15-feet wide, a main street in a land of goat paths.

Stitch reached the junction of the Huntington Trail and the new trail and kept running. Three hundred yards later he came upon Bradford Washburn and a group of six other men from the Harvard Mountaineering Club.

Few people knew the area better than Brad. He'd been fascinated by the mountain ever since he was a boy and while he was still in prep school he wrote *Bradford on Mount Washington*, the story of a 1928 climb he and two friends made during their March vacation. Now Brad was twenty-two years old and president of the Harvard Mountaineering Club, and he'd spent the holiday season with six other Harvards working on the cabin the club was building a mile and a half below Hermit Lake.

Brad climbed to the summit the day before and this morning he'd come down over Lion Head in a 60-mph wind, noticing as he descended that the clouds that settled on the summit at sunset were now down to the 4,500-foot level, near the floor of both Tuckerman and Huntington Ravines. He went on to the Harvard cabin to meet his mates and a little after two o'clock they gathered up their gear and started for Boston. Each of them had a Yukon packboard with 30 feet of rope and they also had a dull axe they'd have sharpened in Boston. A Yukon packboard is a wooden frame with two vertical slats and four cross braces, and remarkably heavy loads can be tied on and carried quite easily. They'd just passed the Forest Service work camp at the junction of the new Tuckerman Trail and the Huntington Ravine Trail when they heard Stitch Callender yelling at them from behind.

If Stitch had been just a few minutes earlier or later he would have missed Brad's crew, but now he told them that Jessie Whitehead and Walter Sturges had fallen in Odell Gulley, that Jessie was badly hurt and still in the ravine, and Walter was also in bad shape but making his slow way down the trail. He said that Brad's group should get back up to the ravine and try to find Jessie because Walter had told him she probably wouldn't survive the coming night without help. They huddled briefly and realized that their strengthened party still wasn't enough, so Stitch ran on down to Pinkham for more help while Brad and his crew headed back up to the accident. There's a level stretch on the Huntington Ravine Trail just before it starts through the boulder field on the floor of the ravine and they found Walter Sturges there. By now he was only semi-conscious and not able to tell them exactly where Jessie was, but he was still moving, so Brad left three of his crew to help Walter down toward Pinkham. The three Harvards remaining with Brad still had their Yukons and ropes and the dull axe, so they cut two slender spruce trees and rigged the trees with their packboards for a lash-up stretcher and started out to find Jessie.

Conditions were not good. After a week of rain the weather had cooled, the rocks were glazed with ice, and new snow had fallen to hide almost everything underfoot. It was this uncertain combination that had persuaded Jessie not to go skiing two days earlier, and Brad found the going more treacherous than even his own large experience would have liked.

Brad's crew found Jessie huddled in the middle of the trail about a hundred yards above the boulder field. In fact, they almost stepped on her, because the wind-driven snow had nearly covered her already. They brushed away the snow and discovered a sight that is still vivid in Brad's memory after sixty-six years: "All the front part of her scalp was bare bone, with her hair upside-down on the back of her skull — a dreadful sight. She shrieked in pain as we untangled her and got her onto our little stretcher, to which we tied her with another of our packboard ropes."

They made Jessie as secure as they could and started down over the boulders and the ice and the snow. Jessie was conscious and in terrible pain, so they were as careful as they could be, but it was very tough going through the boulders. The shortest day of the year was only just past, the sun was long gone behind the ridge above them, and they'd only gotten as far as the trees on the floor of the ravine when night began to fall. They had almost three miles to go.

When Stitch Callender got to Pinkham, "Itchy" Mills and Wendell Lees were just driving out of the parking lot with the AMC truck, headed down the notch to meet the train in Glen. Stitch yelled and they turned around to join Joe Dodge and Johnny Hall in a dash up the mountain. They met Brad and his crew just below Huntington Ravine, moving slowly. Jessie recognized Joe and she said, very clearly, "Joe, give me a drink of milk and take me to the hospital. I'm sick."

The combined forces shifted Jessie to the stretcher that Joe's crew had with them, but the carry didn't get much easier; the terrain was rough, the dense spruce growth was only cleared for single-file hikers, and their wide carry kept crowding them off the trail.

Johnny Hall was coming up behind Joe's group and he had blankets and another stretcher, and when he caught up with Joe and Brad he realized that they had the situation in hand. He'd passed Walter Sturges on his way up and he decided that his equipment could be put to better use by the three Harvards helping Walter, so he turned around to find them. This left Brad and Joe Dodge and seven other men, enough to shift off as they carried Jessie. Joe's group had flashlights and with this improvement they decided to cut across to the new Tuckerman Trail; it would be somewhat longer but certainly faster than continuing down the old Huntington Trail to the lower junction. As they were working their way through the woods the deep laceration on Jessie's neck hemorrhaged, so Joe stuffed handfuls of snow into the wound and stopped the bleeding. Most of the men knew Jessie and now they were dumbfounded. All through the jolting carry down the mountain, Jessie cursed volubly and loudly, with nary a stammer or a stutter anywhere in her litany of pain.

By now they were out of the wind vortex churning down from the ravine and even though the temperature was approaching zero they felt warm enough to strip to their shirt sleeves. They'd left most of the clouds behind, too, and a quarter moon was showing through. They reached the wide avenue of the new Tuckerman Trail at about 8:30, and now their progress over the thin firm snow was as rapid as anyone could hope for. They reached the lower junction of the Huntington Trail in twenty minutes and found the toboggan and some blankets that Joe's party had left on the way up, so they put Jessie's improvised litter on the toboggan and reached Pinkham at 9:25.

Meanwhile, Walter Sturges had used up the last of his strength, so Johnny Hall and three Harvards carried him more than a mile and a half from the crossing of the Raymond Path down to Pinkham. Teen Dodge, Joe's wife, gave him hot tea and turkey soup and put a hot-water bottle under his feet; then, just as Jessie was brought in, Walter was started down the road to the hospital seventeen miles away in North Conway.

Jessie's injuries dictated all possible speed to the hospital. By this time she was struggling against her pain and her restraints, so the rescue party swaddled her in blankets for both warmth and bracing and put her in the back of the AMC truck. Wendell Lees climbed in with her and held her head steady while Joe drove the truck as fast as he could down the Pinkham road, but with the winter conditions, the primitive surface and marginal maintenance, it was about like driving crossways over a farmer's plowed field. Later Joe said, "I can't understand it. We were rougher than a son of a bitch with her — had to be. But she lived."

The AMC had no telephone in Pinkham Notch, so someone had gone to the Glen House to call Harold Shedd, the principal doctor in the North Conway hospital. He heard the ring just as he was walking down the steps of his house on his way to visit his wife in Boston.

Dr. Shedd was typical of the medical arts in his day: no matter what the occasion or the details, if care was needed he provided it. After he'd treated Jessie's most threatening injuries he called her family in

Cambridge and told them that she was out of danger, but there was one disturbing consequence: when she came out of the anesthesia there was a neurological problem he had not expected: she had a severe stutter. Jessie's family told Dr. Shedd not to worry about it, she'd stuttered all her life.

Jessie was admitted to the North Conway hospital shortly before midnight on January 2 and she was discharged on May 16, a stay of 136 days. The hospital charge was one dollar a day, with home-cooked meals; surgery and various other attentions added about $100 more.

AFTERMATH

$\mathcal{T}$wo months after Jessie was released from the hospital she was back up on Mount Washington, looking for her ice axe and anything else she might have lost. She continued to work at Widener Library and she continued her year-round trips to the mountains, sometimes staying in her cabin on Chocorua, sometimes with Joe Dodge in Pinkham Notch, and sometimes with us in Jackson.

When father finished telling us the story of Jessie and her terrible fall in Huntington Ravine, he'd tell about Jessie and the King's Broad Arrow Pine.

The King's Pines were the trees that the quartermasters of George III marked in colonial days. Europe had used up its supply of trees suitable for the masts of ocean-going ships, so the virgin forests of the New World were a critical military and commercial resource. The mast trees were marked with a broad arrow cut into the bark, and if any colonial yeoman used such a tree for his own purposes he was severely punished. It was known that some of these trees survived the age of sail, and it was rumored that even 150 years later they were sometimes found by determined explorers of the deep woods. Jessie was just such an explorer, but she'd never yet found one of the King's Pines in her many lonely hikes. Still, though, she kept trying.

Then the great hurricane of 1938 struck New England. It came ashore on Long Island, it went straight up the Connecticut River, and when it reached Jackson it was still so strong that it lifted our four-car garage off its foundations. Vast tracts of the mountain forests were knocked flat and Jessie was heartbroken; she was certain that there must be a few of the King's Pines still standing in some undiscovered glen and she was determined to find one. Now it seemed obvious that she had lost her last chance.

It was not obvious to Jessie. She was sure that a certain distant corner of the forest still had a colonial relic and the summer after the hurricane she went there and was unreported for many days. The destruction was terrible and one day she was crawling on her hands and knees, trying to get through an endless blowdown. Jessie's sweater snagged on a broken branch and she twisted around to attend to it. As she looked up, she saw above her head the mark of the King's broad arrow.

CHAPTER TEN

WRONG-HEADED
FROM THE BEGINNING

There was a time when the source of misfortune lay outside of ourselves; it might be the result of a curse, or a poison philtre, or a misalignment of the stars, which is the origin of the word disaster, but it was not of our own doing. My father did not believe in such fancies, he always said that people got into trouble because they didn't use their head.

Father was certainly right when it came to Simon Joseph and his two friends in 1933. Their plans for a Mount Washington climb were wrong-headed from the beginning, a textbook of accumulating errors, the inevitable misfortune created a great stir among New England climbers, and its many consequences still mark the Presidential Range. All this, however, came too late for Simon Joseph.

• SIMON JOSEPH •
JUNE 1933

*O*n Friday, June 17, 1933, Simon Joseph, Gerald Golden, and Charles Robbins took the train from Boston north to the station at the top of Crawford Notch. They were all college age; Simon was nineteen and a sophomore at Harvard. They planned to sleep in the woods near the Crawford House that night, get food at the hotel, and then hike across the Southern Peaks to the Lakes of the Clouds Hut.

The site of the Crawford House had deep memories of hikers; the patronymic Crawfords built the first trail to the summit of Mount Washington in 1816 and it began here, and Frederick Strickland started his 1849 climb from the family's inn here. In 1933, the most recent edition of the hotel loomed like a great white ocean liner anchored at the top of the notch and it had become a rather starchy place that sheltered five presidents, assorted captains of industry, and P. T. Barnum.

The three boys from Boston were intent on saving money and they were not provided with starchy clothing. History is silent on this point, but it seems likely that they hoped to get something to eat in the help's dining room next to the kitchen. The hoteliers thought otherwise and told the boys that they could find food at the store maintained by the proprietor of the Willey House, at the site of the disaster celebrated by Nathaniel Hawthorne in *The Ambitious Guest*. This was a three-mile walk down the steep Crawford Notch road and then back again, and the trio decided they didn't want to make the effort. They each had two blankets, so they curled up to sleep in the woods, though it wasn't a very comfortable night: the temperature was down near 40° and there were fairly heavy spatterings of rain. The next morning they again tried for some food at the hotel and they were again turned away. Thus prepared, they started the hike of 6.8 miles along the Southern Peaks to the Lakes of the Clouds.

The Crawford Path is one of the most delightful outings in the White Mountains and the terrain is easy. The Northern Peaks were sharply cut by the glaciers and they're jagged pyramids above the main ridge. The ice sheet slid over the first five of the Southern Peaks, so they have rounded summits joined by moderate depressions in the ridge; only Monroe has a jagged outline. The Crawford Path was graded for horse travel. It rises by easy grades to Clinton, then turns north along the ridge to Pleasant Dome, which may be avoided by following a bypass. Franklin has so small a rise that it hardly seems like a separate summit at all, and there's another bypass around the sharper summit of Monroe.

The Southern Peaks are generally lower than the Northern Peaks and the Crawford Path flirts with timberline for almost its whole length as it climbs toward Mount Washington. The easy grades and long views, the quick access to the shelter of dense spruce, and the connecting trails back to the valley, all make it an excellent climb for a day of dubious weather.

Sunday, June 18, was a day of dubious weather. Simon Joseph and his two friends left warm early-summer days in Boston and they did not anticipate the climatic difference their northerly trip would create. This morning the temperature at the Crawford House was still in the 40s, wind-driven rain was falling when they started up the trail, and they had not brought anything beyond the clothes they'd need for a summer evening.

The trio had no food with them and they knew the Lakes of the Clouds Hut was not yet open for the season, but they thought there would probably be some other hikers staying in the off-season refuge room at the hut who would probably have some extra food they'd pass around to new arrivals. If that didn't work out, Joseph and his friends planned to break into the closed part of the hut; surely there would be some nonperishable food left from the previous summer.

The hikers were in the clouds long before they reached timberline on Mt. Clinton. Charles Robbins was getting along better than the other two, so at some point after they reached the crest of the ridge he hurried on toward the Lakes Hut. The conditions up ahead would not improve: the 8:00 A.M. readings at the Mount Washington Observatory showed a temperature of 33° with a northwest wind gusting to 75 mph and carrying sleet and snow.

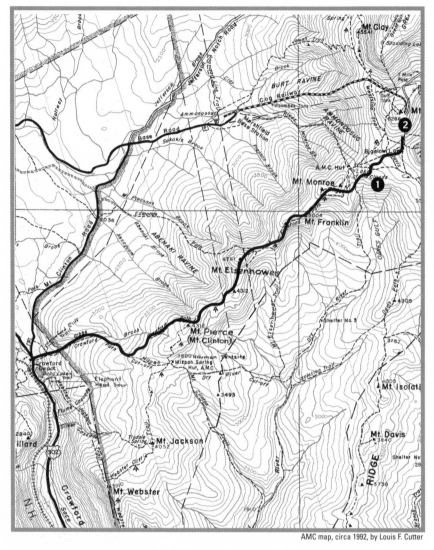

AMC map, circa 1992, by Louis F. Cutter

1 Missed turn to Lakes Hut
2 Died just short of Southside Trail

There was indeed a party of hikers in the refuge room at the hut. Five youngsters from Massachusetts had come in Saturday night and stayed on through Sunday, pinned down by the weather. Several other hikers came in during the morning and ten more came by at about noon, heading down the Ammonoosuc Ravine Trail and the quick shelter they'd find there, but first they left a note in the logbook saying that conditions up on the summit cone were very unpleasant. Their retreat was wise and time-honored; the original name for the Ammonoosuc Ravine was Escape Ravine.

The next entry in the logbook shows that Charles Robbins came in at about three in the afternoon, very much reduced by the weather and by the lack of any food since early in the previous day in Boston. The group waiting out the storm in the Lakes refuge room spent twenty minutes getting him warmed up, then John Ellsworth and Don Plympton started out to find Simon Joseph and Gerald Golden. They headed south along the Crawford Path and found Gerald on the bare, rocky terrain between Monroe and Franklin, about a mile from the hut. He seemed lethargic, but he was on his feet and moving in the right direction and they asked him where the other fellow was, meaning Simon. Gerald said that his friend was ahead of him on the trail, so the two rescuers turned in that direction, back toward the hut.

The Lakes of the Clouds Hut did not exist when the Crawford Path was laid out, so the bridle path followed the height-of-land along the rounded ridge that leads from Mt. Monroe to the beginning of the summit cone of Mount Washington. The lakes are west of the height-of-land and about 150 feet lower, so when the hut was built in 1915 the Crawford Path was redirected toward the lakes. The new trail turned sharply west on the flats at the northeast edge of Monroe and the original location was abandoned. The old path was still visible, though; rocks were rearranged to make a better footway, conspicuous depressions were worn into the terrain in many places, and grass and moss had not yet covered the wear of eighty years. The two rescuers were hurrying to find Simon and in their haste they missed the abrupt turn and continued straight on along the old path. John Ellsworth quickly realized the mistake and they went back to the junction and down to the hut, where they reported that they'd found Gerald Golden, but not Simon Joseph. So ended Sunday.

Monday brought somewhat more tolerable weather and a group from the refuge room finished their trip and went down by way of the AMC headquarters in Pinkham Notch, which did not yet have a telephone. They reported that a fellow seemed to be missing up near the Lakes Hut, but they were not good on the details. Meanwhile, Gerald Golden and Charles Robbins had recovered some strength and they joined two of the stay-overs and went looking for Simon. The hut was scheduled to open for the summer season that day, and at about 4:30 in the afternoon AMC hutmen Ellis Jump and Don McNaughton arrived and started putting things in order. Soon Gerald and Charles returned with the two other searchers and no news of their missing friend, so they went up to the summit and found Alex McKenzie at the weather observatory and told him that their companion was unreported for a whole day.

Alex was a member of the crew that established the observatory the previous October and he'd been there through the winter. Now he was a bit skeptical. He remembered several times when winter hikers came in with dire reports of lost companions and each alarm proved to be unfounded. Nevertheless, he took two steps. The observatory crew had improved the time during their long winter isolation by building a twenty-pound two-way radio and they sent this breakthrough unit down to the hut to see if it would help with the search. Alex also opened the radio link to the Forest Service office in the town of Twin Mountain, twelve miles west of the summit, and the district ranger said he'd organize a search party and come up to the hut the next day, which was Tuesday.

Tuesday was election day in Twin Mountain and the district ranger could find only one person who wanted to climb the Southern Peaks on the chance that someone was missing. The two of them searched the middle section of the trail the boys had taken and found nothing. They returned to their office in Twin Mountain that evening and called the district supervisor in Laconia, who authorized funds for a ten-man search party. While this was going on, the two hiking partners of Simon Joseph also went down to the valley and hitched rides another eighteen miles to the Willey House in Crawford Notch, where they made a telephone call to Simon's parents. Their son had now been missing for two days and this was the first time they'd heard about it. Mr. Joseph immediately called the governor of Massachusetts, who organized a search party and dispatched it to the northern mountains.

On Wednesday, these two groups converged on the Lakes of the Clouds with a total of nineteen men. One group was led by District Ranger Spinney of the Forest Service and New Hampshire State Fire Chief Boomer. They took the Edmands Path up the west flank of the ridge to join the Crawford Path between Pleasant Dome and Franklin, then turned north and searched the middle section of the Crawford Path. The other group was led by District Ranger Van Alstine; they climbed the Ammonoosuc Ravine Trail to the Lakes Hut and searched southward toward the other group. No one found any trace of Simon Joseph.

On Thursday, Assistant State Forester Hale reached the hut with a third search party, but the morning brought thickening weather and the searchers stayed inside the hut. The air cleared later in the day and all three groups renewed their work. At the same time an airplane made repeated low passes along the length of the Southern Peaks and over the slopes at the head of Oakes Gulf, which runs the length of the ridge on the east side. Mr. Spinney and Mr. Boomer led their groups back to the areas they'd been searching on Wednesday, while Mr. Hale's group went out along the Camel Trail leading from the hut eastward across the head of Oakes Gulf.

At 4:00 Thursday afternoon, Mr. Hale's group found the body of Simon Joseph near the old Crawford Path. He had indeed been ahead of Gerald Golden and he'd gotten to the place where the new section of the Crawford Path turned left toward the hut, the place where John Ellsworth and Don Plympton had briefly followed the old path, then corrected their mistake.

Simon Joseph followed the old path, too, and he did not correct his mistake. The bridle path ran fairly straight along the crest of the Southern Peaks, in fact, today's trail is hardly changed at all from the first location. The old path continued straight at the junction by Monroe and ran about twenty yards across a pebbly flat, then it wandered and curled across the broad saddle for more than half a mile until it reached the Davis Path. This route makes no sense except for horses; the Crawford family liked to keep their animals on the soft tundra-like soil as much as possible, and they stayed away from ledge and areas of loose or rough rock.

That old location had been officially abandoned after the new trail was built to the Lakes of the Clouds Hut, but the old footway made by the horses was still much more obvious than the new route. Simon must have been well aware of his surroundings at this point because he kept on the crooked path, stepping on the very place where Father Bill Curtis died thirty-three years earlier, but he finally ran out of strength forty paces short of the anchor bolts remaining from the refuge built after the Curtis-Ormsbee episode. At this point the strong northwest wind would have been hitting Simon on the left side of his face, so he turned away from the icy blast and made his way twenty paces across a grassy patch to an outcropping of rocks on the lee side of the ridge. There's a high-walled split in the rocks here; it's floored with grass, a soft and well-sheltered spot, and Simon lay down to rest on this bed.

After two days of uninterrupted bad judgment, Simon had finally done something right in finding this shelter. But those who believe in star-crossed enterprise would note that if Simon had looked left instead of right as he stood on the Crawford Path he would have seen the Lakes of the Clouds Hut only a few easy minutes away. Moreover, if he'd kept going for a few moments longer he would have found the Camel Path just beyond the iron bolts and a sign there directing him to the hut a quarter of a mile away. Simon did not get up from his rest, though, and he died on that grassy bed with his blankets still rolled up.

AFTERMATH

$\mathcal{N}$ews of the complex situation surrounding Simon Joseph's death spread quickly, and the results were both immediate and long lasting.

The first concerned radio. As the nineteenth century turned, virtually nothing of what we think of as modern times had emerged. One of the first hints of the world we now take for granted was the amazing device put together by a young Italian named Guglielmo Marconi, who successfully transmitted a wireless telegraph signal for about a mile in 1896, what would become known as radio. But Marconi was not a disinterested scientist; he was more like an electronic entrepreneur and he had his eye out for the main chance. This came in the fall of 1899, when that year's edition of the America's Cup yacht races were scheduled for the ocean off Sandy Hook, at the northeast corner of New Jersey. James Gordon Bennett was the editor of *The New York Herald* and he thought it would be a splendid thing if up-to-the-minute news of the races could be flashed from the offshore excitement to his downtown editorial offices. So he sent the proposition and an offer of $5,000 to Signor Marconi, who came to America to cash in both the check and the publicity and create the world's first ship-to-shore radio contact.

It was an important moment. From the wine-dark seas of Homeric legend until that day, ships at sea had always been alone. Ocean communications were limited to line of sight with flags or lanterns; beyond that they were at the mercy of the many gods of the sky and the deeps. Now they could send messages over the horizon, but, perhaps following Marconi's commercial impulse, ship-to-shore telegraph was seen as a novelty, a way to send birthday greetings and other such trifles, and operators were licensed by the Marconi Company as if the Italian meant to keep radio as a proprietary account.

One licensee was Jack Irwin, at the Marconi station at Siasconset on the eastern shore of Nantucket. Another was Jack Binns, the Marconi operator on the White Star liner *Republic*. On the night of January 23, 1909, the *Republic* collided with the *Florida*, inbound from Italy, and received a mortal wound. Marconi operators did know of a distress call, but it had never been used; it was CQD, standing for "Seek You — Danger." Now Jack Binns sent that code and Jack Irwin picked it up, and for the rest of the day the rescue of the *Republic*'s crew and its 1,500 passengers was directed by radio. This proved the true usefulness of Marconi's novelty, but CQD was an awkward series in Morse code, it was (–.–. – –.– –..). So it was changed to the simpler (... – – – ...), which was SOS, a letter-clump standing for no words but easier to transmit under stress.

The rescue of the *Republic*'s passengers created an enormous sensation and Jack Binns was the unwilling hero of autograph seekers, tabloids, popular songs, and a fictionalized film by Vitagraph. Jack fled home to England and grateful White Star executives offered him the most prestigious Marconi job they had, but at the last moment he fell in love and asked for a later posting. This cost Jack Binns his chance to sail with the *Titanic*.

In the coming years Guglielmo Marconi continued to devote more time to his reputation than to his laboratory, and the effect was to freeze the official dogmas of radio at the rather primitive stage represented by his low-frequency transmissions. It wasn't that higher frequencies were not known or the necessary equipment was too difficult to make, the problem was that the sainted Marconi had not gone in that direction.

This led to a curious situation in which eager youngsters building high-frequency radio sets at their kitchen tables were often considerably ahead of the industry. They formed a loose sort of juvenile federation which they named the Radio Club of America, or RCA, and Joe Dodge was in that loop, reassuring his aunt that he didn't have to open the window to let in the radio waves.

The Mount Washington Road

This splendidly hyperbolic view of the Presidential Range was published in 1872. The foreground shows the eight-mile carriage road to the summit of Mount Washington and the sunlight picks out "Camp House" in the lower right. (Bartlett town library)

The Southern Presidentials, as seen from Mount Washington. (Photograph by Robert Kozlow)

Mount Washington, with Tuckerman Ravine on the left and Huntington Ravine on the right. (AMC collection)

The Northern Presidentials as seen from Mount Washington over Great Gulf: Mounts Clay, Jefferson, and Adams, with the beginning of the summit ridge of Madison on the far right. (Photograph by Robert Kozlow)

Nineteenth-century gentlefolk like to climb their mountains sitting down, as in this Winslow Homer view on the Crawford Path up Mount Washington. (Mount Washington Observatory collection)

Crawford Notch, circa 1860. Early settlers had no way through the major mountain ranges of northern New Hampshire until a narrow gap was found in 1771. Today the gap is U.S. Rte. 302. This picture shows the route at about the time Frederick Strickland stopped at Thomas Crawford's hostelry, just beyond the rocks on the right. (Mount Washington Observatory collection)

The only known photograph of Lizzie Bourne, used as the basis for the portrait painted three years after her death. (Mount Washington Observatory collection)

The Thompson Bridle Path, built up the east side of Mount Washington in 1851 and later converted to a carriage road leading to the summit. In 1855, Lizzie Bourne and Dr. Ball both took shelter here in the Camp House, which housed workers. It later became known as the Halfway House. (Mount Washington Observatory collection)

Lizzie Bourne's final resting spot years after her death, just yards from the safety of the Tip Top House. Baldwin Coolidge, photographer. (AMC collection)

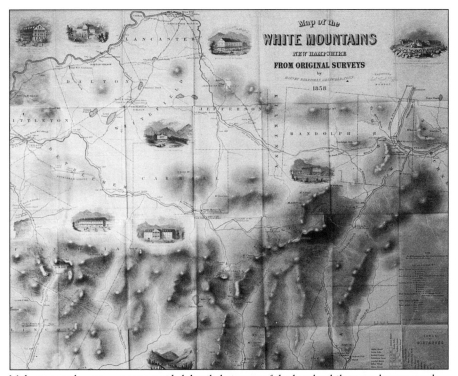

Mid-nineteenth century maps provided detailed pictures of the hotels while vague humps stood for the Presidential Range. Dr. Ball had no map at all when he started to climb Mount Washington in October 1855. (Mount Washington Observatory collection)

Tucker Sno-Cats descending the summit cone on Mount Washington toward the flats known as "Homestretch" circa 1960. Dr. Ball mistook this area for the summit and nearly perished before heading down toward two more days of peril. (Mount Washington Observatory collection.)

His mouth too cold to melt snow, Dr. Ball drank from water collected in these glacial basins. (Nicholas Howe)

The immensely popular "snow arch" in Tuckerman Ravine became a destination for hikers and in 1886 it killed Sewall Faunce. (AMC collection)

"Father Bill" Curtis and Allan Ormsbee approached the AMC meeting on the summit by way of the 8.2-mile Crawford Path. They encountered a fierce storm and took shelter by burrowing into this clump of dwarf spruce. (Nicholas Howe)

This cross marked the spot where Allan Ormsbee perished. (Mount Washington Observatory collection)

Until it was stolen by vandals, a brass plaque marked Father Curtis's final resting spot. (AMC collection)

The deaths of Curtis and Ormsbee led the AMC to create the first hiker's shelter on the upper slopes of Mount Washington in time for the 1902 summer season. It was purposely made too oddly-shaped and uncomfortable to appeal to anyone not in dire straits. (Mount Washington Observatory collection)

Specialized clothing for recreation is a very recent innovation as the mountains count time. In 1915, Sheldon Howe, the author's father, leads the way in white shirt and tie, with his sisters Louise and Harriet in the middle, dressed in bloomers. Few people had rucksacks in those days, so Harriet has dropped her sandwiches down her bloomers and they're visible at her knee. (Howe family collection)

An early rescue along the Mount Washington Carriage Road, circa 1912. (AMC collection)

Two winter hikers survey the rime ice covering a trail sign, circa 1905. (AMC collection)

An AMC group at the original Madison Hut, spring of 1890. (AMC collection)

In 1908 a fire destroyed most of the summit buildings atop Mount Washington. An astonishing new hotel was planned, shown in this prospectus, to be served by an electric trolley. Survey work for the trolley began in 1911 but was stopped in 1912. On one of the last days of work, John Keenan disappeared in a cloud near the summit and was never seen again. (Mount Washington Observatory collection)

Joe Dodge found his life's work when he arrived at the AMC base camp in Pinkham Notch in 1922. Over the next 36 years he'd change the lives of countless hikers and save the lives of no small number of them. (Dodge family collection)

Mountain rescue used to be straightforward; here Joe Dodge carries a disabled hiker off Mount Washington. He's just passing "Lunch Rocks" in Tuckerman Ravine and he has almost three tough miles to go before reaching the AMC base camp at the highway. (Dodge family collection)

"The Stage Office" on Mount Washington housed the first year-round weather observatory in the 1870s, it was used again when observers re-occupied the summit in 1933, and Max Engelhart was serving snacks here when a storm overtook him in October 1926. (Mount Washington Observatory collection)

"Shelter" must be understood conditionally on the heights of the Presidential Range. Here snow blows in through a stoutly sheathed wall. Such conditions drove Max out the door and into a ferocious three-day ordeal. (Dodge family collection)

Joe Dodge's search for Max Englehart was greatly hampered by the snow drifts that form on the heights of the Presidential Range. (Mount Washington Observatory collection)

Sylvester Marsh's cog railway reached the summit on July 4, 1869. The first engine was officially Hero No. 1, known as Peppersass (seen behind several newer models on the summit). In 1929 Peppersass was brought out of deep retirement for one more ceremonial climb, which would prove fatal for Daniel Rossiter. (AMC collection)

Jessie Whitehead (left): scholar, early champion of high-achieving women, and an ardent mountaineer. In January 1933 she fell 800 feet down Huntington Ravine and lived, which did not surprise people who knew her. (Courtesy of George Cleveland, photo by Jean Smith)

The Intercollegiate Outing Club Association chose the Great Gulf shelter as their camp for their annual September hike in 1934. After a torrential rainstorm the tiny stream in the foreground flooded the shelter. The river just behind the photographer rose correspondingly and cost Jeremy Pierce his life. (Guy Shorey photo, Mount Washington Observatory collection)

Simon Joseph reached the end of his strength on the exact location of this photographer's stance. If he'd turned to the left he would have seen the AMC's Lakes of the Clouds hut, but the wind was blowing from that direction and exhausted hikers rarely turn into the wind. (Nicholas Howe)

Instead, he took a few steps downwind and lay down to rest on this sheltered patch of grass, where he died without unrolling the blankets he was carrying. Mount Washington is in the background. (Nicholas Howe)

In January of 1954, Philip and Polly Longnecker and Jacques Parysko climbed up to Tuckerman Ravine and fashioned a dugout at the base of the headwall. Polly returned to the valley, Philip and Jacques stayed in the ravine. Here Polly watches from the foreground while the recovery team digs trenches in the avalanche debris while searching for her brother's body. (George Hamilton collection)

In the 1950s, bodies were brought down from the region of Tuckerman Ravine by army-surplus Weasel. Joe Dodge is sitting astride the headlight, George Hamilton is driving. This is at the beginning of the trail to Tuckerman Ravine and hikers pass three signs warning of avalanche danger. (Dodge family collection)

Mount Washington looms over the AMC encampment in Pinkham Notch. (Photograph by Jerry Shereda, AMC collection)

Signs posted by the USFS along the Crawford Path warn hikers about the physical dangers that lie ahead. (Photograph by Robert Kozlow)

The Presidential Range makes its own weather, a result of the convergence of two jet stream tracks over the area and the sweep of prevailing winds driving warm valley air upslope into the cold air on the heights. This can create sudden and completely unexpected fog that has brought many hikers into serious trouble. (AMC collection)

A winter hiker armed with modern gear pauses before tackling the Crawford Path. (Photograph by Robert Kozlow)

The Alpine Garden spreads just below the summit ridge of Mount Washington and in the fair weather of summer enthusiasts come from all over the world to study the tiny flowering plants that have found a way to survive there. Winter conditions are often beyond the endurance of the strongest man to survive and many have died in the near vicinity. (David Stone photograph)

An observatory crewman climbs the section of the auto road known as Five-Mile Drift circa 1935. (Mount Washington Observatory collection)

The Stokes litter was developed later in Joe Dodge's tenure. Six carriers are required in each shift, with two or three shifts waiting to relieve them. These rescuers are making their way through a dense fog above timberline. (AMC collection)

In January 1984, Hugh Herr and Jeffrey Batzer climbed a gully in Huntington Ravine, then pushed on for the summit of Mount Washington in the face of rapidly worsening weather and lost their way. A large-scale search was set in motion and this group from the all-volunteer Mountain Rescue Service is huddling at the 7-Mile marker on the summer auto road. These men could go no further and they made their way down safely. Albert Dow was with another team of MRS men and he was killed in an avalanche this same afternoon. Hugh Herr and Jeffrey were found in Great Gulf and they survived. (David Stone photograph)

MacDonald Barr collapsed on the summit of Mt. Madison in the great storm of August 24, 1986. His son Tavis was able to reach the patch of dwarf spruce just above the hut and it took two crew members 40 minutes of hard work to bring him in from there, but they could not help his father higher up. (Dodge family collection)

Alex McKenzie was another of those inventive youngsters, and he and Joe stayed with it. By the early 1930s, they were leading spirits in establishing the weather observatory on the summit of Mount Washington, a place with something very much like the old isolation of the silent ships at sea. The observers rarely came down the mountain, Joe Dodge and the AMC camp in Pinkham Notch was their nearest contact with the outside world, and there was only fitful highway traffic and no telephone in Pinkham.

Joe had been one of the first few Americans to contact Europe with short-wave radio; he'd been working a short-wave set in Pinkham Notch since his summer-only tenure before 1926, and when the summit observatory opened he had a line-of-sight link to the summit. Now the plan called for the observatory to make radio contact with the Blue Hill Observatory four times a day and transmit weather data on the same schedule.

Radio traffic from Marconi sets traveled in relatively long waves and, given the practice of the day, the antennas were correspondingly long. Ocean-going ships in the days of the *Republic* and the *Titanic* usually transmitted on the 100-meter band with antennas that stretched most of the length of the ship. This was still the model in 1933, and it presented an immediate and obvious problem for operations on the summit of Mount Washington: the antenna wire would be too long to mount inside the observatory building and an outdoor antenna would be destroyed by the very reason for its existence, the violent summit weather.

The observatory crew decided to try a higher frequency and they put the shorter antenna in a stout wooden box bolted to the summer water tank on the highest point of the summit settlement. Accepted Marconi practice indicated that the higher frequencies could be used only in line-of-sight transmission and Blue Hill was over the horizon, but Joe and Alex were right: the Blue Hill transmissions were successful and a page was turned in the theory and practice of radio. Closer to home, Joe Dodge maintained daily radio contact with the summit station from opening in the fall of 1932 until war-time restrictions were imposed in 1942, then he resumed the contacts until the hour he left Pinkham Notch in 1959.

Many years later, Alex McKenzie thought back to those times. He realized that the scatter effect and bending capacity of the troposphere had been greatly under-estimated in 1933, and the success of the summit transmissions forced an important reconsideration in this area. Furthermore, the position of the antenna box on the tank was fortuitous; they'd faced it toward Blue Hill, which seemed obvious, but they didn't realize that the steel hoops and curved back wall of the water tank might work as reflectors and reinforce the signal. Furthermore, their Blue Hill schedule gave them a self-contained index to the effect of weather on the propagation of radio waves. In further contradiction of prevailing electronic wisdom, the summit crew discovered that their signal could reach New York City on certain days. This was much farther down the curve of the earth than Blue Hill and, putting this together with their weather maps, they realized that high-frequency signals were reinforced by traveling along a weather front and were also boosted by traveling through bands of certain temperatures, a method whales use to send their sonic messages across thousands of miles of ocean water.

The more immediate result of the Simon Joseph episode was the success of the twenty-pound portable unit the summit crew sent down to the Lakes Hut to help coordinate the search.

Radios of those early days were imposing. They had heavy metal frames and coiling cables and ranks of glowing vacuum tubes and black boxes, with numerous separate elements ranged along the shelf; this is why a complete radio was called a "set," a term that survives in today's television market. So when the observatory crew of 1933 made a twenty-pound portable, they achieved an important breakthrough.

The AMC was so impressed by reports of the Joseph episode that their high-elevation huts — Lakes, Madison, and Greenleaf — were equipped with portable two-way radios against the needs of search and rescue. Word spread, and by 1938 the Swiss were equipping their mountain refuges with thirty-pound portables.

The most immediate and visible result of Simon Joseph's death was the project to rebuild all the cairns marking the trails above timberline on the Presidential Range: the cairns on the more popular trails were raised to a height of four feet and the interval was tightened to fifty feet. This enormous job was done by members of the Civilian Conservation Corps, "CCC boys" as they were always called.

The CCC was one of the earliest of President Franklin Roosevelt's New Deal initiatives. Roosevelt took office on March 4, 1933 and on March 5 he convened a meeting of the secretaries of labor, agriculture, interior, and war, the director of the bureau of the budget, the judge advocate general of the army, and the solicitor of the department of the interior. They roughed out the plan for the CCC, the enabling legislation went to Congress on March 21, it passed on March 31, and on April 7 the first of four-million CCC boys signed up.

About two months later, a troop of CCC boys was assigned to work on the cairns of the Presidential Range. They were bunked three apiece in the AMC huts at Madison Springs on the Northern Peaks and at the Lakes of the Clouds, and two or three of them stayed in the summit hotel on Mount Washington. This caused some concern. The CCC was organized along distinctly military principles and soon after the CCC boys were on station, an army captain blustered into Joe's office in Pinkham Notch and inquired, with some heat, if there was enough air for the boys to breathe up there above timberline. Joe assured him that air was supplied in pretty generous quantities up there.

That summer the U.S. Forest Service put up the first generation of yellow metal signs on all trails that led above timberline: "STOP: This is a fine trail for hiking, but be sure you are in good physical condition, well rested and fed, have sufficient clothing, emergency food and equipment. Travel above timberline is hazardous. Climatic changes are sudden and severe at all seasons."

There were further consequences. Simon Joseph was the thirteenth person to die on the Presidential Range, and the New Hampshire State Development Commission launched an initiative designed to prevent further deaths. They sent word to the Appalachian Mountain Club, the Dartmouth Outing Club, and the Mountain Hotel Proprietors Association asking for their help in a crusade to educate hikers. One of the leading elements in this idea was that all people planning to climb Mount Washington should be examined by an official who was competent to judge the state of their clothing, their boots, and their health, and to test their knowledge of the mountain. A similar proposal went to the New Hampshire legislature, but it did not gain enough support to merit a vote. Neither of these precautionary measures was ever heard from again.

The CCC boys did their work so well that the cairns they built have lasted to the present day with very little additional maintenance, and the yellow signs still guard trails leading above timberline.

CHAPTER ELEVEN

A DEADLY CROSSING
IN GREAT GULF

*S*eptember of 1934 was not a good time to be starting college. The Great Depression was five years old and its grip was still growing tighter on the land; President Roosevelt's myriad New Deal agencies were everywhere, but they had not lifted the stock market out of the low 40s. On the other hand, more Americans were going hiking than ever before.

Several factors were at work. For one thing, the growing number of good roads in North America and increasingly reliable automobiles made backwoods outposts more accessible. Beyond that, the Depression did not close schools. Indeed, this was a period of large growth in private schools and the faculty had secure jobs, a relatively high income, and more than three months of vacation every summer. The hidden lesson here is that the more comfortably fixed American families kept their money. Finally, there was an unprecedented burst of exploration and mountaineering in North America that was discovering new mountains in the high ranges of Canada and Alaska and making first ascents that loomed large in the pages of publications such as the AMC's semi-annual *Appalachia*. Bradford Washburn led many of these expeditions, and for entry-level excursionists there were the more familiar reaches of the White Mountains with the AMC huts and dozens of *lean-to shelters to welcome them.*

My father taught at Deerfield Academy in Massachusetts, and he was the resident faculty member in the Saxton House, which was an academy dormitory with our family on the first floor and students on the second floor. In 1933, one of the students was John Pierce, conspicuous because his fine and enthusiastic singing voice could be heard all over the house. The Saxton House was not very large and my bedroom was a space under the stairs just large enough for a cot bed, and I was too young to remember John's singing.

In the fall of 1954, I was visiting Goddard College in northern Vermont as a prospective student, and when the tour was over I was deciding that I didn't like it very much. My mother had driven up with me, and while I was making the official tour she was making herself politely scarce in a far reach of the campus. She heard singing and followed the sound until she saw a man weeding a flower garden. He was on his knees in the corner of an L-shaped building, facing inwards, and my mother came up behind him and said, "John Pierce?"

It was. He was on the faculty at the college and he kept this garden in order because he could see it from his office, so he took me in hand and told me about the real Goddard. Mother and I returned to Deerfield and I packed a supply of clothes and went straight back to Goddard. I stayed there in one connection or another for eight years.

John Pierce became my closest friend on the faculty, and he and I and some other students often went hiking together. There was a chip in one of his front teeth and after I'd known him for a decent interval I asked what happened to it. He said that happened years earlier during a camping trip in Great Gulf, over on the Presidential Range. He said he'd been diving in the river and hit an underwater rock, and he never had the tooth fixed because it was a reminder. John never told me any more than that, and forty-four years would pass before I learned what happened in Great Gulf.

• JEROME PIERCE •
SEPTEMBER 1934

$\mathcal{T}$he Intercollegiate Outing Club Association was a vigorous force a generation or two ago and they published a song book, actually, *the* songbook, what everyone called the IOCA book. This was the collection that had all the verses of all the songs — *Abdulah Bulbul Amir, The Eddystone Light, Oola Ski Yumper from Norway, Juanita, Who Threw the Overhauls in Mrs. Murphy's Chowder* — and all the other favorites in the days when skiers and hikers actually did gather around the fire to sing. It was an institution and the catch was that no one wanted to be seen using the IOCA book, it was a point of honor to know all the words without it.

In September 1934, the IOCA had their annual College Weekend. This year there would be hiking on the Presidential Range; forty-two people signed up for the outing and fifteen of them were staying at the Great Gulf Shelter, which was also an institution. The first small refuge on the site was built in 1909, then replaced in 1927 with a new one rated at twenty-two hikers.

This shelter was a sort of grand central station for Mount Washington and the Northern Peaks. It was on the Great Gulf Trail, which is most conveniently entered from the Glen House or the AMC camp. The trail leads uphill from the shelter to the summit of Mount Washington and downhill to the highway, and the shelter was a quarter of a mile from the spot where the Wamsutta Trail led up Mount Washington on one side of the Gulf and the Six Husbands Trail led up Mt. Jefferson on the opposite side. Two other trails branched off Six Husbands soon after it left the floor of the gulf, one was the Adams Slide Trail up Mt. Adams and the other was the Buttress Trail to Mt. Madison and the hut there.

Spaulding Lake lies high up in Great Gulf, a glacial tarn named for the first keepers of the Summit House, the family who tried to restore life in Lizzie Bourne. The West Branch of the Peabody River starts at the lake and flows 6.8 miles out to the main river in Pinkham Notch, running close to the Great Gulf Trail all the way down. The sides of the gulf are uniformly steep and they hold very little soil, the terrain is mostly ledge with an overburden of rough rock broken loose by millions of cycles of frost and thaw, and there's a thin mantle of soil and moss. This combination does not absorb much water and after a rainstorm the many streams running down the sides of the gulf quickly swell the West Branch to a torrent.

The IOCA group reached the Great Gulf Shelter Friday afternoon and found a considerable number of hikers already in residence. Nothing daunted, John Pierce and Hartness Beardsley built a snug little hemlock lean-to for Harty's sisters Mary and Connie and three other IOCA girls, and they improvised poncho shelters for themselves. The Pierces and the Beardsleys were neighbors back home in Springfield, Vermont, and they all knew each other very well.

An easterly wind had been blowing all day, which is an alarm bell for veterans of the Presidential Range. It brought intermittent rain on Friday, then during the night the wind moved into the southeast and a torrential downpour commenced in the hours before dawn. John and Harty kept getting up during the night to keep their campfire going, but the rain soaked everything else. A small stream runs down off Mount Washington and passes a few steps from the shelter, so small a stream that it would more properly be called a rill — two or three people with pails could move as much water. On Saturday morning, it had risen two and a half feet and threatened to flood the IOCA campsite.

The college crew decided to stay with their plans; this was, after all, the last weekend before the semester began. The Beardsley-Pierce group, along with a few friends, was going to start by climbing Mt. Adams by way of the Adams Slide Trail, which meant that they'd have to cross the West Branch immediately.

The course of the river is steep all the way down the gulf, mile after mile of rapids and falls studded with rocks ranging from the size of a plum to the size of a cottage. There are many trails and many streams in the gulf and the crossings are not difficult, most of them are a matter of hopping from one rock to another. The usual crossing from the Great Gulf Trail to the Adams Slide Trail requires from three to six hops, depending on length of leg and zest of hop, but the river is quite flat here and in normal times a dry crossing is routine.

The morning of September 9 was not normal times. The air had cleared by 10:00 A.M., but the West Branch had risen far above its normal level and the crossing to the Adams Slide Trail had no stepping stones showing at all, just a flood of churning water. Some other place to cross would have to be found if the IOCA crew was going to make the climb they'd planned for that day.

It probably would have been a better idea to change their plan. If they turned right instead of left at the Adams Slide junction they could go 1.6 miles up the Wamsutta Trail to 6-Mile on the auto road, a wonderful hike that gets above timberline quickly and opens spectacular views of Great Gulf and the Northern Peaks. If they wanted to go farther, they could connect there with the Alpine Garden Trail across the head of the ravines or up the Nelson Crag Trail to the summit of Mount Washington. Alternatively, they could continue along the Great Gulf Trail and on up the headwall to the Gulfside Trail, then follow this route two miles along the ridge to the Sphinx Trail down into the gulf and thence back to the shelter. Any of these choices would be easier and more interesting than the relentlessly steep Adams Slide Trail and would not involve major water crossings. Instead, the IOCA group stuck with their original plan.

Jerome Pierce had just graduated from high school in Springfield and at seventeen he was the youngest fellow on the trip. He'd come along with his older brother John, who was going into his junior year at Middlebury College in Vermont, and Jerry would follow John to Middlebury the week after the trip was over.

John and Jerry both had strong personalities. John was assertive and apt to think that his view of any situation was the correct one, a quality which gained emphasis by the discovery that he usually turned out to be right. Jerry shared the assertive part but the edge was softened by his friendly and engaging character, and he was very popular with everyone who knew him.

Jerry was a good friend of Mary Beardsley. She was sixteen years old and an ardent hiker, and she liked to go on long walks with the Pierce boys or anyone else who shared her enthusiasms. People underestimated Mary at their peril and whenever she was out hiking it wouldn't be long before the others would be yelling, "Slow her down!" Mary and her family hiked the whole length of the Long Trail in Vermont, one section at a time, the ridgeline traverse of the Green Mountain from Quebec to Massachusetts. Mary was only partway through the Dana Hall School in Wellesley, Massachusetts, but her family let her come on the IOCA trip with her brother Harty because, it seemed to her, they'd let her go anywhere with her older brother.

The first day in Great Gulf certainly wasn't what the IOCA crowd had hoped for, but after cooking the best breakfast they could under the circumstances, John and Harty started working on the problem of high water in the West Branch. They thought they could build a bridge across the stream, so they took an axe and went looking for spruce trees that would be suitable for civil engineering.

Jerry Pierce had other ideas and, perhaps eager to prove his mettle to the college men he'd soon join, he went looking for his own place to cross the West Branch. The stream is quite flat below the trail crossing and all possible stepping stones were deep under the flood. There wasn't any possible footing just upstream, either, but about forty yards farther up he spotted a large pool with a curious waterfall above it. A room-size boulder jutted out from each bank and just above them a third boulder was securely lodged. The whole content of the river divided around the upper boulder and the two lower boulders forced the streams together again in two falls that met in a 45° angle. This appeared to be the only place to cross, because the river widened and flattened again just above this barrier and all the low rocks were covered.

These three boulders were so large that they rose above the flood and the space between them seemed a reasonable two-jump way to cross the river, so Jerry tried it. He missed his footing on the first jump and fell into one of the angled waterfalls. Two of the boulders, the center one and

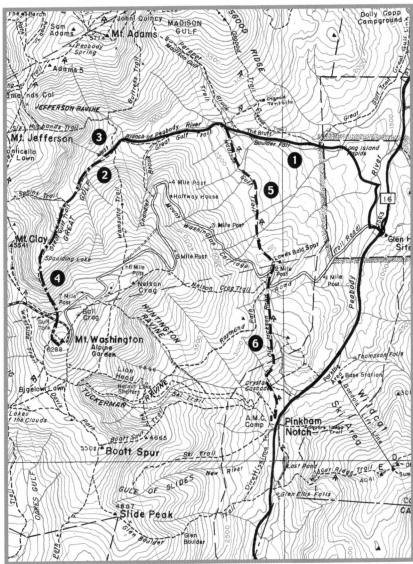

AMC map, circa 1992, by Louis F. Cutter

1 & 2 Up Great Gulf Trail to Great Gulf Shelter

3 Fell just above crossing

4 Ran for help up Great Gulf headwall to summit

5 & 6 Mary Beardsley and companion continue to Pinkham for help via
Madison Gulf Trail and Old Jackson Road

the far one, sloped inward on their downstream side and the massive force of the two opposing falls pushed him back into that undercut.

The IOCA boys immediately formed a human chain and on one try they got close enough to feel Jerry's head about three feet below the surface, but they could not pull him free, he seemed to be caught in the rocks and an old log under the waterfall. They found a slender spruce tree and quickly trimmed it and tried to use that to get Jerry free. They tried again and again, but the pool below the boulders was eight feet deep, the force of the stream swept them away again and again, and the full-body push of the water quickly stole their strength. They kept trying until they were exhausted, and then John kept diving and diving, trying to reach his brother at the base of the falls. John was being badly battered by the crushing falls and the underwater rocks but he kept trying and trying until at last he, too, had gone beyond his strength and his friends pulled him to shore.

Meanwhile, Mary Beardsley and one of the Middlebury students ran down the Great Gulf Trail and turned off on the Madison Gulf Trail and then the Old Jackson Road to find Joe Dodge at the AMC headquarters, an urgent dash of four and a half miles. As always, Joe dropped everything, gathered a crew at Pinkham, and headed for the trouble.

One of the other IOCA boys climbed 3.3 miles and 3,038 feet up the headwall of Great Gulf to get help from the summit of Mount Washington. CCC boys were billeted on the summit and at the Lakes of the Clouds and Madison Springs Huts and they'd been put to work at useful jobs on the range. Now they were back for their second summer and they'd become used to pitching in on unexpected jobs. The IOCA call was answered by three CCC boys, two men on the hotel staff who had worked in the AMC huts, and several other volunteers, and they all headed down into the Gulf.

The summit group got there first. Some of them cut several long poles in the woods while the rest of the hands piled rocks in the channel of one of the facing waterfalls to divert the flow into the other channel and take the criss-cross pressure off the rocks down below. They jammed the pole under the waterfall and anchored it on shore, and then they worked their way down the pole and groped around under the fall and in the whiteout of the foam.

They found that Jerry's feet were wedged between two rocks so his head was held underwater, and it was obvious that the IOCA group never had any chance of pulling him free. Now the group from the summit retrieved his body and they'd just started down the trail when they met Joe Dodge and his group coming up with a stretcher to complete the carry to the Glen House.

Mr. and Mrs. Pierce had been notified and they drove up to the Glen House. Many of the others on the IOCA trip were there, and Harty Beardsley went to the train station in Gorham and took his friend's body home to Springfield. John was at the Glen House, too, and didn't want much company. Instead, he found a piano and sat there for a long time improvising quiet laments in all the minor keys he knew.

AFTERMATH

Not long before the trip to Great Gulf, Jerry Pierce gave his mother subscriptions to all her favorite magazines. That way, he thought, she wouldn't be so lonely when both her sons were away at Middlebury College. After the news from Great Gulf, she never let the subscriptions lapse.

The two Beardsley girls returned to school the week after the trip, Mary to Dana Hall and Connie to nearby Wellesley College. Church attendance was required and Dana Hall did not have its own chapel, so on Sunday the girls went to the services at Wellesley. The minister was Boynton Merrill, and when he rose for his sermon on the first Sunday of the new term he chose the Great Gulf accident as his text. Mary was stunned, and her sister was so upset that she had to be taken back to her dormitory.

The Great Gulf Shelter was the place of my own first overnight hike, in 1947. Later on, smaller companion shelter was built nearby and then another one further down the Gulf, then all three were demolished when the Great Gulf was designated a Wilderness Area and all human additions were removed except for the trail signs and the trails. The old clearing is still there beside the small brook, and it's still used by campers as a tent site.

John Pierce carried the memory of the IOCA trip for the rest of his life; he was haunted by the thought that the bruise on Jerry's head was from the pole he used when he tried to free him from the waterfall, and that was the cause of his brother's death. John named his first son Jerome, and he died before I found the doctor's report showing that the bruise came from a fatal impact on the rock before Jerry went into the water.

CHAPTER TWELVE

THE CHOICE
OF PRESIDENTS

*he Northern Peaks and the Southern Peaks of the Presidential
Range are joined by Mount Washington, but that's about the only
thing they have in common.*

*The Southern Peaks start with Webster, which isn't so much a
mountain as it is one wall of Crawford Notch, and Webster wasn't a president
anyway, he was either Daniel, the man who debated Lincoln, or Noah, the
man who wrote dictionaries. Next comes Jackson. He was the sixth president
and the first one who didn't seem vaguely like a king.*

*Jackson didn't seem at all like a king, after he was inaugurated he had a
party at the White House where he shook hands with people, and crowds from
his hometown tracked mud all over the fine carpets. The mountain named for
him has a lovely all-around view and although there's a steep scramble up the
south side of the summit, the trail goes through a swamp just past the summit on
the north side, which isn't what one expects on a mountain ridge.*

*Then there's Clinton, and for most of my hiking life there wasn't a
President Clinton, either. Now that there is, the peak is supposed to be called
Pierce. It's a brisk 500 foot rise up the south side but there's no summit, just the
end of a ridge leading north.*

*Next comes what we always called Pleasant Dome, and so did
everyone else for most of its history, and it's the only one of the Southern Peaks*

that really stands up from the ridge. Then, without warning, the name was changed to Mount Eisenhower. This was because the military hero started toward the White House in the New Hampshire primary and, being a military man, he was the first president who had a chief of staff. This was Sherman Adams of New Hampshire, a peppery little wood chopper turned governor who quickly became known as the president's No man and brought his edibles to the White House in an old-fashioned woodsman's lunch pail, then patrolled the dining room to see how much time the rest of the staff were taking off for lunch.

Next past Pleasant Dome/Eisenhower there's what we always called Franklin Pierce; we thought it was actually named Franklin, but the venerable kite-flyer was never president, so we called it Franklin Pierce. Most people don't recognize that as a presidential name, but we knew he was the only president who came from New Hampshire. At any rate, this presumptive summit is so low it's easy to miss as you hike over it.

Finally there's Monroe, a crest that we admired because we all learned the Marine Corps Hymn during World War II, the service song that told about the halls of Montezuma and the shores of Tripoli, and it was president Monroe who sent the marines to the shores of Tripoli to smite the Barbary Pirates.

The sun always seems to be shining on the Southern Peaks, the trail along the crest flirts with the sweet shrubs and moss of timberline all the way, and the quirky elements of their topography and nomenclature and the pleasant trails that reach the crest of the ridge have always been the signals of a friendly nature.

The Northern Peaks seemed serious to me right from the beginning. There is no easy way up Madison and Adams and Jefferson, they leave timberline far below them and they drop straight from their sharp summits into the Great Gulf. This is what the nineteenth century artists had in mind when they contemplated the sublime acclivities and the dreadful abyss, and even the fairest days up there are tinged with threat.

In 1938, three friends were already weak when they began their climb up the Northern Peaks and they chose one of the most difficult routes to reach the heights. They made it through their traverse to the Southern Peaks, but not by much. Then things got worse.

• JOE CAGGIANO •
AUGUST 1938

$\mathcal{J}$oe Caggiano and Frank Carnese lived near each other on Long Island, New York, Phillip Turner lived near Boston, and when the three friends left for a week of hiking in the White Mountains they were thinking of ways to save money. The stock market hit bottom at 40.22 in 1931, when they left for their trip seven years later it had climbed 7.68 points to 47.90, and during their four days in the mountains there was good news from the railroads, which lead a strong advance of 0.7. But still, the three friends didn't have much money and they decided to economize on food and accommodations during the trip they planned.

There was some hiking experience in the group, but not much. Joe was seventeen years old and he'd hiked on the Long Trail in Vermont. Frank was twenty and he'd done some hiking on Bear Mountain, north of New York City. Phillip was twenty-two, he was a student at the New England Conservatory of Music near Boston, and had a job at Jordan Marsh in that city. He and Joe had met two years earlier on the Long Trail. Phillip was born in New Hampshire and he'd climbed Chocorua several times and had hiked a little further north once. None of them had any experience with conditions above timberline.

This trip would be a climb on the Presidential Range during the last week of August and the boys decided to travel light, so they saved weight by bringing a minimum of clothing. Sleeping bags were not yet widespread among hikers and the few types in the market were very expensive, so all three boys were using blanket rolls with rubberized ground cloths tied to their rucksacks, clumsy and inefficient loads that ranged from forty to sixty pounds.

The trio boarded the train on the afternoon of Saturday, August 20. Their first stop was Mt. Chocorua, where they'd make a sort of shakedown hike to test their kit and their condition. Chocorua is thirty-five miles south of Pinkham Notch and it's one of the most popular mountains in the Northeast. It has a rich Indian legend, it's right beside the main road, and the towering summit ridge of bare rock is framed by a stand of birch trees and reflected in a lake, a favorite with artists and calendar-makers everywhere.

The three friends reached Chocorua late Saturday evening and climbed three miles to a shelter on the upper shoulder of the mountain, where they camped for a rather short night. On Sunday morning they climbed another mile to the summit, then came down and got a ride to the AMC headquarters in Pinkham Notch. They hardly paused at Pinkham, though; their plan was to spend the night at Crag Camp, on the northwest side of Mt. Adams and eight miles of stiff climbing from Pinkham. So they started out on the trail called the Old Jackson Road, connected with the Madison Gulf Trail into Great Gulf, and climbed on up the headwall of Madison Gulf.

This made a very long day, little less than a hiking frenzy. Each of the boys had been working at sedentary in-town occupations and Joe was just getting over a lingering illness; he weighed only 123 pounds and he was in reduced condition. The headwall of Madison Gulf is forbiddingly steep, all three of them had been feeling a bit ill since morning, and they'd eaten very little. So they gave up on their plans for Crag Camp and slept in the open at the top of Madison Gulf.

Hikers on the Presidential Range had enjoyed fair weather for the previous three days, with moderate wind and mild temperatures, but that was changing as Joe and his friends climbed the headwall of Madison Gulf. The Mount Washington Observatory is four air-line miles from the place the hikers slept, with the chasm of Great Gulf intervening, and the observatory records show that the wind was shifting from the northwest around into the south with a rise in humidity to 91 percent at midnight, sure signs of less pleasant things to come.

On Monday, Joe and his friends packed up their overnight gear and crossed the plateau to Madison Springs Hut, but in keeping with their economies they didn't partake of its comforts and services. They "hovered about," as one of the hutmen put it, then they climbed up the rocky slide on the shoulder of Adams and continued along the Gulfside Trail to

Thunderstorm Junction at 5,500 feet before descending to Crag Camp, perched on the very edge of King Ravine at about 4,300 feet. The portents of the evening before had come to pass, and they'd been in clouds almost all day with temperatures in the low 50s and dropping into the 40s.

They'd been above timberline and fully exposed to a cold wind for all of this day, so the boys finally got comfortable at Crag Camp, their first good rest since leaving home three days earlier. Indeed, Crag Camp was very much like home. It was one of the private cabins built in the golden age of the Randolph Mountain Club, a quite improbable house pinned to a ledge overlooking King Ravine and fitted with a kitchen and bunk rooms, a fieldstone fireplace, a cast-iron kitchen stove, a library, and a parlor organ.

The weather broke in the hours surrounding midnight and a brilliant aurora borealis lit the sky, but the fair promise of morning faded and the fog closed in again as they climbed back to the crest of the ridge. The Gulfside Trail stretched 5.5 miles across the Northern Peaks to the summit of Mount Washington and the temperature was in the 40s all day long and the wind rose into the 50-mph range. The observatory calculates wind in two ways: momentary velocity and total miles passing the instrument in twenty-four hours. During the previous day there were 337 miles of wind, this day there were 1,058. Conditions were so unpleasant that the boys spent the afternoon in the Summit House, then at about 5:00 P.M. they started down the Crawford Path to the Lakes of the Clouds Hut, 1.4 miles away and still above timberline.

They didn't stop there long, however, they went on another mile or so along the Crawford Path and made camp in the scrub growth just above timberline on the Southern Peaks, near the place Father Bill Curtis and Allan Ormsbee took refuge. They were not abundantly provided for this, but they found a soft place on the stony ground and made what Phil described as "a good supper," then they spread their blanket rolls on their ground cloths and lay down.

About midnight, it began to rain. They huddled under their ground cloths for two hours and waited for it to end, but it didn't end and at 2:00 A.M. they gave up. They left all their gear where it was and groped their way a mile back up the ridge to the hut. One of the hutmen heard them, so he got up and gave them some blankets and they lay down on the floor.

It was a short night and an uncertain start for the next day. The rain had broken into their first sleep, and the hutmen and early-rising hikers began moving around at first light. Phil Turner hiked back to their camping place and brought in their sodden gear, and when he returned Joe Caggiano realized that he'd left his knife where they'd camped, so he and Phil went back to look for it, without success. When they were all back at the hut the crew offered to fix a late breakfast for them, but the boys declined the chance. They each had a cup of coffee and a piece of leftover corn bread and started back across the range, retracing their ridge-top steps of the day before, but under far worse weather conditions.

This was a curious plan. If they'd kept going down the Crawford Path past the Lakes of the Clouds, they would have been hiking on new and much easier terrain and seeing new views on the Southern Peaks, and they would not have had large verticals to deal with. If the weather continued wet and windy they'd have the shelter of thick spruce trees for a large part of the way, and they could look forward to the snug comforts of Mizpah Springs shelter at the end of a moderate day's hike.

Instead, they turned north again, and it was not a good start. The only dry clothes they had were at the bottom of their packs — shorts, sweaters, and low socks — and that was not what was needed for this day. The rain turned heavy at 8:00 A.M. but the boys persisted and got on the trail two hours later, still in heavy rain with the temperature dropping into the 30s and winds gusting to more than 50 miles an hour on the summit just above them.

The Westside Trail skirts the summit cone of Mount Washington, then meets the Gulfside Trail to cross the Northern Peaks to Madison Hut. As before, the boys planned to turn off at Thunderstorm Junction and go down to Crag Camp. They were virtually retracing their steps, but this day was cold, wet, and windy, with dense fog settling onto the range early in the afternoon, so it was slow and treacherous going over the slippery rocks.

The embattled hikers fell again and again, but they kept going. In fact, they tried to go as fast as they could on the theory that the exercise would keep them warm. It didn't, it made them more tired and more unsteady on their feet. Now there was sleet mixing with the rain as they crossed the saddle between Clay and Jefferson. Here the trail starts to climb toward Monticello Lawn below the summit cone of Jefferson. In fair weather this is one of the sweetest places in the mountains, so level and grassy that in earlier years there had been a croquet set for the pleasure of passing hikers.

This was not a day for croquet. Joe and his friends met two other hikers on Monticello Lawn, hurrying to get out of the storm. They saw that Joe Caggiano was, as one of them said, "blue from the knees down," and they urged the boys to turn around and come with them down the Sphinx Trail, a quick and well-protected one-mile descent to the floor of Great Gulf, then an easy 0.6 to Great Gulf Shelter. They boys said they were getting along all right and they'd get warmed up and dried out when they reached Crag Camp.

Joe and Phillip and Frank stayed together until they were skirting the summit of Jefferson and heading for Edmands Col. They'd been exposed to cold, wet weather and the full force of the wind ever since they left the Lakes Hut, they'd been sleeping in unfamiliar outdoor beds for four nights, they did not have warm clothes, and they hadn't had anything to eat since the coffee and corn bread at the Lakes.

The Gulfside Trail is steep and rough as it pitches down into Edmands Col, difficult footing even in good weather. Somewhere on this stretch, one of the straps on Joe's pack broke. Frank stopped to help him, but Phillip Turner didn't realize what had happened and he kept going. He wrote later, "The wind was so bad, the fog was so thick and the wind so heavy, biting into us with a chill that turned us limp and weak, that we couldn't see more than ten or fifteen feet and, somehow, despite our best efforts, we lost sight of one another."

This is a terrifying situation. Everything turns gray and even a person who grew up on these trails, someone who knows exactly where he is and where the next trail junction is and which is the quickest way to

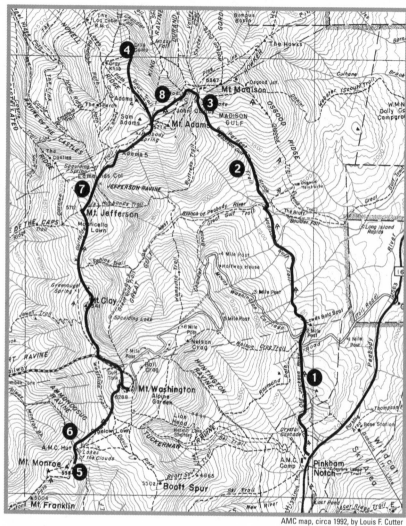

AMC map, circa 1992, by Louis F. Cutter

1 & 2 Up Old Jackson Road and Madison Gulf Trail

3 Spent first night near Madison Hut

4 Spent second night at Crag Camp

5 Across Gulfside Trail and Crawford Path to start third night near trail below Mt. Monroe

6 Forced to Lakes Hut by rain in middle of night

7 Began faltering near Edmands Col

8 Collapsed near Gulfside Trail above King Ravine

shelter, someone who is *at home* on the Northern Peaks, even someone like that will feel a kind of sudden dread.

These three flatlanders had none of those advantages but all of the dread. Later, Phillip wrote, "Joe and Frank were walking ahead of me near Edmonds Col, picking their way slowly and carefully — and then they were not there. The wind was so terrific and the rain and sleet were so weakening that I was nearly all in. A great terror came over me, I didn't know which way to search for Joe and Frank. Again and again I shouted their names. All I heard in answer was the fearful howl of the gale. Whenever I stopped to get my bearings, I nearly froze. My feet were so heavy they were like lead, my head was pounding terribly, and I began to wonder if I'd ever make shelter. I kept struggling along, half in a coma, and every step took all of my will power." Phillip was ahead of his companions as he descended into the wind tunnel of Edmands Col, but he didn't know it. He went on through the col and followed the Gulfside Trail up the long shoulder of Adams toward Thunderstorm Junction.

As badly as Phillip's day was, it was worse for Joe and Frank. Of those two, Joe was in greater difficulty. Slight of frame and weakened before the trip began, he did not have much reserve strength to call on. Joe's pack was the heavier of the two, so Frank took it and they reached the bottom of Edmands Col and headed up the south slope of Adams, still facing into the worst of the storm. Their packs were very difficult to manage and seemed to contribute to their frequent falls, so when they reached Peabody Spring, about a mile and a quarter from Madison Hut, they dropped their packs and their extra clothing and their blanket rolls.

Half a mile farther on Joe fell and cut his knee badly. Frank was not doing much better, but he managed to get his friend back to his feet, then after a few more steps Joe staggered and fell again and this time he couldn't get up. Frank decided that the best thing to do was leave Joe and go on to Madison Hut for help, so he found a grassy place between two rocks and put Joe in that meager refuge and headed for the hut.

Phillip Turner had already reached the refuge: "Even when by good fortune I found the Madison Springs Hut looming before me, I had all I could do to finish the last few yards. I couldn't have gone another ten feet. They told me that at the hut, and I knew it. I managed to stammer out that my two companions were up on the trail."

It was now mid-afternoon and the hut was full of hikers waiting out the storm, with hutmen Bob Ohler, Fred "Mac" Stott, and Ernie Files keeping an eye on things. One of them put Phillip in a bunk, wrapped him in blankets, and gave him something hot to drink, but Mac Stott had an uneasy feeling. It seemed to him that Phillip was in pretty good shape and not saying much about his friends, and Mac wondered if he'd become separated from them by accident or if he'd left his friends behind.

There was no time to extend these thoughts now, though, so Mac and Ernie recruited one of the weather-bound hikers, gathered up their emergency gear, and made ready to start up the Gulfside to find Phillip's companions. Just as they were leaving the hut, Frank Carnese staggered out of the wind-driven fog and collapsed in the dooryard of the hut. The crew carried him in and, with the last of his strength, Frank told them that Joe Caggiano had fallen, that he couldn't go on, and that he'd left him in the lee of a rock about half a mile up the trail.

Mac Stott and Ernie Files and their recruit took off up the Gulfside at a fast trot. This left only crewman Bob Ohler at the hut, but "The Red Shirts" were there, a hiking club of twenty ministers from Massachusetts, and they had a helpful and steadying effect in a situation that was becoming difficult. Addison Gulick was another guest, he was a professor in the geology department of the University of Missouri and he asked what he could do to help, then he started down the Valley Way to the Ravine House, where he called Joe Dodge at the AMC headquarters in Pinkham Notch.

As the Gulfside Trail leaves Madison Hut it crosses a patch of stunted spruce, then rises sharply up a stretch of loose rocks to the ridge and begins a long rising traverse across the northwest side of Adams to Thunderstorm Junction, a mile from the hut. Mac and Ernie and their volunteer went all the way to the junction and found no sign of the fallen hiker, so they turned around and spread their forces: the volunteer stayed on the trail, Ernie went upslope about thirty yards and Mac went downslope the same distance, as far as they could go without losing sight of the man in the middle. Then they started back toward the hut.

They found Joe Caggiano at 3:30 in the afternoon. He was about half a mile along the Gulfside from the hut and 150 feet north of the trail and he was wearing only shorts and a light sweater with his boots. He was not in the sheltered place Frank had described; he'd used the last of his strength to get a few yards farther along toward the hut, and then he died.

Just as they found the body, Sumner Hamburger came running by on the Gulfside. He was on the crew at the hut and he was coming back from days off. He kept running and brought news of Joe's death to the hut and said they needed a stretcher up on the ridge. Madison Hut was provided with tiers of fold-up pipe-frame bunks, so one of these was unbolted and a crew of volunteers went up to retrieve Joe's body.

They took the body into the kitchen by the back door. Bob Ohler was a medical student at Harvard and he said they should prepare Joe's body for the carry down to the valley before it began to stiffen up, so they tied a prune crate to a packboard, put Joe's body on this makeshift seat, wrapped it in blankets, and tied it to the packboard. "Then," as Mac Stott remembers, "in absolute silence, we carried him through the main room and out the front door. Four of us alternated in the carry and halfway down the Valley Way we met Joe Dodge leading a dozen rescuers. The next morning's *Boston Herald* carried it on page one."

Frank Carnese and Phillip Turner rested overnight at the hut. During those hours the wind veered into the northwest; it was the classic pattern for a northwest clear-off on the range, and the next day dawned so brilliantly fair that the ocean was visible from the summit of Mount Washington. This weather had come too late for Joe and his friends, so the survivors went down the Valley Way to the Ravine House in Randolph. Phillip's two brothers drove up from Boston and started them on their way home. They were still traveling as economically as they could, with severe costs.

AFTERMATH

*A*s often happens, this accident led to counsels and plans in the AMC and the Forest Service. The AMC's Committee on Trail, Hut and Camp Extensions took up the questions left by Joe Caggiano's death and their report was published in June 1941.

"In view of the number of diverging trails which lead to shelters," they wrote, "it is obvious that there would be little danger if trampers would only use reasonable judgement and descend one of these trails in case of trouble. The Committee felt, however, that they could not ignore the safety of the many trampers who will not use such judgement." As a result of this reading of topographic and human nature, "public safety makes a refuge of some sort desirable." Given the length of the Gulfside and the layout of trails on the Northern Peaks, it was persuasively obvious that such a shelter should be in Edmands Col on the Gulfside, just above timberline on the crest of the ridge and equidistant from almost everything.

All the AMC huts had a refuge room left open in the off-season, but despite this convenience, hikers repeatedly burned everything flammable in the place and stole the few utensils left for their convenience, and sometimes they broke through stout defenses and got into the main hut to do more damage there. So the committee decided on a minimalist approach and recommended that, "Unless such a refuge could be in charge of a caretaker, it should be so constructed as to discourage camping and any use except in case of emergency. It should be built of stone with a non-combustible roof supported on steel rafters. No wood should be used in its construction, and it should contain no equipment whatsoever.

"Regardless of the erection of a refuge, conspicuous signs should be placed at important junctions on the Gulfside Trail indicating the direction and distance of the nearest or best shelter in case of emergency."

For most of remembered history, the nearest refuge to Edmands Col was the Perch, 1.2 miles down the Randolph Path from the col. J. Rayner Edmands himself built it for his own convenience in 1892, a curiously elaborate shelter tucked in well below timberline and next to an unfailing stream. The Randolph Mountain Club took it over and it had been a great favorite of hikers ever since. But the Perch eventually fell into disrepair and the RMC announced that it would be abandoned. In light of this development, the AMC committee recommended that if a new refuge was not approved for Edmands Col, a standard lean-to shelter should be built on the site of the Perch. The report was approved by the club and a copy was sent to the Forest Service.

The United States entered World War II six months after the report appeared, all work on the range was suspended, and the 6.3-mile span of exposed ridge between Madison Hut and relief on the summit of Mount Washington or at the Lakes Hut remained without any shelter until 1956, when a refuge was built in Edmands Col.

This was Spartan beyond anything the committee could probably have imagined, and if the 1901 refuge on Bigelow Lawn was "far too uncomfortable to attract campers," the refuge in Edmands Col positively repelled such visits. It looked like half of a large corrugated steel pipe bolted to a concrete pad, there was a crawl-in entrance and the dark interior dripped moisture and rattled with metallic echoes. But hiker traffic on the range was rising sharply in the 1960s and '70s and the Edmands Col refuge became an overnight destination despite its uninviting characteristics. The Forest Service decided that this non-emergency use was blighting the grand setting and delicate environment, and every trace of the refuge was removed about 20 years after it was built. The high Northern Peaks traverse has been pristine ever since, but, happily, the RMC had succumbed to the pressure of its own history and the Perch was rebuilt in 1948.

CHAPTER THIRTEEN

DEATH COMES
IN SMALL PARTS

*A*s my generation of Overlook cousins grew up, our summer *hikes grew also. The greatest trips were on the Presidential Range and we'd watch as the trees got smaller and smaller as we climbed until the last of them were squashed into moss and there was only rock and sky in front of us. There was a metal sign about here on every trail, bright yellow with black lettering:* STOP: Weather changes above timberline are sudden and severe. Do not attempt this trail unless you are in good physical condition, well rested and fed, and have extra food and clothing. Turn back at the first sign of bad weather.

This meant that we were getting into serious territory. We'd always known that people died up on the heights, and now we were up on the heights ourselves. My brother had worked for Joe Dodge for many years; he was on the crew at Madison Hut and I could think of no higher aspiration than to follow in his footsteps. Finally I was old enough to work for Joe myself and there was no doubt in my mind where — I'd work at Madison.

The Gulfside Trail began at the hut and not long after it topped the first crest there was a brass plaque beside the trail. It marked the place where Joe Caggiano died in 1938 and this brought an immediacy to the times of peril and heroics that I'd never felt before. Up until now, those stories had been stories that someone told and the names were places on the list of fatalities on the wall down in Porky Gulch. Ever since our earliest visits, we'd go over to that list and read all the names again and feel a distant surge of danger, but standing by Joe Caggiano's marker was standing on the very rocks that were in those stories, this death was the closest in both time and distance to our bunks at Madison and we thought about it without really knowing what we were thinking. It would not be long before we became one of the stories ourselves.

• RAYMOND DAVIS •
AUGUST 1952

$\mathcal{A}$ugust 23 was a major event in the hutman's calendar. This was "Guinea Day," established some years before to celebrate the birthday of Vincent LaManna, who was chief of the storehouse in Porky Gulch and affectionately called "Vinny the Guinea." His birthday was late in the summer and provided a convenient occasion for a party to mark the end of the season.

That August week in 1952 brought very severe weather. On the twenty-first, clouds thickened steadily on the heights, the wind backed into the southwest and, curiously for that heading, the temperature on the summit of Mount Washington did not rise out of the 40s all day. The upper reaches of the range remained in the clouds all the next day and the wind veered into the northwest and rose from the 20-mph range in the morning to a peak of 71. The temperature settled from a morning high of 46° down to 32°.

Early the next day the trails on Mount Washington and the Northern Peaks were closed to hikers, so extreme a measure than no one could remember such a step being taken before. The wind was out of the west and blew steadily in the 40-60 mph range all day at the observatory and rose to 76 after supper. The summit temperature was nailed at 30° all day, with snow and sleet collecting on the ground.

Bad weather or not, about twenty-five hutmen got to the party in Pinkham Notch. It was always a spaghetti and beer bust, and momentum gathered quickly. Suddenly a young woman appeared. She was wet, muddy, and out of breath; she said she was a nurse and a man had collapsed up above Tuckerman Ravine. Her companion, another nurse, had stayed with him.

Joe Dodge's example taught us that there was never a moment of hesitation at times like this, so we put down the spaghetti and the beer and took off up Mount Washington at a trot. The clouds closed in on us, the rain turned to sleet partway up Tuckerman Ravine, then ice was gathering on the rocks. It was the weather those signs warned about and it was tough going, but at nineteen you are not only invincible, you are immortal, and we were all nineteen. When we got to the man, he was dead.

Most of us had never seen death so close and many had never seen death at all, we hadn't learned that when lifeless flesh is pressed, it does not rebound, it does not press back. This man seemed extraordinarily large, too heavy to lift, and we learned the meaning of "dead weight," a weight that doesn't help you at all. We could barely keep our feet as we headed down over the headwall of Tuckerman Ravine; we half-dropped our burden several times and we did drop it several times. Some laughed, saying we should just let him slide down the dizzying slope, he wouldn't mind, and we'd catch up later; others wondered if the spaghetti was getting cold. That, apparently, is what you do when you're at the height of your powers and carrying a dead man you can hardly lift.

Being tall, I was at the downhill end of the load. One of the man's booted feet was flopping right beside my shoulder, just flopping there with an absolute limpness I'd never seen. The nurse who stayed behind said she'd found a prescription for heart medicine in the man's pocket and I kept wondering what he was thinking when he passed the sign telling how the weather changes above timberline are sudden and severe, and how the upper trails are now closed. I wondered if he meant what was going to happen, and I kept looking at the boot laces on the foot flopping on my shoulder. They were tied with a double bow knot and I kept thinking the same thing over and over, that when he tied that bow this morning he was looking forward to the day.

They were beautiful boots, carefully greased for waterproofing and flexibility. All our boots were leather and they were part of us, our link to the ground. Now here was this man's beautiful boot, flopping at my shoulder. Like us, he'd taken out the cloth laces and replaced them with leather, also greased for strength and longevity. I kept looking at the bow knot, thinking how carefully he'd tied it that morning, so it wouldn't come undone. As it turned out, that was not the weak link.

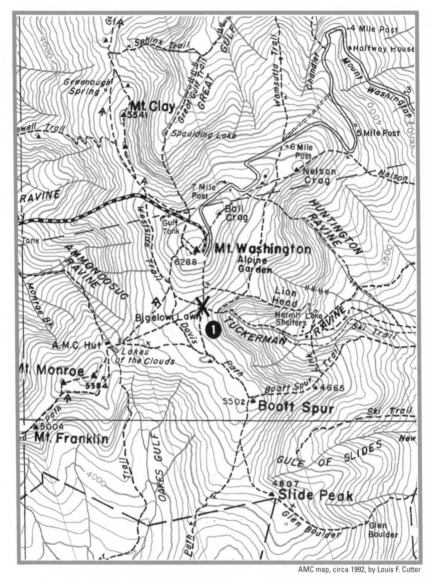

AMC map, circa 1992, by Louis F. Cutter

1 Route of hike unknown; he died at Tuckerman Junction

My friend Chan Murdoch was level with the man's arm and he told me later that all the way down he could only think of how the man's limp elbow kept nudging him as he struggled with the carry, just that persistent mindless nudge. When Chan said that, I realized that we'd both seen our first death in very small parts.

For Joe Dodge, there was other business to attend to. He lived with emergency like his own shadow and he'd led the charge uncounted times. So when we got to the AMC headquarters at the bottom of the trail, Joe made the call. It appeared, however, that the person at the other end of the line insisted on hope. Finally Joe said, "Hell no, lady, it's worse than that. The poor son of a bitch is dead."

CHAPTER FOURTEEN

THE SUMMIT AS HOME

*T*he Presidential Range is unique among the major mountains because the highest point has been an outpost of civilization from the earliest days. The first party to spend the night on the summit of Mount Washington went up in July 1784 and the mountain they climbed had been called, variously, Agiococook, Waumbekket-methna, Christall Hill, and Trinity Height. When they came down it was called Mount Washington, because the six climbers had gone up for a christening to honor the man who would soon lead the new nation. In the same festive vein, five of the men named the river flowing out of the great eastern ravine after their companion Dr. Cutler.

The first shelter on the summit was a primitive stone hut built by Ethan Allen Crawford. That was in 1823 and, pleased with his work, he immediately built two more. Always alert to a commercial future, the epochal mountain pioneer installed a sheet of lead upon which visitors could scratch their names. Needless to say, they often scratched more than that. Samuel Cowles, of Farmington, Connecticut, started toward the summit with Thomas Crawford on June 10, 1823, and reached the top the next day. He was the first to leave his trace on the register, but he saw very little beyond that, an experience that would be repeated many times over in the years to come. "The Creator," he wrote, "had spread a veil over the grandeur and beauty of His works."

The summit of Mount Washington proved to be a dependable source of inspiration. Many American citizens never went beyond their letters and numbers, but those who did often became intimates of the classics. Not only could they explain without hesitation the distinctions separating elocution and rhetoric and oratory and declamation, but if surviving diaries are to be believed, outbursts of eloquence threatened to overtake them at every pleasing prospect. On July 8 of the same summer, a visitor spent an uncomfortable night in one of the Crawfords' stone huts, but found that the morning made up for it:

> The Muses' most inspired draught,
> From Helicon's pure fountain quaff'd —
> What is it to the rising sun,
> Seen from the top of Washington!
> Canst thou bear a dreary night?
> Stranger! go enjoy the sight.

Spiritually rewarding as the heights might be, the Crawfords' stone tourist court was a financial failure because the huts did not keep out very much weather and visitors soon discovered that the summit of Mount Washington had a variety and a force of weather entirely beyond the experience of most mortals.

Mr. Crawford already knew about that. An early commentator wrote that his stone cabin "was ever by the winter's storms rendered a most desolate object, though sheltered behind a bold crag. The shingle roof, split down in the woods on the mountain side and packed up on the backs of men, was scattered to the four winds. The levers of the frost, and the wild hurricane, tumbled down the thick stone walls; and every spring a roofless heap of ruins, with a rusty old stove, and the iron chest, was left to tell a sad story of the invisible power that over these towering summits stretches the arm of destruction."

Undeterred by these elemental setbacks, Mr. Crawford abandoned his stone cabins and put up a tent, thoughtfully equipped with a wood stove to keep out the damp. This innovation brought the windy nature of life on the summit into sharp focus, and the first good blow ended the era of canvas on Mount Washington forever. Ontogeny recapitulates phylogeny, it always does, so the Crawfords continued to compress the whole history of lodgings into this short time and small span and they built a tiny shelter made of wood. This proved inadequate to their large commercial vision, so in 1852 they caught up to the present with a handsome and substantial building of wood, masonry, anchor bolts, and steel cables. This new hostelry promised so much that they named it the Summit House.

Nothing succeeds like success and that same year Samuel Spaulding built a larger hotel called the Tip-Top House. A contemporary guide wrote that "cement and iron hold this monument of daring enterprise, in proud defiance of wind and storm, to the most bleak top crag of Mount Washington." The new hotel measured twenty-eight by eighty-four feet, and it was provided with a telescope on the roof and fresh dairy goods in the kitchen, the latter supplied by hardscrabble cows tethered about a mile below the summit in the Cow Pasture. Many lodgers rode to the summit on horseback, using the four bridle paths that had been built by then. Work on a carriage road up the eastern flank was begun in 1855 and then the cog railway on the western flank reached the top in 1869, and the larger throngs they brought required a larger hotel. This was an even grander Summit House, a full-service installation to meet every need for 150 summer lodgers. By now there were also buildings to serve the needs of patrons of the carriage road and the railroad, a large three-story observation tower, a building for the U.S. Army Signal Service, and a building for the editorial staff and press gang of *Among the Clouds*.

Everything except the Tip-Top House burned in 1908. By 1915, the third-generation Summit House was open, a lovely heavy-timbered place with twenty-two double guest rooms and every amenity the stylish traveler could desire. In 1924 a small cabin was built near the Summit House and named Camden Cottage to salute an admired employee of the cog railway who slid down the 3.25-mile track on a board in only three minutes. This refuge was for climbers and it was left open all year round, partly to deflect the attention of cold-weather visitors who might otherwise break into the hotel.

The U.S. Army Signal Service served as the national weather bureau and a detachment of soldiers set up an observatory on the summit of Mount Washington in November 1870, using a building with two heavy chains run up over the roof and anchored to bedrock.

Heavy and reassuring as the construction was, there were times when the men thought it might not be enough. Consider, for instance, the experience of Private Doyle in January 1877. As the account of that year describes it, "Anticipating, from the aspect of the heavens in the afternoon preceding the gale, when the clouds spread for miles around — an ocean of frozen vapor — and became, late in the day, so dense as to reflect the colors of the spectrum, that some great atmospheric disturbance was impending, the observers made everything snug for a storm."

Night came on and the wind rose to 100 mph, driving sleet so thick the men dared not make their outside observations. At midnight they recorded winds of 120 and the thermometer stood at -24°. The small building was heated with a coal stove and this night they stoked it until it was red hot, but water froze less than three feet from its glowing sides.

By one o'clock in the morning the wind touched 150 and blew through the sturdy building so freely that the carpet floated a foot above the floorboards. Soon one of the windows collapsed. There were only two observers on summit duty and they struggled mightily to close the inside shutters, but the repair held for only a few moments before the wind burst through again. As described in the account of that year, "After a hard tussle, they again secured the windows by nailing a cleat to the floor and using a board as a lever. 'Even then,' said Private Doyle, 'it was all we could do to force the shutters back into place. But we did it. We had to do it.'

"The remainder of the night was spent in an anxious and alarmed state of mind, as was but natural when they did not know but that at any moment the building would be carried over into Tuckerman Ravine and they swept into eternity with it." Private Doyle and his fellow observer were increasingly confident in this unpromising forecast, so they wrapped themselves in blankets and quilts secured with ropes and then they tied on iron crowbars lengthwise as further strengthening against the long fall that seemed inevitable. Thus encumbered, they attended to their duties until the storm abated.

The Signal Service recorded temperatures down to -59° and wind as high as 186 mph and they occupied the summit year-round until the fall of 1887 and summers-only until 1892, when the government closed the observatory. The warm-weather population remained strong, but year-round occupants did not return until the International Polar Year was announced for 1933.

Joe Dodge led the campaign for a new weather observatory on the summit and four observers moved up in the fall of 1932, getting along as well as they could in what was known as the stage office, a building remaining from the carriage trade. It had been built for summer use, but the thick accumulations of rime ice on the outside walls helped keep out the wintry blasts. A good thing, too, because these observers recorded the all-time record for surface winds on the earth at 231 mph. A new facility was built in 1937, it was framed with 9 x 10-inch timber bolted a minimum of four feet into bedrock, and it was reported to be the strongest wooden building in the world. Borrowing an old trick from coastal fisheries in Maine, it was insulated with seaweed.

This new building was equipped with thick plate-glass windows covered with heavy steel grates, and it had a full kitchen and a chemical toilet adjacent to the kitchen. All plumbers know about the need for vents built into their pipes and the summit contractors did not neglect this duty. They also knew about the summit winds and they inquired as to the least likely direction for severe storms, then they placed the plumbing vents so they would have maximum protection from all the other directions. The direction they left with the least vent protection was southeast.

The great Thanksgiving hurricane of 1950 was one of the worst sustained storms ever to strike the summit, and it came out of the southeast. The observatory records wind speed on a revolving circular chart;

the wind averaged 120 for an hour and then the pen went off the chart at 162. This wind was blowing straight into the plumbing vents, which argued for caution when using the chemical toilet.

It also suggested an experiment. One of the observers noticed a bottle of child's soap bubble mix on a shelf; nobody knew how it got there, but there it was. So the next time there was a lull in the wind he poured the whole bottle into the sink drain and washed it down with a hearty dose of hot water. When the wind speed went back into three digits there was a demonstration of bubble-making power that set an entirely new standard for this once-gentle art.

Given Joe Dodge's inclinations, radio loomed large in the lives of summit personnel. Electronics made a major move to the summit in 1940 when a transmitter, tower, and domestic facilities for experimental FM broadcasting were built there. This forced the issue of water. Ever since the cog railway trestle reached the summit, water was pumped up from the base station for summer use. The new observatory had an open-top wooden cistern in the cellar and just before the railway closed in the fall the cistern was pumped full, then replenished with ice when the original supply dwindled. This was sufficient, and the observers learned not to think about it too much — when the cistern was drained in the spring a startling variety of drowned rodents would usually appear on the bottom.

A new age dawned with the FM building. When the concrete floor was finished, an artesian well rig was driven up the road and parked on the concrete. Then it started to drill. Water was finally hit 1,112 feet down, just slightly above the surface level of the Lakes of the Clouds, and when the drill was removed the water rose to about 240 feet below the cellar floor. Full happiness was not realized, however. Some time afterward, one of the crew was pumping fuel oil from the storage tank to the cellar tank and he forgot to shut the valve when the cellar tank was full. This oversight was not discovered before a considerable amount of oil ran out onto the floor and down the artesian well. Every theory and effort was applied to ridding the well of the noxious slime, but a distinctive taste remained in the water for as long as the well stayed in use.

World War II accelerated scientific research, as wars always do, and Mount Washington contributed its weather to the cause. The benchmark research for cloud seeding was done by the observatory crew, aircraft wing sections were tested up there, and when jet engines were being developed for military use a prototype of each model was hauled up the road in the fall. This was a joint project by the navy and air force, and at first a whole navy Phantom carrier fighter, minus the folding part of its wings, was mounted in the building, so it was called the "hanger." Then only the engine was mounted, freeing so much space that a second mount was built in the hanger. At first it was anti-icing tests, then production engines were being tested to see if they met their specified performance. The hanger was an immense block-like building at the end of a former parking lot and there was an even more conspicuous dormitory building on the level section of road called Homestretch which is just below the summit, the place where Dr. Ball wandered to such poor effect 100 years earlier.

The dormitory had beds for sixty and this new age brought flood tide in summit population. Previously there were two men in the electronics transmission building and three or four in the observatory, but the military and engineering presence of the 1950s and 1960s put as many as sixty-five men in winter residence, boom times that brought amenities never dreamed of by the pioneers as they braced against the wintry blast in their blankets and crowbars. For instance, two of the engineers set up a bar and imported liquor and beer from the valley which they sold at a favorable rate, though not neglecting their own profits. They also brought up several slot machines to extract pocket change from their summit mates, but it must be said that the slots were set to pay off at a generous rate.

The jet testing program also brought an adaptive response by the summit cat. This was Felony, a beast of such remarkable dimension that his tail could be brought forward over his head and tucked under his chin. Felony began life at John Howe's house down in Jackson, where he liked to spend the night outdoors. Winters were cold down in the valley, and year by year the frost chewed away at Felony's ears until there were hardly more than stubs. Then Felony moved to the summit, where he liked to sleep in the jet building. The grease made it difficult for Felony to keep his coat in good order, but he slept in the hanger and hardly seemed to notice when the engines ran up to full throttle. The effect of Felony's blighted ears on his acoustic defenses was never adequately studied.

Nome also spent most of those years on the summit. He was a malamute dog and, like Felony, he adapted. He lived in the observatory, he was a well-brought-up fellow, and he made his visits outside as required and regardless of the prevailing conditions. One of Nome's most admired achievements was the technique he developed for dealing with the winds of winter and the accumulation of rime ice during these outings, but it was lonely up there and, unlike the other men, he had no scheduled days off. So Nome carried on a long-running romance with Joe Dodge's faithful and very attractive dog Tanana and, when the spirit moved, Nome would go down to visit her. The observatory would know when he left and Joe would note the moment when he arrived, and on the next radio contact they'd calculate Nome's elapsed time. The ardent canine would regularly achieve all-weather descents in times that approached free-fall.

In the pioneering days of winter residency, the summit crew understood that they were on the frontier and it was only natural that they endure hardships whether they were indoors or out. They took it for granted that they'd hike up and down the mountain as needed and meet the hazards as they found them.

These assumptions could not be made in the later days of winter occupancy, these residents were scientists, not adventurers, and their regular jobs were often in the aircraft industry of southern California where the temperature on a chilly winter day was usually warmer than midsummer on Mount Washington. This situation promised trouble, so a series of refuge shacks was built along the upper half of the auto road. The first ones were built in the 1940s and more were added as the summit traffic increased until there were shacks at five and a half mile, six mile, six and a half, seven, seven and a third, seven and two-thirds mile. These shelters were about ten feet square inside, with a heater and a telephone and army surplus K rations. These accommodations would be barely sufficient by most standards, but under the circumstances, barely sufficient was good enough.

One early test came on February 19, 1946. Vernon Humphreys was in the last stages of his military service and the army loaned him to the observatory to finish an intensive study of rime ice. There had been two days of remarkably fine weather and he started to hike up the road for what promised to be an enjoyable outing. Marshall Smith was a member of the regular observatory staff and he started down the road to meet Vernon.

The weather held fine, but there was a brutal cold front closing in and it hit the two men just before 4:00 P.M. when they were half a mile above the 6-Mile refuge. They realized that the day had turned against them, so they retreated to the refuge hut, chopped away the ice on the door without difficulty, and closed it behind them. They started the heater and called the summit and the valley to report their situation, but all the emergency food was gone except for a can of grapefruit juice. They set up an hourly phone schedule with the outside world and then, attuned to thermal physics as they were, the observers rigged heat shields to absorb the energy of the heater for later release.

The cold front proved violent indeed and the two men stayed in the shelter through the night, all the next day, and through the next night. The storm eventually blew itself out, and at about noon on the third day two men from the observatory arrived with hot tea and soup, then they escorted Vernon and Marshall the rest of the way to the summit and set a meal before them that was entirely adequate to their great need. That is to say, both the observers and the emergency shelters worked exactly as they were meant to.

Lacking bad news from Mount Washington, New Hampshire editors looked for other sources of excitement. *The Berlin Reporter* was the nearest newspaper and it ignored the saving features of the auto road huts, but it did report that the 4-H Wide Awake Club was meeting on schedule and that the stock market had taken its biggest drop in six years, with losses ranging from one to nine points before closing at 76. The plunge continued the next day and the Dow fell to 74.6.

The next-nearest newspaper was *The Littleton Courier*, and the editors ignored the Mount Washington story, too, although they did provide a lemon recipe that should help with rheumatism. The *Manchester Leader*, the state's flagship paper, took a pass on the story in favor of stronger stuff: Jack Dempsey was in town to referee an evening of boxing, Russian spies were causing worry, and children were told to find amusements for themselves.

The winter population of the summit peaked before the perfection of winter transport, but mountaineering enthusiasm could not be assumed among the engineers arriving from Los Angeles and San Diego. Veterans of Mount Washington work worried about this. There was the day, for instance, when the chief of the permanent testing group started up the road with ten or twelve new arrivals from the sunny shores of southern California, and as far as anyone knew the most difficult hiking they'd done was from their desk to the water cooler. So they got to the bottom of Mount Washington and fitted out with clumsy cold-weather gear from the military stockpiles, then they started up, a long line of them. The weather turned bad above timberline and the chief was in the lead group, so he kept going until he hit such strong winds on Cow Pasture that the only way he could move was to lie down on his back and kick himself along toward the summit with his crampons. All of the rest of the new engineers had holed up in twos and threes in the refuge huts behind him. They spent the night in these minimalist accommodations and were rounded up the next day, not much the worse for wear.

By now it was obvious that some way had to be found to manage wintertime shift changes that was less punishing and less dangerous than muscles and crampons. The first serious attempt at mechanization involved Weasels, the tracked vehicle developed during World War II by the American army's Tenth Mountain Division. Passenger comfort was not a priority in wartime; in fact, Weasel design made almost no provision for passengers at all. The troopers wanted something like a snow-qualified jeep and Weasels had no significant heat and only a flimsy canvas top, and the ride they provided on the wind-chopped road up Mount Washington was about like a rowboat in an ocean storm. More to the point, Weasels had very little sideways traction and threatened to slide away downhill on the drifted side-hills of the auto road.

The first mechanical snow traveler of the postwar era clanked out of the back room of the Tucker household in Medford, Oregon. That was in 1945 and one of the continuously improved editions of the Tucker Sno-Cat reached Mount Washington by the early 1950s. It had a roomy interior and it was well heated by mountain standards, but the center of gravity was so high that one of them actually capsized. Furthermore, the drive train was fragile and when it broke the vehicle was in free-wheeling. Nevertheless, the orange Sno-Cats worked the summit schedule for many winters.

One persistent problem was the sidehill drifts on the out-and-back traverse pivoting on Cragway Turn. It was a mile and a half long and no track-driven vehicle could hold the sidehill slope of the drift, so a sort of notch had to be bulldozed to make a negotiable surface. Visibility is always a problem above timberline, fog and wind-whipped snow reduce visibility to almost nothing and erase all contrasts in the light, and the bravest traveler becomes almost helpless. Phil Labbe was the full-time summit driver for three decades and even he was frequently blinded by these white-outs. One early and memorable entry came in the winter of 1953 when he was bulldozing along the Cragway drift to make a level surface when the light went flat. He tried to keep going, but it was bulldozing by memory and by Braille and eventually he simply abandoned the tractor. For a long time after that, the record of his effort was visible from the valley, an increasingly wayward trace punctuated by the abandoned bulldozer at the end. Finally they got a Sno-Cat up to the end of his bulldozed stretch, then something broke and it stayed there for the rest of the winter.

The Tuckers were not the only internal combustion vehicles on the winter road. The first Polaris "Sno-Traveler" was made in 1954, a spidery little device with a track on the ground, an engine in the rear, steering skis in front, and a seat for the driver — the prototype snowmobile. Six Polaris Sno-Travelers made a successful ascent of Mount Washington in February 1962 and hope surged, the snowmobile might be the key to quick personnel travel on the winter road. It turned out that the drifts and ice were too tough and the one-man one-machine format was too risky, and the age of the snowmobile for summit workers ended almost before it began. Finally the Thiokol aerospace company in Utah developed their line of snow tractors and these became the standard winter transit for summit personnel. The summit road, however, still wasn't main street.

At least one group thought it could be. This was the Mercedes motor works of Germany, and they were bringing out a new line of rotary snowplows. Someone in their U.S. marketing company wanted something spectacular to launch the new line, and what could be better than clearing the road up Mount Washington? So early in April they brought three models to New Hampshire, the medium-sized one, the big one, and the huge one.

The man in charge was from Germany and he looked the job over. It had been a good snow year on Mount Washington and there had also been a considerable amount of rain, so the snowpack was both deep and solid. The head plowman said they'd take a day to clear the road to halfway and the next day they should be able to get to the summit. The summit regulars thought the Mercedes people had bitten off more than they could chew, and maybe more than they could bite.

On the third or fourth day a veteran of the summit crew went down to see how they were getting along. The surface was the kind of very hard boiler-plate that summit people know so well, but he was using crampons and an ice axe and he got along all right. The Germans were not doing quite that well. They'd gotten as far as the five-mile grade and the long sidehill drift that Phil Labbe learned was impossible terrain even for a bulldozer to notch. This is the reason the Cut-off was made, a winter-only tractor route from 4.5-Mile to 6-Mile that does not suffer from too much drifting.

The Germans meant to clear right down to the surface of the road and it was heavy going. They had four or five people out in front driving stakes into the snow to show where the road was, though this had to be mostly guesswork because all they had to look at was a sidehill drift. Not only that, but they had no crampons and their work was punctuated by many quick and desperate scrambles. If the scramble failed, a man would not slow very much until he hit timberline far below.

So the scouts would set their stakes and the huge rotary would back up about twenty feet from the frozen wall that marked its farthest advance. Then the driver would gun the engine, gather speed, and hit the wall with a mighty crash. The work advanced about six inches per crash. The hours were passing, the wind was picking up, and snow was coming on, so the observer found the German's crew boss and told him that neither the weather nor their progress was very promising. The Mercedes marketing campaign looked elsewhere for their triumph.

Phil Labbe survived every imaginable winter situation. One memorable entry came on the Cow Pasture in 1983. This is a sort of summertime oasis, an acre or more of smooth and level green in the rocky desert above timberline, there's even a small fresh-water spring conveniently placed in the middle of it. Samuel Spaulding's herd of cows was presumably happy here during their days of service with the Tip-Top House kitchen, but the cows are many generations gone. Now there are two roadside parking lots near Cow Pasture and it remains a popular place for summertime road passengers to take a fair-weather stroll.

The weather was not fair on a winter day when Willy Harris and Marty Engstrom were due for their shift change. They were waiting on top to ride down with Phil Labbe, but Phil did not arrive at the summit at his usual time, which was rare enough. He didn't arrive later than his usual time, either. In fact, he was lost.

The problem was on Cow Pasture. There were guide stakes all along the road, but they weren't working as planned. The stakes were set on both sides of the road so the driver would go between them, but when the weather was very thick it was difficult to tell the difference between two stakes on one side of the road and a stake on one side and another stake on the other side. This meant that if the driver got ninety-degrees off line he could pass through the expected pair of poles and not realize he was headed for the trackless wastes. Phil had more experience with bad-weather winter transits on the road than any person who ever lived, but he did make that mistake; he got ninety-degrees off line and soon realized that he couldn't see any stakes at all, he was lost.

A Thiokol is a very large piece of equipment, so rather than drive it blindly into an even worse situation, Phil got out to see if he could find any stakes nearby. He couldn't find any stakes. Then he couldn't find his cottage-size orange tractor. Phil did the difficult thing, he kept his head, and he was able to find his way back to one landmark, then to another, and then to his tractor. After this close call, all the stakes were put on the same side of the road and a tether was rigged for anyone who went out looking for the route.

John Howe took a job with the observatory in the fall of 1950 and, with a few absences for other meteorological duties, he worked on the summit until 1988. He was an observer of the old school, he preferred hiking to mechanized convenience under almost any circumstances, and his standards for hiking weather were considerably beyond those of most men.

The large postwar military presence on Mount Washington included another visit from what was now called the U.S. Army Signal Corps, but they were not on the summit. They were working on designs for automated weather stations and they built their research facility on what is known as Cape Horn, a rocky spur of the mountain known by earlier generations as the Ledge. It's just above timberline and the auto road loops around this promontory above 4-Mile.

One shift-change day in March 1952, John started down the road with full winter clothing and his crampons and ice axe, and he also had his skis and poles lashed to a packboard for days-off skiing in the valley. The wind was blowing so hard that he had to crawl across the Homestretch flats, then the situation eased a bit and he was able to get along with his crampons and ice axe. Then just below 6-Mile it suddenly worsened a lot. The wind grew violent — lull and gust, lull and gust. John was getting along by keeping his back to the wind and sitting down into it when a gust hit, then the strongest gust yet hit him and he couldn't sit down into it quickly enough. It tipped him over the edge of the road and he started sliding on the boiler-plate surface of the snow. He was immediately going too fast to catch himself with his ice axe or crampons, and he knew that the only way to stop was to hit something. There was one rock sticking up above the ice below him, and he hit it.

He took the force of the blow under his left arm and his shoulder dislocated, but he did stop. His goggles were broken and he'd lost his mitts, but he managed to get out of his pack harness and chop and push and scrabble back up to the road and he kept going down to the Signal Corps station on Cape Horn. The men there were due to make a trip down in their Sno-Cat, but the weather was so bad they decided against it — their wind recorder showed that the gust that tipped John over registered 125 mph on Cape Horn, which was 1,200 feet lower than his knock-down. The army crew was not very sympathetic until the sergeant in charge found John squirming around on the floor of one of the back rooms, trying to find a position where he could stand the pain. After that, they started up the Sno-Cat and took him down to the valley. I was working for the AMC at Pinkham Notch and I got to the bottom of the road just as he was brought in. John is my brother and all he said was, "Don't tell mother about this."

I didn't, nor did I tell her about the time the Sno-Cat left him behind in a whiteout near Cow Pasture. It took a lot to stop a shift-change trip to the valley and this one was right at the limit: the summit wind hit 180 that afternoon. Phil Labbe started the Sno-Cat down in the morning when the wind was within travel tolerances at about 80 mph. The air was a fury of blowing snow and visibility was almost nil, so when Phil got to Homestretch he asked John to get out and walk ahead to guide him. John was familiar with the territory and the surface was fairly good for crampons, so he kept Phil on course until the end of Homestretch, then he got back in. They pushed on through the storm until they reached the drift that forms just above Cow Pasture and Phil drove out onto the drift by feeling his way through the steering gear, and suddenly the Sno-Cat slipped sideways six or eight feet. Phil didn't know if he was still on the road, so he asked John to get out again and see where they were.

"Which I did," says John. "I determined where we were and then I turned around to go back to the machine and I couldn't see it. Then the blowing snow cleared and I saw it and at the same moment I fell, a gust of wind toppled me. I must have gotten disoriented or something, because I was watching the machine — I could still see it — and it drove off. There was no question in my mind, it drove off, heading down. So I thought, Well, Phil must have seen where I was and he just wants to get off that little sidehill. So I walked on down across Cow Pasture cross-lots and found the road down at the other end and came back up the road. No machine. I got to where I thought I'd last seen it — no machine. So I did it again, I made three trips down Cow Pasture and on the last trip I missed the road. It was getting worse, the wind was probably getting close to a hundred. I ended up over at the beginning of Nelson Crag and I thought, Well, I better get out of here before it gets worse — we knew it was going to get worse. So I just walked down.

"I was just getting to the flats down in the valley by the Glen House and here came Phil with the Sno-Cat. They'd been worried to death and finally they'd given up and called my wife to say that I was missing, and Phil stopped beside me and said, 'Never, *never* leave the machine like that!' And I said, 'Phil, you left ME!' Actually, they hadn't moved, it was a visual illusion."

As Private Doyle and his embattled companions learned a hundred years earlier, life on the summit of Mount Washington is never certain.

CHAPTER FIFTEEN

FROM HOMESPUN
TO HIGH TECH

*O*n *November 30, 1954, a Northeast Airlines plane crashed while approaching the airport near Berlin, New Hampshire. It was a DC-3 and it hit the crest of the Mahoosuc Range on Mt. Success, just south of the city. Hugh Gregg was the governor, he was energetic, and if there was trouble anywhere in the state, he liked to go there to see if he could help. Now he was standing with a group of men at the airport as they were discussing plans for a rescue, and as they talked he learned that the pilot was Peter Carey, who'd been a classmate at Yale. The topography of the Mahoosucs is complex and although the wreckage had been spotted by a search plane, no one seemed sure exactly where it was on the map or how to get there. More to the immediate point, there was no official state organization to attend to the work of search and rescue.*

Paul Doherty was there, too. He was the district game warden with the New Hampshire Department of Fish and Game and he was an activist, he was always pushing into distant reaches of his territory and learning the ways of the woods. Paul was standing near a man with a radio who was talking to the search plane and trying to get a ground location for the plane. A friend of Paul's was there too, man named Claude who was an old woods boss for the Brown Company, the largest timber operator in the area.

Claude said he thought the plane was right near the Labonville cutting, up in Leadmine Brook country. Several others in the group said they didn't agree, but Paul told them that if Claude thought it was near the Labonville job, that's where it was. Not only that, but Paul had already organized a group of woodsmen and the necessary equipment and they were ready to go. So Paul and his crew followed Claude's advice and found the plane right where the old woods boss said it would be.

The whole episode was reviewed at a meeting in Pinkham Notch that evening and Governor Gregg was there. He was impressed by the young game warden's initiative and personally grateful for the result, and when he was back in his office in the capital he signed an executive order that put the field force of the Department of Fish and Game in charge of search and rescue. Then the governor promoted legislation that gave Fish and Game the primary and permanent responsibility for people lost in the woods, for drownings, for ground searches in air crashes, and similar emergencies.

The Forest Service was widely seen as the active agent in the New Hampshire mountains, but it was dependent on a federal budget that was under increasing pressure from Cold War concerns, and cutbacks in its White Mountain operations started in 1950. Fish and Game was a state organization that raised its own money from fishing and hunting licenses, a source so abundant that it usually ended the fiscal year with a large surplus. Furthermore, this thrifty reward was not turned back into the state's general fund, Fish and Game kept it.

One other force was at work. In those days, almost every one of the officers in both Fish and Game and the Forest Service was a combat veteran of World War II: of six wardens in the North Country, two had been paratroopers, one was a marine in the Pacific campaign, one was an air corps armorer in the Pacific, another was a B-24 bomber pilot, and Paul Doherty was a marine doing underwater demolition in the Pacific.

This combat experience meant that they were accustomed to taking orders and giving orders and when the orders wouldn't suffice they knew how to improvise. That was a major factor in World War II; the organization of both German and Japanese forces was rigidly vertical and the lower ranks could not make a move without the proper orders. American forces were accustomed to fighting by the book, but when the book ran out they did whatever worked. These habits paid large postwar dividends in the mountains.

So as the century moved into its second half, the emergency format was perfected in the White Mountains and in many ways the sequence reveals the evolution of mountain sensibilities in New England. In the earliest days, no one venturing onto the heights expected any help; this was the frontier, it was wild country, and if they got into trouble they expected to get out of it by themselves or not at all. As improving highways and railroads brought the mountains closer to the population centers to the south, a sense of collective responsibility grew among the keepers of hotels and boarding-houses and the guides and woodsmen who sustained the new age of tourism. News of trouble would call out any number of willing hands, but they were only organized by word of mouth and equipped with their heavy clothes and what equipment they could find in the barn, and their expertise was limited to the best they could do.

These homespun efforts changed forever when Joe Dodge took over the AMC encampment in Pinkham Notch. This provided a communications center and a cadre of devoted young men working for Joe, and when he passed the word they'd drop their hammers and cookbooks and hit the trail. In winter, the Mount Washington Volunteer Ski Patrol was the first line of response to difficulties in Tuckerman Ravine. The MWVSP was a noble organization in the long tradition of amateur rescue and it stood as a bridge between the old and the new on the Presidential Range, something like the passage from the colonial to the federal in our country's organization.

Tuckerman Ravine, like the rest of the White Mountains, had been in the national forest since the earliest days of organized woodland care, but as the number of hikers and skiers increased, the governmental presence did not. As far as hikers were concerned, the White Mountains were a sort of AMC protectorate and Joe Dodge was the territorial governor. Skiing was taking hold in the ravine by the end of the 1920s, but there was no source of emergency help other than skiers themselves.

The Forest Service shelter was built on the outer floor of the ravine in 1937, but to call it by that name does not carry quite the right force. It was built at flood tide of the architectural period that might be known as Federal Rustic, and that original building compared to a shelter as the Sphinx compares to a sand castle at the beach. Those were the days of President Roosevelt's New Deal, and make-work projects spread across the land; it was a time of starvation glory in the halls of Congress, when the whole point of building something was to use as much material as could be found and put as many men and women to work for as long as possible. Timberline Lodge on Mt. Hood, Oregon, was built in the same spirit but not the same shape. Timberline was in the style of a French chateau, but the low outline and broad sloping roof of the new building in Tuckerman Ravine bore a strong resemblance to another refuge springing up in unexpected places, and the shelter in the ravine was known forever after as Howard Johnson's.

It was not manned during the early winter, because the weather was too fierce and the snow in the ravine was too unstable for any human purposes. Skiing in the ravine began to get good when most other ski areas were closing down, the high season began in March and usually ran into mid-June, but skiers don't seem to have been at the center of Forest Service concern when they built their outpost in the ravine. The reason for its construction might be found in nomenclature. The tractor route which led from the highway up to the shelter was known to habitues as the Fire Trail, so historians may postulate that the name came from a Forest Service desire to have a base of operations at this midway point on Mount Washington, operations which would not have a winter component. Skiers, presumably, could take care of themselves.

As spring skiers reoccupied the ravine after World War II, they'd fill up the spaces in the Hermit Lake shelters at the top of the Fire Trail and then they'd spread out in the woods and pitch their tents, sometimes a hundred or more camps on a favored spring weekend. Joe Dodge came up now and then, and if he thought the campers were too numerous or too careless he'd cut the guy lines on their tents, and that was about as much organization as most *people thought the ravine would ever need.*

The numbers kept growing, though, and in 1947 Bill Putnam and Henry Paris thought, separately but simultaneously, that skiers in the ravine might need more help than a random distribution of emergency skills might provide. They pitched the idea to Cliff Graham, the National Forest supervisor, and he said they should raise a volunteer army, so the Mount Washington Volunteer Ski Patrol began with a core of men whose dedication and longevity were remarkable.

Henry "Swampy" Paris was one of the stalwart leaders and the moniker did not denote vagueness of purpose, he earned it when he went to work for a florist and got his truck stuck in a wet place in the gardens. He was almost never seen on Mount Washington without Clinton Glover at his side, but no one knew Mr. Glover by that name. He was, to one and all, "Kibbe." Nelson Gildersleeve and Sam Goodhue were two more regulars, and most weekends would find eight or ten of the MWVSP on duty.

Sam was an engineering student at the University of New Hampshire and he took the lead in setting up telephones for the ski trail descending from the Gulf of Slides, adjacent to Tuckerman Ravine, for the Sherburne Ski Trail from the ravine down to the highway, and for the Wildcat Trail across the notch. The MWVSP didn't really have a budget, so Joe Dodge scrounged wire from the Army Signal Corps test station above 4-Mile on the Auto Road, but it didn't work very well; rodents found the insulation tasty and there were windfalls on the wire and shrinkage breaks in times of deep cold. Then Bruce Sloat, Joe's hutmaster at Pinkham Notch, bargained for another batch of wire from engineering interests on the summit. It proved to be less nutritional and more durable, and it served for many years.

Kibbe Glover had been a ravine habitue since 1932, a tenure only interrupted by the war, and his stories define the era. He reached the front lines at the beginning of the Pacific campaign and went in with the invasions of Guadalcanal and Bougainville, and he was under enemy fire for thirty-six months; on Guadalcanal his unit was bombed for ninety-six nights in a row and it took them six tries to get all the way through a showing of It Happened One Night, the classic comedy with Clark Gable and Claudette Colbert.

It was difficult to get Kibbe's combat presence into focus. He was a small, almost gnome-like fellow of boundless energy and unflinching good cheer, and a typical moment lives in memory. When the war was over, Kibbe and many other veterans of service with the military and with Joe Dodge came back to unwind for a season or two in the mountains. One fellow's mother came up to Pinkham to see her son and one afternoon she was sitting on his bunk and mending his socks, as mothers are wont to do. Suddenly Kibbe tumbled in through the window from the porch roof outside. Surprised to find an unknown middle-aged woman in his bedroom, he reached into his rucksack and gave her an apple.

Kibbe was an avid storyteller, and one evening in his old age he was perched on top of a laundry dryer in the cellar at Pinkham, tapping his thumbs against his finger tips and remembering how service in the MWVSP worked.

There weren't any interstate highways in those days, or even any firm assurance of winter traction. Route 16 was the main line from eastern Massachusetts to Pinkham Notch and, as far as skiers were concerned, the southern anchor was Colby's Restaurant near the railroad station in Rochester, New Hampshire. The Eastern Ski League counted more than twenty-five clubs, and throngs of the faithful would meet at Colby's on their way north. The manager seemed to know where they all lived, and if one group or another didn't show up at their usual time he'd call the state police and tell them that there must be trouble on the road at such and such a place, so get the plows and sand trucks over there.

"We'd collect at Colby's," Kibbe said, "sometimes Friday evening, sometimes Saturday morning, and sometimes after early Mass on Sunday. No matter if it was raining or hot or whatever, we'd get over the top of that big hill in Rochester and see Mount Washington seventy-five miles away and say, 'Oh yeah — a little foggy,' but we'd go.

"We used to drive up in a phaeton, big four-door convertible with no heat, fur coats on and sometimes a red setter for extra warmth. Sometimes there'd be about one-hundred-fifty cars at the bottom of Wakefield Hill waiting for a sand truck and then we'd slide that big car off the road in the pines by Chocorua and somebody'd stop and pull us back onto the road — keep going — keep going. On the way home we'd stop at the Eastern Slope Pharmacy in North Conway for a frappe, get down to UNH and stop for a frosted root beer, stop at Colby's again and write all that stuff in a big book, and, Boom — we'd be in Haverhill."

At the beginning of a new winter, MWVSP regulars would each claim a piece of floor space in the attic of Howard Johnson's, a stoop-way place known among initiates as "Chamonix." They'd keep their gear up there and crawl in to sleep, and during the day they'd do whatever had to be done in the ravine. "You've got to take care of each other," Kibbe said, "you got to take care of each other."

Other sources of help were gathering nearby. The navy and air force and the signal corps were all busy on Mount Washington, and the Army Quartermaster Corps set up camp in the old CCC buildings a mile and a half north of the AMC headquarters in Pinkham Notch. They were developing cold-weather equipment and passers-by on Route 16 could watch in wonder as awkwardly clad fellows made their way across the Glen House meadow to the frozen Peabody River, chopped a big hole in the ice, and jumped in.

Perhaps most important for the future, they had Weasels. We have always lived in cold places and we've always tried to find a way to travel over snow that is less punishing than foot and boot. Military forces needed more than that, and in the early 1940s the army developed their doughty little tracked vehicle. When World War II ended, several surplus Weasels were used by the Mount Washington summit interests, Joe Dodge had one, and the quartermasters at their camp in Pinkham Notch had a small fleet of them.

Other dawns were breaking, too. Gentlefolk of the down-country precincts had generally considered winter in the mountains to be a desperate time best left to fur-bearing trappers and hibernating bears. But the spur of wartime necessity drove a postwar surplus bonanza of warm clothing and improved camping equipment not known by earlier generations; for instance, sleeping bags were rarely seen before the war. This led Americans to the snowbound mountains as never before, and this migration was especially strong among veterans taking some time to unwind and among forward-looking enthusiasts in college outing clubs. Most recently, the urge to the difficult mountains had been reinforced by a series of widely publicized mountaineering triumphs. In 1953 an American expedition almost reached the summit of K2, the world's second-highest mountain, the British made the first ascent of Mount Everest the same year, and in 1954 an Italian expedition conquered K2.

I have personal markers on this epochal passage. When I was a teenager my mother made me a heavy shirt from an old woolen blanket. I thought it was splendid and that, with Levis and long underwear, seemed enough armor for any imaginable winter activities. By 1951 I was on the AMC's winter crew in Tuckerman Ravine and I'd added an army-surplus windbreaker, army-surplus mukluks, and a new sense of possiblity — all the winter-proofing I'd ever need.

In the fall of 1952 I went west to seek my fortune. Gabardine ski pants replaced Levis, and the army windbreaker gave way to a single-layer nylon parka, and I wound up with a dream job on the ski patrol at Sun Valley, Idaho. That winter also brought the first quilted parkas I'd ever seen; the ski school instructors at Sun Valley had them, and in my second year at the Valley I had one, too. Wearing it brought one of the most startling experiences of my outdoor life: after just a few minutes outside in the cold Idaho air I began to feel feverish and thought I must be coming down with something.

I wasn't coming down with something, I was warm! It had never occurred to me that such a thing was possible.

All of these streams converged at the end of 1954, when Philip and Polly Longnecker and Jacques Parysko left Cambridge, Massachusetts, for a winter weekend on Mount Washington.

· PHILIP LONGNECKER ·
· JACQUES PARYSKO ·
JANUARY 1954

*S*aturday night dinner was a major event in Pinkham Notch. Fred Armstrong was the cook and he'd learned his trade in the old-time lumber camps, where just one of a woodsman's meals might fuel an ordinary citizen for a week. Saturday was roast beef night in Pinkham, and George Hamilton usually found himself in the area at just that time.

George spent his childhood with oceanic enthusiasms around his home in Marblehead, Massachusetts, and he started hiking on the high ranges of New Hampshire when he was in summer camp before the war. He was mustered out of the air corps in 1946 and, remembering the mountains, he went to work for Joe Dodge. George though he'd like to do as many things as possible in his life, so he joined the New Hampshire Department of Fish and Game in 1950 and was assigned to the White Mountain region. On the evening of January 30, George was doing his best to finish Fred Armstrong's roast beef dinner and three young women were sitting near him at the table, they seemed to be college students from Boston.

One was a notably lively person and she was telling her companions about how she and her brother and a friend climbed up to Tuckerman Ravine on Friday and made camp and spent the night there. She said it seemed like a bad idea, she'd been frightened so her brother came down with her this morning and then he went back up. He and the other fellow were going to spend the weekend up there, it seemed as if they were trying to prove something.

George listened to all this and it alarmed him. A west wind had been blowing all day on Mount Washington and it was rising sharply as evening came on. It had been snowing steadily all week and it snowed all this day and the temperature was moving down through the single digits. Anyone who was familiar with Mount Washington knew that this combination maximized the snow-fence effect in the east-facing ravine and there'd be a great deal of new snow hanging on the headwall. George was in his Fish and Game uniform and he leaned toward the young woman and said, "Let me be sure I understand this — they're up in the ravine in a little igloo or hole and they're going to sleep there?" She said, "It's something like that."

Joe Dodge was sitting at the end of the table near the kitchen; he always sat there when he was having a meal with the guests. When dinner was over George told him about the ravine campers and said that he didn't like the sound of it. Joe didn't either, and he said, "Well, Jesus, at this time of night there's not a hell of a lot we can do about it." George was living down the road in Jackson and he told Joe that he wouldn't be doing anything tomorrow that he couldn't postpone, so if there was a search he'd be available, give him a call. Joe said he'd have to find out more about this and he'd let him know.

The summit observatory recorded -5° at midnight and the temperature sank all through Sunday morning. That afternoon Wallace Barnes came into Pinkham with an unsettling story: he'd been climbing the Sherburne Trail on skis and he found a figure of some kind half buried in the drifting snow up near Windy Corner. He poked at it with his ski pole and saw that it was only partly clothed and stony hard. It seemed like the kind of mannequin you'd see in a store window, and he couldn't imagine how it had gotten there.

The Sherburne ski trail runs from the ravine down to the AMC camp, and Windy Corner is about a mile and a half from the bowl. A party was sent up to investigate and they found that the "mannequin" was the body of a young man who looked as if he'd just gotten out of bed: he was wearing a light shirt and pants and nothing else. His ankles were heavily scratched and there were footprints leading back up the trail toward the ravine.

The track staggered and wandered, suggesting that the man who made them was *in extremis*. The search party followed the trace up to the foot of the Little Headwall, where it disappeared in the snow, then they brought the frozen body down to Pinkham and the arrival caused a stir.

The young woman George had talked to was named Polly Longnecker and when she saw the body she screamed; it was her brother's friend.

Philip Longnecker and Jacques Parysko were in the Harvard graduate school, but they were not members of the mountaineering club. Phil had gone to Colorado College and he'd done some climbing and camping in the mountains out there, but Jacques had no climbing experience at all.

This impulse put them in abundant company, it was flood tide of unrestricted camping and on a good weekend of spring skiing in the ravine there'd be throngs staying in the two lean-tos near Hermit Lake and in campsites in the woods around Howard Johnson's. It was a frozen Elysium, tinctured with the fragrant smoke of evening campfires and the tang of balsam boughs fresh-cut to make mattresses for the night. The weekend Philip, Jacques and Polly climbed to the ravine was not a time for rusticated idylls. January brings such extraordinarily harsh weather on Mount Washington that few people venture into the ravine for any purposes at all.

Phil's group did not stop in the woods where everyone would be camping three months later; they kept going up into the bowl of the ravine. Every canon of physics, mountain wisdom, and common sense would argue against this plan, and signs at the base of the trail warned hikers of avalanche danger in Tuckerman Ravine. There were more signs up near Howard Johnson's and at least one person and maybe two advised Phil not to camp up there and not to try to climb on the headwall because of the unstable snow, but no one knew their plans in any detail and no one knew where they made their camp.

As it happened, they could hardly have chosen a worse place for it. They made their way over the floor of the ravine to the beginning of the headwall, where they dug a hole and built a sort of roof out of crusted snow and ice. They were in the left center of the headwall, below the section that skiers call the Chute, and there was deep snow everywhere. In this situation, avalanches are not just probable, or even likely, they are inevitable.

Sunday afternoon was partly gone when Jacques' body was identified. The early season, bitter conditions and high avalanche danger in

• PHILIP LONGNECKER •
• JACQUES PARYSKO •

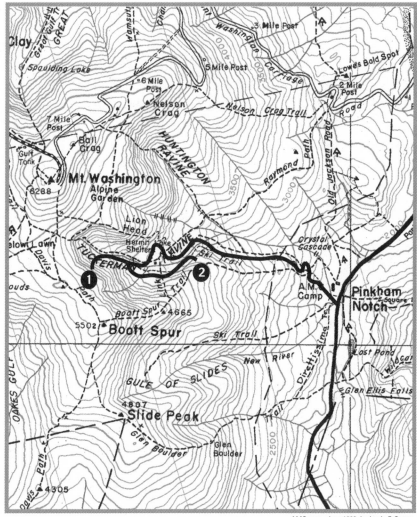

. AMC map, circa 1992, by Louis F. Cutter

1 Longnecker died in dugout near base of Tuckerman Headwall
2 Parysko died near Windy Corner on Sherburne Ski Trail

the ravine meant that no skiers were up there, but the men of the Mount Washington Volunteer Ski Patrol were keeping watch at Howard Johnson's. As soon as Jacques Parysko's body was identified down at Pinkham, Joe Dodge said, "I'll call the goddamn fish cop."

Fishing was Joe's one great release from his 24-hour days in service of the mountains, and he regarded it as an art form of such noble lineage and exquisitely difficult practice that it should not be encumbered by very much in the way of statutory restraint. This meant that Paul Doherty was Joe's natural enemy on warm-weather waters, but in every other respect he held the game warden in the very highest regard and they worked shoulder-to-shoulder on more rescues than either of them could count.

Soon Joe and Paul and some other experienced men started up the Fire Trail to look for Phil Longnecker. They joined the MWVSP men at Howard Johnson's and headed up into the bowl of the ravine.

The conditions were brutal, the high winds and the snowstorm were still on the mountain and new snow was accumulating rapidly. The afternoon is still vivid in Paul's memory: "It was so frigging cold and windy and snow blowing up there that you couldn't do a goddamn thing." They did find a bundle of the slender green sticks used for slope marking. This was a lead, and they probed on that site but found nothing except four feet of new snow. Even this hard work was not enough to keep the men warm; the temperature was down to -10° and the wind was up to 60 mph and they realized that the cold was biting too deep. Joe said they'd better get out while they still could, so as the early darkness of January came on they called off the search and went back down to Pinkham.

That evening Joe Dodge called Mack Beal, who first worked for him before the war and was very familiar with the mountain and AMC practices. Now Mack was living ten miles down the road in Jackson and he, too, had joined Fish and Game and currently worked as an executive assistant. Mack called a cadre of rescue workers and Joe called Major Peterson, commander of the quartermaster camp in the notch.

On Monday morning the snow had stopped and a crew was assembled: Joe and a team of AMC hutmen working at Pinkham were reinforced by Mack Beal, George Hamilton, Paul Doherty, Major Peterson, and seven quartermaster troopers. This kind of interdepartmental effort was new in itself, and it was accompanied by another new arrival. These woods had known the rhythmic crunch of snowshoes for many years, but now they resounded with the roar and clank of two army Weasels and a third that Joe Dodge had. Joe was not a primitivist, he'd be the first one to recognize any advance in equipment and this was the first mechanized search party. Polly Longnecker rode up with Major Peterson so she could help find the dugout.

Snow travel in Weasels was not all the army hoped it would be. Besides the problems of lateral traction, they tended to chew into snowdrifts rather than climb over them, so the combined forces on the Fire Trail had to do considerable digging to clear the way. When the group reached Howard Johnson's they parked the Weasels and put on snowshoes and skis to climb the Little Headwall to the bowl of the ravine. Progress slowed here. So much snow had drifted onto the slope that snowshoes wouldn't hold and the men's progress was often more like upward floundering than a steady ascent.

Paul Doherty loved backwoods tales and as he struggled up the Little Headwall he thought of the days almost 100 years earlier when gold-rushers climbed up the endless, heartbreaking pass outside Juneau, Alaska, heading for the Klondike. Those men wore whatever they found in their closets at home or in the outfitters' stores in Juneau. Now some of the men around Paul were wearing outfits better suited to skiing, Joe Dodge had a cold-weather navy jacket and Alaskan mukluks on his feet, the soldiers had the cold-weather gear they'd been developing at the quartermasters' base, and George Hamilton had an arctic outfit developed for the navy. Mack Beal's turnout was particularly notable. He'd been a radioman in the submarine service during the war and when hostilities were over his boat was sent to the far north Atlantic near Thule, Greenland, where he'd acquired a pair of Eskimo boots made in the traditional way with chewed leather and finished with beautiful sewing and insulation made of arctic grass. Mack's father was a textile broker with special interests in long-staple fibers, so Mack gave him a very fine parka made of Egyptian cotton that was virtually windproof. Mack eventually got it back and he paired it with his Eskimo boots for this day's work.

Paul Doherty was well equipped, too. The quartermaster men had an advanced base in the old Halfway House, four miles up the auto road, and they accumulated a considerable store of experimental clothing there. Paul understood the hardships that army rations can inflict, so he'd bring venison steaks up to the men and in return they'd provide him with the best in new cold-weather gear, sort of an inter-service relief program.

Monday was still bitterly cold, but the clouds had lifted to the upper reaches of Mount Washington and the ravine was clear. The combined forces totaled twenty-five and when they reached the ravine they saw that the whole headwall had avalanched. There was a deep fracture line about two-thirds of the way up the headwall and Joe knew that more snow could break loose at any moment, so the first thing he did was station a man farther out on the floor of the ravine to watch for more slides. The search party realized that the new slide reduced their chances of success and new snow was still drifting in, so any kind of low shelter would be buried under a smooth surface that gave no hint of what was underneath.

Polly Longnecker had never been in the ravine before this week and she'd only seen it through a disorienting blur of blowing snow when she was up there with her brother and Jacques. George Hamilton felt a sort of brotherly sympathy for her; she seemed like a genteel young woman and totally out of her element in the winter mountains, and now her brother was probably dead. She was obviously apprehensive, but George thought she seemed reassured by having Joe Dodge and his AMC crew and the game wardens and the army on her side — this was the varsity team. Polly tried to get a sense of where they'd made the dugout and pointed the search party to that spot. It was on the first rise of the headwall, the kind of place that would suggest itself to novice winter campers who wanted a snow shelter without all the work of building an igloo; here, they could dig into the slope and geometry would do part of the work for them.

The men of the rescue party started at the left side of the likely area and dug four long trenches, each about four feet deep. This effort did not uncover the shelter or any camping debris, so they probed the spaces in between with aluminum rods. This is subtle work; the probers have to interpret the feel of the push to know if resistance means a change in snow texture or a scrub spruce or a rock or campsite debris or a body. This is the first part of the ravine to lose the afternoon sun, and as the shadow slid down the headwall to cover them a cutting wind sprang up. Soon after 1:00 P.M. they struck the wrecked campsite. In that same hour Durban Longnecker, Phil's father, reached Pinkham after flying from Toledo, Ohio. Major Peterson had driven a fourth Weasel up to Howard Johnson's and Polly rode back down the mountain to join her father.

Up in the ravine, the men found an orange, then an ice axe and then a pair of crampons, then boots, a small gas stove, a hunting knife, a pair of pants and some food — all scattered through the packed snow like the relics of some lost civilization. Finally they came to the body of Philip Longnecker, and at 1:30 P.M. word was radioed down from the ravine and Durban Longnecker learned that his son was dead. The roof of the dugout had collapsed and Jacques Parysko's empty sleeping bag was next to Phil, and his boots and his socks and his mittens and his warm pants and his jacket were next to his sleeping bag.

Four feet of densely-packed snow rested on top of the camp. The men dug straight down through this burden to clear the campsite, and as they worked they noticed that the snow face they cut did not show the mixing pattern that would be expected in the remains of an avalanche. It was evenly stratified all the way down to the broken snow of the camp preparations. The first and most obvious assumption was that the dugout had been swamped by an avalanche of new snow hanging on the slopes above them, but the stratification was typical of an undisturbed snowfall and suggested that this had not happened.

Thirty feet farther down the slope, the rescue party found more of the marker sticks the MWVSP men had seen the previous afternoon; in fact, they were probably from the same bundle. It was important to learn the cause of the young men's death, so the rescuers dug sample holes near the sticks. They cut down through almost six feet of new snow before they hit the old crust and the upper levels were stratified but the lower part, more than half of the total, was not. This bottom layer also held irregular pieces of ice and frozen snow, and these could have been torn loose from some place higher up the slope or they could have been part of the roof the campers built over their dugout.

The men of the rescue party studied the contradictory clues and worked out a sequence of events that made sense. Joe Dodge thought that a rather small slide of new snow had come down during the night and swept past the camp but not directly over it. There was enough mass in the slide to knock loose the roof of the dugout, but it was at the edge of the slide and the volume of snow wasn't a large enough to bury the camp. Then a larger slide came down later and buried the site.

Published accounts of the accident reported that there was a heavy block of ice on Phil's head and he died from the impact. Those who were most closely involved in freeing his body do not remember any block of ice or any sign of trauma on his head. On the contrary, they were struck by how peaceful and composed he looked, as if he was in an undisturbed sleep.

This suggested a different cause of death. The snow on the head-wall was very cold and powdery. When a slide of this type comes down there's a pressure blowout on the sides, and if the slide brushed the camp as Joe supposed, a dense mist of snow would fill the dugout and Phil would breathe it in, but he would not breathe it out. One of the officers involved in the rescue remembers that the coroner found water in Phil's lungs; from a medical point of view, he drowned.

Opinion was divided on what happened to Jacques. Some thought he'd gotten up to answer a call of nature just before the slide and he was out of the way when it hit. Then, terrified beyond reason, he ran for help without pulling on any clothes or looking to see what had happened to Phil. There was a problem here. He might answer the call without getting into his heavy clothes, but he'd probably pull on his boots. This suggested a different scenario. According to this theory, Jacques woke up in the midst of the slide and his only thought was to get away as fast as he could, so he jumped out of his sleeping bag and ran away downslope in a panic.

In either case, dawn was far enough along so he could see and he ran out across the floor of the ravine and on down over the Little Headwall and down the Sherburne Trail to Windy Corner before he collapsed. This desperate flight took him past three emergency telephones that connected to the AMC base camp, and he died within shouting distance of ten more people staying in the Harvard Cabin just off the Sherburne Trail.

Jacques had seen all these sources of help during the previous days, but they did not register with him in that awful dawn. The rescuers also realized that if the two campers had made the extra effort of digging a cave into the slope instead of covering over a hole with loose debris, they would have been protected by a roof of smooth compacted snow, and the small slide would have passed them without any damage. There was another alternative: they could have listened to the advice of the people they met and heeded the signs warning them not to go into the ravine.

The afternoon was almost gone when the men finished their work at the campsite, so they lashed Phil's body to a toboggan and headed for the Little Headwall. They could sit on their snowshoes and slide down the headwall much faster than they'd climbed up that morning, but the slope was too steep to manage the toboggan very well, so they wrapped a rope around an ice axe driven into the snow and snubbed their burden down to easier terrain.

The Weasels were loaded with the searchers and their sad discovery, and the machines made heavy work of it on the way down to the highway. True to their reputation, one of them slid over the edge of the trail on a sharp turn and seemed certain to capsize, but the army driver kept the momentum going and the Weasel scrabbled back onto the trail. Another quartermaster Weasel went over the edge, too, and it hit a tree and caught one of the soldier's boots. The man pulled his foot free, but the Weasel proved to be more intractable and it had to be retrieved the next day.

Phil owned a jeep and he'd driven his sister Polly and his friend Jacques up to Pinkham to start their days on Mount Washington. Before Durban and Polly Longnecker left for Toledo they gave the jeep to Joe Dodge and it served many useful years at Pinkham.

CHAPTER SIXTEEN

A QUESTION OF LIFE
OR DEATH

*W*e try to make our lives safe. For every hazard there are warnings and barriers, for every bold assertion there are fallback positions, for every fallible device there are back-up systems and redundancies. Children go forth to play girded with armor for their head, face, teeth, elbows, knees, and any other part that may suffer assault. I've seen a step ladder with eighteen warning labels pasted to it, another with a six-part lesson on how to avoid falling off, with attendant diagrams. If all else fails, we go to court; when a piece of bridge masonry fell through the top of a convertible, the driver sued the car company for making a cloth top that wouldn't keep out falling masonry. So when we talk about questions of life or death, we usually don't mean it.

There do come times, though, perhaps only once in a lifetime, when we're really up against it, when there's no manual or guide or precedent, when we really do have to answer a question of life or death. The crew at Madison Hut had to do that one evening just as they were serving dinner to a full house, they were all college age and they were up against it.

• MacDONALD BARR •
AUGUST 1986

*M*adison Springs Hut is one of the great rallying points on the Presidential Range, few places can match its spectacular location and none can be reached by so many trails — there are eleven direct routes to the hut. On August 24, however, MacDonald Barr was primarily interested in climbing to the summit of Mt. Madison, which rises 556 feet above the hut.

Don Barr was serious about this kind of thing, and as he started up the trail in Randolph that day he was a candidate for his Ph.D. in geography from Boston University. Beyond that, he loved it. As his wife Yvonne said, "He was the kind who would go the extra steps for a big view or to just see the stars. The mountains were an extra dimension in his life."

The gentlefolk of Randolph's classic age would understand. As Don Barr started up the Valley Way, he was directly across a broad meadow from the site of the Ravine House, which was the home away from home for the generations of vacationing Boston academics who spent their summers in Randolph and built that extraordinary network of trails on Madison and its adjoining peaks on the Presidential Range. They'd go anywhere for a pleasing outlook and a pretty waterfall, which is why they built so many trails.

Don came from a long line of military men. He'd grown up on a number of military posts in far-off climes, but his home base was in Pueblo, Colorado, and he learned the vigorous life there; in fact, he had a reconstructed kneecap as a reminder of an early rock-climbing fall. He settled in Brookline, Massachusetts, to make his own life and after his first college degrees he worked as a civil engineer and city planner for about fifteen years. He continued to believe in the active life, and as a member of the Brookline Town Meeting during the 1970s and as a city planner he pushed for the development of bike paths around Boston. He also went whitewater canoeing and hiking and rock climbing in the nearby Quincy quarries when he could. He and his wife had a daughter, Heather, and a son, Tavis, and as the children grew up these outings were an important part of their family life.

But on this late August day they hadn't made their big summer climb yet. Don had been busy that summer finishing his PhD in geography and looking for work in the new field of geographic information systems, and he'd be taking another job soon. The Barrs had already taken a combined business and family trip to the West, and the Madison trip was probably their only chance for a New England hike this year.

Don was acquainted with the White Mountains and their upland lodgings. He'd taken Tavis on a hike up the Southern Peaks and they'd stayed at Mizpah and Lakes of the Clouds Huts, he'd taken Heather on a different Mount Washington trip, and planning for family hikes was careful and enjoyable, it was actually the beginning of the trip. They began thinking about this year's White Mountain hike before they went west, and while plans were afoot Don called the AMC to see which one of their huts would have room for a party of three on the night of August twenty-fourth. Madison Hut would, and he made the reservations.

Heather Barr was in Germany that summer, so the three would be Don and Tavis Barr and Christian Steiber, a German exchange student living with friends of the Barrs. Don and Tavis didn't know him very well, but he was added to the roster so he could see another part of American life before he went home. Don was fifty-two, Tavis was thirteen, and Christian was sixteen. They got an early start from Brookline on the twenty-fourth and reached the parking lot at the beginning of the Valley Way Trail at about noon. Don knew that the weather report was not promising, and he and the boys got their gear organized under lowering clouds.

Up on the heights, the weather was treacherous. On the twenty-third, the Mount Washington Observatory recorded mild southwest winds in the teens and 20s rising to a peak gust of 53 a little after 6:30

P.M., but the temperature ranged from 47° down to 39°. This is the kind of summer weather that can presage trouble for hikers who confuse August in the valleys with August on the Presidential Range. In fact, it was on August 24, 1938, that Joe Caggiano died near Madison Hut, and on August 23, 1952, Raymond Davis hiked across the range to his death above Tuckerman Ravine.

On the twenty-fourth, the summit observatory recorded a wind moving steadily into the northwest with a morning average in the 50 mph range. This is a veering wind and it's a good sign; an old sailor's adage promises, "Veering is clearing." My father always called it a northwest clear-off, a promise so eagerly awaited that my generation saved time by calling it an NWCO. This was not the pattern that was developing this day.

The usual plan for an overnight climb to the summit of Madison is to hike up one of the many trails to the hut, spend the night there, and then go to the summit and down to the valley the next day. Don knew the weather report was not promising. Thinking back to that day, Tavis says, "He felt that if we didn't see the summit that day, we wouldn't see the summit. I think maybe he wanted to leave in the morning for somewhere else." So Don decided to climb to the summit of Madison in these marginal conditions before they got worse, then descend to the hut for a good dinner and a cozy night and see what the next day would bring.

Only two trails lead directly from Randolph to the summit of Madison. One is Howker Ridge, which starts almost a mile east of the Valley Way and follows the high arc of the ridge to the summit. It's a spectacular trail, but it's four and a half miles long and would take about that long in hours, too. The only other direct route is a combination of three trails: the Valley Way, the Brookside, and the Watson Path. This route is three-quarters of a mile shorter to the summit of Madison and, like the Howker Ridge Trail, the last mile would be along rough terrain above timberline, with no protection at all from the weather. And, again like the Howker Ridge, there would be another rough and fully-exposed half-mile down to the hut.

Given the late start and the poor weather, the prudent approach would be to stay on the Valley Way, which provides the shortest, easiest and most sheltered route to the hut; in fact, it stays below the crest of the ridge and also below timberline until about 100 yards from the door. Then Don and the boys could see what the next day brought; and even if the weather went against them, they'd have a wide choice of trails back to the parking lot where their car was. They wouldn't get to the summit of Madison, but it would still be a fine and memorable hike. The three of them talked this over and Don decided to stick with the Watson Path.

The Watson Path turns off the Brookside, which turns off the Valley Way. The beginning of the Valley Way is enchanting. It leads over very moderate grades through a cathedral grove of ancient evergreen trees, with the many pools and cascades of Snyder Brook just a few steps away on the left. Remembering the day, Tavis says, "It wasn't raining, but just kind of humid, but in almost a nice way, a blanketing kind of humidity. It wasn't very steep and it was very pretty."

After almost a mile they came to a seven-way junction of trails, an eloquent testimonial to the enthusiasms of those nineteenth-century academics in their summer pursuits. The Brookside is one of the choices. True to its name, the trail runs along the brook up Snyder Ravine and the AMC *White Mountain Guide* mentions its "views of many cascades and pools" and calls it "wild and beautiful, with cascades, mossy rocks and fine forest." It's a mile and a half long and the early going is right beside the brook; then the trail joins an ancient logging road relicked from the original forest cutting early in the century. It follows this easy grade for more than half a mile through a beautiful mature birch forest, the usual succession after a timber clear cut.

The Snyder Ravine finally pinches in, the logging road ends, and the Brookside runs close to the brook and becomes more of a scramble. Soon the trail turns away from the brook at Salmacis Rock and becomes steep and rough. The Watson Path enters from the right on a short and almost flat connection from the Valley Way, and Don Barr's group could have made this quick change to a sheltered trail better suited to the day, but they didn't. Typical of the Randolph Mountain Club's affection for natural curiosities, the Brookside soon comes to Bruin Rock and then Duck Fall, and after a few more strides the Lower Bruin departs on the right for another chance to join the Valley Way, and the Watson Path bears away left. Don Barr turned left.

So far, the hike was a damp but enjoyable riparian reverie, but then everything changed. The Watson Path is a misleading choice. The contour lines on the AMC trail map do show that it's the steepest of the alternatives to the Valley Way, but the 100-foot contour interval is necessarily an average calculation and it does not show that the steepness comes in clumps and the footing is much rougher than any of the neighboring trails. The climb out of Snyder Ravine is the price hikers pay for the gentle walk along the old logging road down below; it's an exhausting and frustrating grind, and not often chosen for a repeat visit.

By now it was mid-afternoon and on Mount Washington the wind was in the 70 mph range; the summit temperature dropped from 49° early in the morning to 32° at noon, it held steady at freezing all afternoon, and the heights were in the clouds with intermittent rain. Madison Hut is above timberline in the col between Adams and Madison, four miles across Great Gulf from the summit of Mount Washington, and conditions at the hut were not much better: afternoon temperature sank into the 30s, the wind was in the 50-60 range, and there was a harsh driving rain. Hikers arriving at the hut were severely chilled and their numbers climbed into the forties as prudent people caught above timberline on the range made for shelter. The numbers rose to the hut's capacity of fifty and the hut crew kept busy warming them and watching for hypothermia.

The Watson Path climbs out of Snyder Ravine on the north shoulder of Mt. Madison, and Don Barr and the two boys kept scrambling upward over the steep terrain with its loose stones and root traps, a tough piece of work under the best of circumstances and a severe test in the rain and cold of this afternoon. About three miles after leaving the parking lot they reached timberline and a stretch of peculiarly discouraging terrain; there's a hump that looks like the summit, then three more crests and then another hump, each of which brings false hope. By now, hikers are wondering if there's ever going to be an end to it. Tavis says, "I don't think the map showed where timberline was. So we looked at the map and saw one major topographical bulge before the summit and then the summit and then the hut on the other side. So we looked and we figured, Okay, this is the first bulge and the next one will be the summit." To make matters worse, the trail leads over large angular rocks that tend to shift and tilt underfoot.

Madison Hut is open from early June to early September with a crew of five, but there's always one person on days-off, so in practical terms it's a crew of four. The line-up had changed on this late-summer day. Liz Keuffel had been the hutmaster, but she left just the day before to return to her teaching job for the academic season; Emily Thayer had been assistant hutmaster, so this was her first day in charge.

Emily was no shrinking violet. She'd grown up in a large and enthusiastic family of hikers; her grandparents and parents and aunts and uncles and cousins and two brothers all gathered at their summer place in Whitefield, just west of the Presidential Range, and her memories of childhood were filled with heroic outings on the heights. Now Emily had finished her junior year at Middlebury College in Vermont, this was her fourth summer working for the AMC, and she'd reached her full strength at 5'8".

Lars Jorrens, Alexei Rubenstein, and Dan Arons had been on the Madison crew all summer with Emily, but Dan was on days-off this weekend. It was a good day not to be at Madison Hut and for those who were there to stay indoors, and Emily kept looking out the windows at the dark swirling mist on every side and wondering about people who were out on the range.

Emily knew about bad weather on the range. During one of her childhood summers a throng of relatives set out from Whitefield to climb Mt. Jefferson. They started up the Caps Ridge Trail, which is the express route of the Northern Peaks; it starts at the 3,000-foot high point on the Jefferson Notch road and runs straight up the ridge 2.4 miles to the 5,715-foot summit of Jefferson, a delightful climb, but one that's studded with the steep rocks of the "caps" and runs above timberline for most of its length.

The weather went bad when they were near the top of Mt. Jefferson and the grown-ups decided that rather than go back down through the weather on the difficult trail they'd come up, it would be better to march the family troop down the summit cone of Jefferson, across the ridge of Mt. Clay, around the headwall of Great Gulf, and on up to the summit of Mount Washington so they could take the cog railway down. A family photo album preserves the image of Emily sitting in the summit hotel, twelve years old, soaking wet, and glumly reflecting that the celebrated wisdom of grown-ups might not be all it's cracked up to be. In fairness to the senior Thayers, it must be said that agile children enjoy steep rocks a lot more than grown-ups do, and they also have an instinctive faith that their skin is waterproof.

Now, eight years after that stormy day on the range, Emily turned on the radio to hear the regular 2:00 P.M. call from AMC headquarters in Pinkham Notch. Hut crews take turns cooking on a daily rotation and this was Emily's turn, all huts have a reservation list so they can plan their meals, and the 2:00 P.M. call provides news of late cancellations or late additions that will require adjustments in the kitchen. This day the call did not include any cancellations and Emily had an immediate thought, almost a reflex: "We're going to be going out — we're going to be going out." That is, they'd have to answer a call from distressed hikers.

It seemed to Emily that there had been an unusual number of emergency calls that summer. Twisted ankles and tired hikers are a matter of course and crews take them in stride, but extra dimensions had been added this summer. There was, for instance, the German shepherd dog. One day a man came in and said that his dog needed help out on the Parapet Trail, that he couldn't walk anymore.

The Parapet is a nasty piece of work. It was cut in 1951 to provide a foul-weather route around the summit cone of Mt. Madison and the 0.7-mile length leads over large angular boulders and through dense dwarf spruce growth. When the 1951 trail crew got through, it was so difficult to negotiate that the Madison Hut crew thought it must be a rough draft, a sketch to be refined and finished later. It was never refined, and Emily's crew loaded the dog into a litter and spent a very unpleasant time hauling it back to the hut. The owner called for a helicopter lift to the valley; he said he'd pay for it, but this was not arranged and the hut crew had to take care of the dog for three days while the

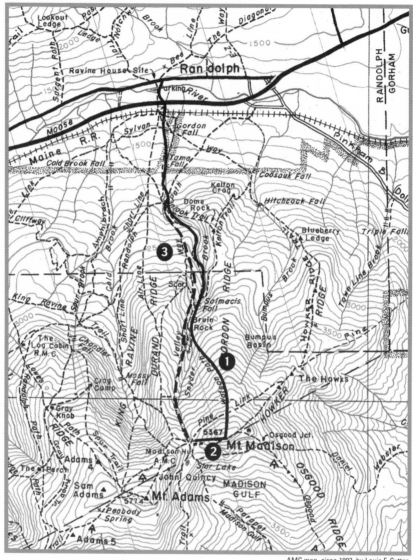

AMC map, circa 1992, by Louis F. Cutter

1 Up via Valley Way, Brookside, and Watson Path
2 Died on summit of Mt. Madison
3 Evacuation via Valley Way

owner went to the valley to look into other arrangements. Finally the dog got a ride down in the cargo net slung below a regularly scheduled supply helicopter.

So 1986 rescue demands on the Madison crew had been heavy, unusual, and not necessarily rewarding. Now, on the afternoon of August twenty-fourth, the people who'd been hiking across the range from the Lakes of the Clouds Hut began coming in. The wind was gaining in strength and they were cold and wet and almost everything they had with them was soaked, so the crew kept busy getting them supplied with warm drinks and putting them into whatever dry clothes could be found; the crew dug into their own reserves of clothing and Emily even contributed her favorite original Chuck Roast fleece jacket, which she never got back.

August twenty-fourth also brought a new crew member to Madison. Kari Geick belonged to an active family in Kent, Connecticut, and she was an equestrienne of very considerable achievement. After college Kari spent four years with the biology department at Tufts University working in animal behavior; then she decided it was time for a career change and planned to relocate in Colorado. She'd hiked on the Franconia and Presidential Ranges and she had a little time before leaving for Colorado, so after she left Tufts she went to the AMC headquarters in Pinkham and asked if they had any openings for end-of-season fill-ins. Liz Keuffel had just left the Madison crew so Kari was hired on the spot and she went right on around to Randolph and hiked up the Valley Way.

Late in the same afternoon, Stephanie Arenalas showed up at the hut. She'd worked for the AMC the previous two summers in several connections, she'd been on the trail crew and on the storehouse crew managing supplies for the huts, but she was not on the roster this summer, so she'd come to the mountains to pay a surprise visit to her friend Liz Keuffel at Madison.

Stephanie hiked up the Madison Gulf Trail, which rises from the bottom of Great Gulf south of the hut and provides the most difficult of all direct approaches to the hut. It's a strenuous but wonderful climb in good weather, but this day the trail was more like a brook bed and the top section was steep water-soaked ledges, so Stephanie reached the hut exhausted, wet to the skin, and severely chilled. Then she learned that Liz had just left. Stephanie knew the ropes, so, in the time-honored tradition of the huts, she stayed to lend a hand.

Don Barr and the boys were still pushing up the Watson Path. Timberline is about 4,000 feet here, with another 1,363 feet to the summit of Madison. The northwest wind was blowing straight onto the ridge and its violence was heightened by the topography: they were climbing the northernmost ridge of the Presidential Range, the terrain turns a corner here, and a northwest wind starts into the long accelerating venturi of Pinkham Notch. Tavis says, "At that point it might have dropped thirty degrees and the winds became a lot faster. It was a little breezy as we were getting up to the timberline but all of a sudden there were the fastest winds I've ever been in. I was out in a hurricane in Boston and the winds on Mt. Madison were faster than that." Don's group was not prepared for this; they had long pants, hats, sweaters and light jackets, but no real protection against heavy weather, and the bare rocks gave them no protection at all.

"We were in the clouds and we kept pushing on," says Tavis, "because we thought we were almost there the whole time, we kept seeing these bulges and, 'Okay, maybe that's it.' You get this series and each one you think, 'Well, that's it, we know the hut's right on the other side.' So that's why we didn't turn back."

There was still a chance for an escape. A little more than halfway up this discouraging summit climb, the Pine Link Trail crosses the Watson Path at a right angle. The Pine Link is almost level here and it continues level and then descends slightly to the hut. Tavis says, "We debated taking that and then decided we were probably close enough anyway that we should just go over the summit and get to the hut, that that would be faster. At that point we were basically guessing where we were based on the topographical markers, and we were wrong about where we were."

Tavis remembered that his father had said where the timberline would be. Don Barr would be interested in that kind of thing, it's something that geographers think about. But it turned out that his calculation was about 300 feet too high, and this is revealing. Timberline averages 4,000 feet all around the range, but it varies with several factors. One factor is exposure, and timberline on the northwest shoulder of Madison is lower than Don expected because the weather is harsher here than in most places, and harsher than he expected.

Don and the boys kept pushing on toward the top, but they were going slower and slower and stopping more and more often. Tavis says, "We didn't have any backup clothing, we had T-shirts and sweaters and windbreakers. I didn't carry along a hat and dad actually gave me his hat and then it blew right off my head."

Tavis was only thirteen, but he was already taller than his father and notably slender, a physiotype well-known among teenage boys in their growing years. Christian had a hood on his jacket, he had a solid athletic frame, and he seemed to be managing the conditions fairly well, so he told Don and Tavis that he was going on ahead and he disappeared in the fog. Now the cold rain was in their faces and Tavis tried to wrap his hands in a bandanna, but it didn't work very well. He also realized that his father had changed, he was panting in a way that he'd never seen before.

Tavis also remembered a video his grammar school class was shown before they went on a hiking trip. "It was on hypothermia and I remembered that at a certain point you stop realizing that you're cold. And I think that's just about when my dad got to that point. I wasn't at that point yet. I had started to go numb, but I was quite aware of my condition. At that point he had difficulty walking or moving. I was kind of the unsteady you are when you're drunk. I could maybe not run in the straightest line, but I could run." Finally Tavis saw a cluster of trail signs — he'd reached the top. His father was about twenty feet behind him so he went back to tell him. All his father said was, "Oh, good."

"We got past the summit together, my dad was at the summit, but not for much after that. By that time we realized that it was really too late. We both knew we were hypothermic, by the time we were at the summit it really was the fastest way to go straight to the hut, but it was just too late. He was still lucid enough to know. I think we stopped for just a second to look around and that's just about when his lips were going white.

That was the sign that he was really in bad shape. I knew I was in bad shape, I could feel it, but I was still — I would say drunk, but lucid."

There was no lingering on the summit of Madison. "My dad was pushing on. If I reminded him that he was hypothermic and needed to keep pushing on, he would say, 'Oh, yeah, I need to do this.' And I just kept saying, 'We need to keep going — we need to keep going.' He kept trying, and there was a point at which he just visibly couldn't walk anymore. He found a crevice and covered himself up as best he could, and at that point I just started running."

The summit of Madison is not a sharp peak like neighboring Adams, it's more of a short narrow ridge with the trail running just below the crest. Tavis sensed that the storm would get worse before it got better, "but it was so painfully obvious that there was nothing that I could do. He was trying very hard to walk and he couldn't. My choices were either to stay there with him or move on and I didn't really see any benefit in staying there with him. There wasn't — I couldn't really — I didn't have anything to give him."

Down at the hut, dinner was almost ready and yet another group of hikers straggled in. They were soaking wet and they were beyond cold, they had the slurred speech and muddled thinking of hypothermia, so the crew put them into their own bunks in the crew room and made them drink fresh-brewed liquid Jello — the sugar and heat of the dessert is a favorite restorative with hut crews.

It was now 6:00 P.M. and the crew turned their attentions to serving dinner to a full house of hikers; actually, a bit more than a full house. They got everyone seated and just as the soup was going out to the dining room the kitchen door burst open and Christian Steiber lurched in.

Kari Geick was surprised, the weather was so nasty that she couldn't get over how anyone would think it was a good day for a hike. Christian was very much reduced and he tried to tell them urgent news, but it was difficult to learn much about the situation because he had a heavy German accent and imperfect English, and he was further choked by fatigue and cold. The crew did understand that there were two people behind him and going slowly, but they didn't learn how far away they were, how bad their condition was, or even what trail they were on.

Trails approach Madison Hut like spokes aimed at a hub and the crew guessed the people were on the Osgood Ridge because that's the only major trail that approaches on the kitchen-door side of the hut. So they got Christian out of his wet clothes and into a crewroom bunk to warm up, and then they waited for a little while.

Here, too, there were complicating factors. The need for help is subjective and it's liable to misreading. For instance, earlier that summer a woman came in to one of the other huts and reported that her mother was out on the range and having chest pains. This is an automatic danger signal and the crew started up the trail at a fast clip. When they reached the afflicted woman, it turned out that the shoulder straps on her pack were too tight.

The crew waited for a few minutes to see if anyone would come in after the German boy, but no one did. Emily was thinking, "Oh God, we've got dinner all underway here..." Then she told Lars to make up a pack of useful gear and see if he could find anyone on the Osgood Trail. Lars pulled on as much wool and polypropylene as he had, then a hat and rain jacket with a drawstring hood, and he put his mittens in his pack along with a blanket and extra clothes. He took the small high-band radio and Thermos bottles filled with hot Jello, and at 6:15 P.M. he started up the Osgood Trail toward the summit of Madison.

Lars was a good person for the job. He was twenty-two years old, he'd been hiking in the New Hampshire mountains since he was seven, he was six feet tall and 155 pounds, and after a summer of packing loads up to Madison Hut he was exceptionally fit and strong. Now he found Tavis Barr on the Osgood Trail about 500 feet from the hut.

Topography is important here. Timberline is not a precise location, it's more like a zone, and Madison Hut sits in an open field of rock and grass and moss that's inside a ring of scrub growth that protects the lowest part of the trail for about 350 feet above the hut. Tavis was sitting on a rock just above the top of the scrub growth.

The boy was completely exposed to the wind and driving sleet. He was cold but he was coherent, and he told Lars that his father was farther up the trail. Lars asked him how his father was getting along and Tavis said he didn't exactly know. Tavis remembers that Lars had quite a number of things with him, and when the hutman tried to give him some warmer gear, he said, "No, my dad's going to need them more than I do." He did take some hot Jello and a pair of gloves, but Lars couldn't learn much more about Don except that he'd been going slower and slower and Tavis thought his father was dying up there and he came on ahead to find help.

Lars judged that Tavis was certainly uncomfortable but not in serious trouble at the moment, and he asked the boy if he could hang in there for a while longer. Then he tried to tuck him into a bit more sheltered position in the rocks and started up the trail. Lars judged the wind to be about 60 mph and the fog had cut visibility to seventy-five feet. Tavis hadn't said how far up his father was, but Lars was familiar with the terrain, it was his summer backyard, so he made a fast climb even though the gusty tailwind knocked him down several times. It got noticeably colder as he came closer to the summit and the rain turned to sleet and added a sandblast effect to the misery.

Don Barr was lying in the middle of the trail on the near end of that short summit ridge, he was in a level place in the trail that gave no protection at all from the wind and he was in very poor condition. Lars couldn't tell if he'd fallen or if he simply lay down, but he was only semiconscious and mumbling incoherently and he didn't seem to understand what Lars said to him. Don's condition had put him beyond reason and he resisted Lars' efforts to help him; he'd stiffen up and try to protect his body, and he wouldn't take the hot Jello and he wouldn't let Lars put any clothes on him. Lars tried to drag him and he tried to roll him, but he couldn't move Don at all. Lars tried to get through to him, he put his face right down with him and tried to talk to him, but Don barely registered the presence of his Samaritan, he'd just groan.

In fact, Lars could hardly manage the extra clothes himself. Don was wearing jeans and a light jacket and they were soaked, so Lars immediately started to pull extra gear out of his pack and the first thing was a hat. The wind tore it out of his hands and sent it spinning away toward the valley.

Lars did not have a large supply of emergency equipment: "I didn't have a tent or anything, no sleeping bag. I brought a blanket to warm somebody if they were moving — I didn't anticipate that the guy would be lying down and not able to do anything. What we understood was that they were coming along and I was just bringing up a Thermos of hot Jello, which is always a good thing. I had a flashlight and a blanket and some extra clothes — I just ran out the door hoping I could get these folks in, so I wasn't equipped to deal with somebody that couldn't move."

This is always the difficult choice: to wait for a while in hopes of getting more information and making a better-informed rescue, or to go out as quickly as possible and see what can be done. Reports of trouble are often fragmentary and vague, the trouble might be a twisted ankle or a heart attack, and Christian had given the hut crew very little to go on.

By now it was 6:45 P.M. and the situation was critical and moving quickly to lethal. The wind was rising into the 70-80 range and sleet was mixing with the driving rain; the sun was still shining somewhere, but the Northern Peaks were smothered in dense storm clouds. Then more bad luck joined the emergency: the radio Lars had with him was not on the same wavelength as the radio at the hut.

Joe Dodge was an expert and enthusiastic promoter of radio since his childhood. He retired from AMC duty at Pinkham Notch in 1959, and, following his lead, the Pinkham office and all the huts were equipped with two-way radios in 1964. In accordance with the standards of the day, this was low-band equipment in rather large cases containing eleven batteries, and there was a solar charging unit. And, since there was only one radio at each hut, they could not be used as base and remote in emergencies.

Twenty years later, the goal was to provide each AMC facility with two new high-band radios of light hand-held design. These, with a repeater on Cannon Mountain, would put all the AMC huts in contact with headquarters in Pinkham and with each other, and they were suitable for base-remote operations. These radios are expensive and the system was being completed piece by piece with money raised through donations and the sale of various small items such as bandannas. In 1986, Madison had one of the new radios and one of the old low-band models, which meant that both their radios could talk to Pinkham but they couldn't talk to each other.

When Lars left the hut he took the high-band radio, and after he'd done everything he could for Don Barr he pulled it out of his pack to call Pinkham and heard an urgent conversation already going on. Two hikers had been overtaken by the storm on the flanks of Mount Washington, they were above timberline and somewhere between Oakes Gulf and Boott Spur, but they were well-equipped and they did the smart thing, they pitched their small mountaineering tent in a sheltered spot, battened down the hatches, and settled themselves to wait for better weather.

These hikers were overdue on their planned arrival and this had been noted, so search parties were deployed and Lars could hear them talking to each other. In fact, the whole hut system was listening. The eight AMC huts are spaced about a day's hike apart and Peter Benson was listening from Zealand, three huts away at the edge of the Pemigewasset Wilderness. Jennifer Botzo was hutmaster at Lonesome Lake at the far end of the chain and she could hear the exchanges clearly. Suddenly she heard someone break into the talk on Mount Washington. "This is Lars on top of Madison," he said, "this is an emergency." Jennifer could also hear the wind roaring around him.

Peter Crane heard him down at headquarters in Pinkham Notch. It was 6:55 P.M. and the main building was filled with the hubbub of a full house at dinner. Peter was carrying a high-band radio and he heard the call from Lars, but the message was indistinct. The problem was not in the electronics, it was in the air; his words were masked by the blast of the wind, but Peter understood that there was trouble on Madison. In keeping with his careful nature, he began a log on the evening.

Peter was one of the ranking veterans on the Presidential Range. In the fall of 1977 he took the caretaker job at the Harvard Mountaineering Club cabin below Huntington Ravine and the following spring he began work with the AMC. He spent three summers in different huts, three off-seasons in remote caretaker positions, two winters at the shelter in Tuckerman Ravine, and in the spring of 1984 he was appointed assistant manager at the AMC headquarters in Pinkham Notch. By the summer of 1986 he was on the "Notch Watch," one of two people detailed in 24-hour shifts to deal with problems that might arise in the valley operation or emergencies on the heights.

Peter brought more than wide experience to the job; he was also a person of remarkable calm. Now Lars said that he'd done all he could for Don Barr, he said he couldn't move him, that he'd tried to drag him and even roll him, but the man just stiffened up and it wasn't working at all.

Hut crews are housekeepers, not ambulance personnel, and Lars was not feeling very confident, but after just a few exchanges on the radio he felt stronger. "Peter was great. I remember his voice being very calm and that was Peter — he was very good for this kind of situation. I summarized the situation and said there was nothing more here, but there's this kid down below and he is still able to move, from what I can see, and I think we need to get him in, and then maybe we can come back up and try to get this guy down the hill, but I can't do it myself. Peter said, 'You make the call. We don't want to lose you up there — you do what you can.' He asked if I could move him and I said I could not." Peter told him to shelter Don as well as he could and get back down to the hut for reinforcements.

Then Peter asked Lars if the low-band radio at the hut was switched on so he could speak to the crew there, and Lars said that he didn't think it was. This was not a mistake; those old units were in semi-retirement and it was not standard practice to leave them on. At this point Emily and her crew had only the sketchy news brought by Christian Steiber and the situation might be relatively easy — a man was a little way back on the trail and Lars could take care of him with hot Jello, a blanket, a helping hand, and an encouraging presence.

When Peter finished his talk with Lars on Mt. Madison he called the weather observatory on the summit of Mount Washington and asked them to try to raise the Madison crew on the observatory's low-band radio, but the summit could not establish contact. Immediately after this, at 7:00 P.M., Lars called Peter again and said that he could not find any place nearby that offered more shelter than the one Don was in, and that he hadn't been able to move him anyway. He emphasized that Don was shaking and convulsive.

Peter understood that they had a dangerous emergency on their hands and the moment Lars' call ended he called the Androscoggin Valley Hospital, eighteen miles from the Valley Way parking lot. The AVH staff is familiar with mountain emergencies, so Peter brought them up to date on the Madison situation and asked them to stand by, and they advised him on treating Don.

That call was at 7:10 and at 7:15 Peter called Frank Hubbell at SOLO, an organization thirty miles south of Pinkham Notch that specializes in training emergency personnel. No live voice answered at SOLO and Peter left a message on their machine. Then he called the Mountain Rescue Service in North Conway; he didn't know how many AMC staff would be available for emergency duty and he wanted to put MRS on standby.

Peter also called Troop F of the state police and asked them to engage the Fish and Game unit responsible for the area. Carl Carlson of Fish and Game called back at 7:25 and said that he was putting additional necessary people in the loop. Then Peter called Bill Arnold of the very active Randolph Mountain Club. Bill was one of the Forest Service men at the Dolly Copp campground on the northern flank of Mt. Madison and Bill said he'd call Gary Carr about further Forest Service involvement. Then Peter called Mike Pelchat, the state of New Hampshire's manager of its interests on the summit of Mount Washington. All that was done by 7:35.

Meanwhile, Janet Morgan was organizing a team of AMC staff in Pinkham Notch. They had warm clothing, rain gear, heat packs, Thermoses, and headlamps with extra batteries, and they also had oxygen to be administered by Brad Ray, the Forest Service ranger in Tuckerman Ravine and a veteran of thirty years of mountain emergencies. Finally, Peter impressed the nature of the situation on the AMC crew, he reminded them of the first rule of search and rescue: that they could not help the victim of a life-threatening emergency if they became victims themselves.

Up at Madison Hut, Lars didn't come back and he didn't come back and Emily was thinking, "Oh man — what is going on?" The Osgood Path rises directly from the hut to the summit, Lars was young and strong and he had good clothes, but as night came on the conditions were so severe on top of Mt. Madison that he was barely able to get back down himself. The wind was in the 70s and gusting into the 80s and it was right in his face. His body did not obey thought, it obeyed cold and wind, and Lars staggered and lurched down the summertime trail he knew so well until he found Tavis.

"He hadn't moved, obviously he was stuck and he was getting pretty incoherent. I thought, 'Alright, I've got to try get him in. It isn't that far to the hut, so give it a try.' I stood him up and I tried to move him but we were getting pushed over, flattened, and we'd be flopping around and I'd try to get him up again. He was very stiff, he was not helping much at all at that point, kind of a dead weight or even worse than that, he was a sort of resisting weight." Lars wasn't sure of Tavis' mental state, "His speech was slurred and I guess he recognized that I came back down alone and he asked 'How's my dad?' and I said we're going to go back up and get him."

Lars got back to the hut at 7:40. He went in through the kitchen door and found Emily and said, "We've got to talk — there's something serious going on out there." The kitchen and the dining room and the crew room were all crowded with people and Emily didn't want everyone in the hut overhearing what Lars had to say, so she hustled him and Alexei down the aisle between the dining room tables and out the dining room door and into the dingle that serves as a wind break, a dank shelter with the space of two telephone booths. Lars said, "There's a guy dying up there." He used a strong intensifier and this all happened so fast that Emily hadn't pulled the door shut behind them. She shot him a warning glance as she latched the dining room door and at the same time she said to herself, "Oh my God — we've got a major thing going on here."

The dingle didn't provide much shelter, so Emily had a hurried conference out there. Alexei was hopeful; he hadn't been out in the storm and he didn't quite believe it could be that bad. The crew had been out in some pretty bad weather that summer and his feeling was, "Come on, are you sure we can't go out there?" Lars was pessimistic about Don Barr's chances and he hadn't been able to move Tavis along either, but the boy was much nearer the hut and in better condition, so that was the priority. By now the guests knew something was going wrong and several of them said they were ready to go out and help, but Emily didn't think she could put any of the guests at peril out in the storm.

Lars called Pinkham from the hut and the connection was still poor, but Peter Crane got more information about the situation on the summit. He learned that there was another person about a tenth of a mile from the hut who was also hypothermic, but could probably walk if he was strengthened against the high winds and slippery footing. Peter backed up Emily's plan that two or three people should help this second person down to the hut. Lars was used up and Emily was needed to keep things moving in the hut and to oversee the developing situation out in the storm, so Alexei and Kari were the ones to go. They'd take chocolate bars, more clothes, and hot Jello, and do everything they could to bring Tavis in.

Alexei had just graduated from high school, he was 6'1" and after a summer at Madison his lean and rangy frame was almost a twin to Lars. Kari was 5'3" and slender, but her many years of riding and the requirements of handling powerful thoroughbreds made her much stronger than her small presence might suggest.

Kari and Alexei left the pots and pans for other hands to finish and got ready for the storm. Kari put on all the pile clothing she had, then wind gear, a hat and gloves, and an extra jacket; then she and Alexei made up a pack with reinforcements for Tavis and took their turn in the storm. There was still enough daylight in the clouds for them to see, but the air was a maelstrom of stinging sleet and the battering wind was still gaining strength. About 500 feet from the hut they spotted Tavis sitting on the rock. He was not on the trail as Lars said he would be, he was a ways off to one side and they were lucky to spot him.

Tavis was so badly chilled that he had difficulty talking, his speech was slow and slurred and Kari remembers that all he said clearly was, "My dad's up there — my dad needs help." Kari felt it was important to stay positive and she said, "We came to help you. You need help now and we came to help you." They got extra clothes and mittens on him, and even though he was having difficulty swallowing they got some warm Jello into him.

Looking back on that night, Kari says, "He had pretty much seized up by that time and he was very, very cold. The winds were very high, it was right around dusk, it was right around freezing and it was raining. The rain was beginning to freeze on the rocks.

"Tavis couldn't walk. Alexei and I could sometimes get on either side of him and haul him along and we did a lot of pushing and pulling and hauling. We kept saying, 'We've got to keep moving, Tavis, we've got to keep moving.' Up on the rocks he would literally get blown over, so we tried to keep a low profile. He didn't have the strength to stand up, anyway."

At first they were out on large, rough and exposed rocks, then the trail entered the scrub. "It was better down out of the wind. We could be on either side of him as much as possible and we tried to get him to walk, but he had extreme cramps in his legs."

As Alexei remembers, "It's not the kind of thing where you hold his hand and walk him down the path, it's a scramble. It was difficult to figure out a method of bringing him down, aside from picking him up and putting him on our backs, because he wasn't able to move very well. His legs seemed almost paralyzed, almost like cerebral palsy.

"So we were trying to encourage him. It was kind of sliding and it was very messy, me pulling on his legs and Kari pushing him from the back, skidding him along." They bumped and scraped on the rocks and tried not to get lost themselves because they had to go where the rocks and wind would let them go rather than where they thought the trail was. Then the terrain finally eased a bit and they got Tavis up on his feet, but he could not stay steady.

It was almost dark, and in the ruthless conditions even the best intentions and surest orientation might not be enough to avoid moving with the pressure of the wind, which would take them across the slope and away from the hut, but the light from the windows was a lighthouse in the fog. The Osgood Trail leads north of the hut, so they cut across the clearing and headed for the kitchen door. Alexei was new to this. "It's August and I didn't maybe think it was a life or death thing, you have this concept that it's summer and he's pretty close to the hut, it's no big deal, but you have this winter storm..."

Lars was worried, he knew what it was like out there and it seemed to him that they were taking a long time for the short distance they had to go. "After a while I was beginning to wonder when they were going to show up. I was full of adrenaline when I came in, and when I finally stopped and rested I was pretty cold and shivery and soaked to the bone, and I wasn't in any shape to go right back out again."

Alexei and Kari spent forty minutes moving Tavis that tenth of a mile back to the hut. Inside, conditions were at full stretch. The two hikers who came in without reservations could not be turned away, so the accommodations were two over capacity at fifty-two and a full dinner had to be served, cleared away, all the pots and pans and table settings washed up, and makings for the next day's breakfast started. There was wet clothing hanging from every projection and nothing dry to put on, there was no heat beyond the stray BTUs that slipped out of the kitchen while the crew was preparing dinner, and the hut had been buried in supersaturated clouds all day. The arrival of Christian and Tavis, both in dire need of restoration, called on an account that had already been fully spent.

Then Stephanie Arenalas took hold. Tavis was hypothermic and barely able to speak, he was soaking wet, his muscles were going into spasm, and he'd been considerably battered as Kari and Alexei hauled him down over the rocks. Beyond that, his father was alone in the storm up above the hut and there was no way of helping him.

The Madison crew room opens off the kitchen and it used to be claustrophobic, with just enough space for two double bunks and a window. Then it was rebuilt and made into a much larger and more comfortable space, with a three-tiered bunk immediately to the left of the door, a double bunk on the adjoining wall, two windows and a table on the third wall, and then a hinged arrangement that's wider than the other bunks and can be used for extra sleeping space or as a daytime settee or folded up out of the way.

Christian was already in one of the bunks, so Stephanie and another crew member got Tavis out of his wet clothes, dried him off as well as they could and gave him warm Jello to drink, and put him into a sleeping bag with blankets over it in that wide folding daybed.

Stephanie knew that Tavis wouldn't get any colder, but he wouldn't warm up very fast either. She knew that the 98 degrees of heat she could contribute were all they had, so she stripped down and got into the sleeping bag with him.

While the hut crew was struggling with the storm, Walter Wintturi of the U.S. Forest Service called Peter Crane and said that he was in contact with Brad Ray and three or four USFS people would probably be available to go up to the heights of Madison. Ten minutes later Dick Dufour of Fish and Game called Peter and said he was in touch with Carl Carlson. Five minutes after that, at 7:50, a radio call came from the hut telling Peter that Alexei and Kari were tending to Tavis.

Up at the hut, Emily and whatever other crew member who wasn't out on the mountain working on behalf of Don and Tavis were keeping things going for the guests. They'd set out the usual bountiful dinner, attended to refills and the other table needs, cleared off, and set out the next course. The hut was not very comfortable. There used to be a wood stove in the dining room, but that was gone now and there was no heat except the propane rings in the kitchen and the natural furnace of the hikers' bodies, but the metabolic fires were running at a very reduced setting and the hut was dank and clammy.

At 8:00 P.M., a team of eighteen people left Pinkham in two vans to drive around to the Valley Way parking lot and start up to the hut. Forty-five minutes later Emily called Peter to report that Tavis was in the hut and being tended to, but he was very groggy and debilitated.

That left Don Barr alone in the night and the storm. Emily was in her first day as hutmaster and she was in a tough spot. The weather was still getting worse at the hut and she knew by way of the Pinkham radio relay that the Mount Washington observatory could not promise any relief that night.

On paper, the crew's main responsibility was the hut, but this night's responsibilities were already off the paper. One consideration was the carry itself. There were only four people on the hut crew, which is not enough for a litter carry. Emily knew about that. There's something about a rescue that fixes the imagination on heroic carries to safety, so when a call came to Pinkham during Emily's rookie summer there, she thought "Whoo...!" and she was quick to volunteer. It was an easy case, someone went lame on the Tuckerman Ravine Trail a short way above Pinkham and that trail is almost as wide and smooth as a country lane. Emily took her first turn at the carry, stumbling along without seeing her feet and trying to stay in step and keep the litter steady and match the level of her grip to the other carriers and it wasn't very long before she was thinking, "Oh man — this really sucks!"

The situation facing her Madison crew was much more difficult. The guests knew there was a tough situation in their midst and several of them came up to Emily with offers of help. They could help with after-dinner housekeeping, but Emily knew she couldn't ask them to go outside. She was thinking of the chaos that could overtake the evening, how there could be people with all degrees of strength and skill out on the rocks of the summit cone and no effective way of keeping track of them or coordinating their work. Even more to the immediate point, there was hardly a stitch of dry clothing anywhere in the hut. The storm was still gaining strength and the hut crew and volunteers alike would be wet and tired and more prone to hypothermia at the start of the rescue than anyone should be at the end of it.

At this point, Emily was the only one among the guests and the crew who hadn't been out in the storm and she was also the most experienced among them, which would make her the best candidate for a rescue team. But at the same time, she was the hutmaster and she was wondering where her responsibility really lay. Should she lend her strength and experience to a rescue effort, or should she stay in the hut to hold things together there?

By now, Christian had gotten up and he was in the kitchen having something to eat. Tavis was in bed in the crew room and he was beginning to recover from his own hypothermia, he was saying, "Where's my father — where's my father?" Stephanie was still with him, she told him that they were doing everything they could to help his father, but at the same time she didn't want to give him false hopes, because his father was still out there on top of the mountain and alone in the lashing storm.

The hut crew was finally all indoors and they knew they were up against it, they knew they had to talk it over, they had to decide about MacDonald Barr. This led to another problem. There were people everywhere in the hut, they were finishing dinner and milling around in the dining room and the bunk rooms and some were lending a hand cleaning up in the kitchen. Christian Steiber was in the kitchen, too, and Tavis was in the crew's bunk room. So where could Emily gather her crew for a serious talk?

Madison Hut is T-shaped, the kitchen and crew bunkroom are at the base of the T, the dining room is the rest of the leg, two big bunkrooms are the left and right arms of the T, and there's a bathroom at the back of each of the bunkrooms, women on the left, men on the right. It was after-dinner hot drink time, so Emily asked a couple of the helpful guests if they could keep the fixings coming in from the kitchen; then she called for attention and said that the crew would be busy for a while and could everyone take turns using the men's bathroom.

Then the crew gathered in the women's bathroom to talk things over. They knew the Mount Washington weather observatory had reported no signs of relief on their charts. On the contrary, the observatory crew said the storm would probably intensify through the night.

Emily and Lars and Alexei and Kari tried to think the situation through. Emily thought most about the wind; she knew it can be raining hard or snowing like crazy and hikers can still be all right; it fact, they can enjoy it. But it was the wind — above timberline the wind simply tears away every defense.

The Madison crew knew that Don Barr was in mortal danger, but mortal danger was everywhere on the mountain that night; once out there, everyone would be equally exposed. Lars remembers, "There was a little bit of bravado — 'Oh, we can try it — it's our job, we're able to do these things, so let's give it a shot.' We'd all been out, though, and I think we quickly realized that all of us except Emily had just been out in the weather and we probably wouldn't be in such great shape to try again."

There was also the matter of numbers. Even in the best circumstances imaginable, even on a walking path in the valley with fair skies and sweet breezes, the four members of the Madison crew would have difficulty managing a half-mile litter carry by themselves. In the cold and dark and rain and rocks and wind, they would have no chance at all. There was no shortage of willing help among the guests in the hut, but they were there to take shelter, not to risk their lives. Beyond that, taking an unknown and untrained group out on a rescue brings its own hazards, both physical and ethical. The first members of the AMC group from Pinkham were already arriving and the Madison crew had seen them. Lars says, "We started seeing these folks coming in from Pinkham in various states of hypothermia themselves and certainly not prepared to go up on the mountain beyond the hut."

All these thoughts were in the women's bathroom and even though not all of them were said out loud, the hut crew knew that they'd decided. It was not a debate. Lars remembers, "We realized at that point we were making decisions to forget any hope of trying to rescue him or bringing him back alive. We knew that was weighing over us. But we also knew that it was ridiculous to try to go up there to get him. The choice had been made before us." No one asked for a vote or tried to persuade anyone else, but they knew that the risk to a rescue group outweighed the benefit to Don Barr, and Emily summed it up for them: The danger is too great, our resources are too small, and we're not going to go out tonight.

The valley forces were on their way, so at 8:55 Peter Crane called Emily for another report from the hut. Peter was in a position to launch the rescue on his own authority, but, as he says now, "Recognizing that there could be more than one answer to the question, I asked if a party would be going out from the hut. It's very easy for someone in a warm building ten miles away to ask other people to go out, and names like Albert Dow come to mind." Albert was a member of the volunteer mountain rescue squad based in North Conway, and four years earlier he'd been killed while trying to help two teenagers whose inexperience had led them into difficulty.

Peter finishes the thought: "But if those people can actually feel the buffeting of the wind and the stinging ice pellets and have to stare out into the dark fog — if they make the decision that that's excessive risk for them, then I think we in our warm places have to respect that decision, even though it could have grave consequences." Emily told him the difficult news of her decision, and he backed her up completely, he said she should not risk anyone beyond the immediate shelter of the hut.

Right after this exchange Peter called the AMC personnel regrouping on the Valley Way. He told them that twelve should continue up to the hut, stay overnight, and go to work at first light if conditions allowed. The other six in the mobile group should return to Pinkham to keep normal operations going, though that number was considerably below the usual complement. The group should be divided so the strongest members would go up to the hut and those with necessary duties at Pinkham should return. After this conversation, he called Don Dercole of the Forest Service and brought him up to date, adding that his personnel might want to stay in the valley overnight and be ready for an early-morning departure rather than squeeze into the overcrowded hut. He also called Carl Carlson at Fish and Game asking for a call-back on the telephone.

Then Peter called Emily again. The contrast between his strong experience and his mild presence can be disconcerting, and he tells of that dreadful night in a voice that is hardly more than a whisper: "There had been more time to reconsider, or perhaps to wind down a little bit on what had happened thus far. After that decision was made, that initial decision, they had the opportunity to rethink, to reconsider, perhaps to have either more worries go through their head that this was the right decision or to gain confidence within that decision, so I asked again if this was something that they still wanted to follow through with. I indicated that this was a very serious decision they were making and asked if they wanted to re-evaluate their situation and the weather conditions." Emily told him that the situation at the hut had not changed, and they would stay with their decision.

Alexei was still cold and worn from his struggle with Tavis, but it was time for his other duties. The next day was his turn to cook, so he was busy with the small things of hut life, he was laying out the bacon and mixing the dry ingredients for the biscuits he'd make in the morning, and thinking ahead to what he'd make for dinner. He decided on the entrée and he'd probably make cheese bread. Emily taught him how to make cheese bread on the first day he cooked that summer, and he liked it so well that it was practically the only kind of bread he ever made.

Meanwhile, the crew was trying to keep Tavis in the picture, but they were being careful not to give him unrealistic hopes or unrealistic fears. He understood what they were doing. "At that point I knew that he was going to die. They made it sound like, 'We'll see if he's okay,' but you know, as a thirteen-year-old kid I thought they were just kind of delusioned. Now I know they were trying to put a good note on it, but..."

At 9:30 P.M. Peter called the Mount Washington Observatory again. They told him that the temperature remained steady at 32° with fog, rain, sleet, snow showers, and maximum visibility of fifty feet; the wind was averaging 79 mph, gusting regularly to the mid-80s and occasionally into the 90s. They expected no change over the next twelve hours except in the temperature, which might go lower. Peter knew that conditions would be only slightly less extreme where Don Barr was on the summit of Mt. Madison.

Peter tried to raise the group of AMC staff on the trail at 9:30, but he couldn't get them directly, nor could he reach them through the RMC relay. The upper sections of the Valley Way run through a deep cleft in the mountain and the topography blocks most transmission angles into it. He kept trying and he finally got through to Charlie McCrave on the trail and brought him up to date; Charlie said that his leading group was pretty well up by now and they'd keep going to the hut and regroup there. Peter had been keeping track of the numbers and he realized that Madison hut was two over capacity before any emergency crews arrived. Now it would be getting critically short of space.

Just then a call came from Troop F of the state police; they had more powerful radio equipment and mobile units on the road, and through them Peter arranged for four Forest Service men and three of his AMC contingent to turn around on the Valley Way and spend the night in Randolph. Ten minutes later he called Carl Carlson, the veteran at Fish and Game, and brought him up to date on the situation.

The regular 10:30 weather transmission from the summit observatory reported no change in wind or temperature, with intermittent snow and heavy icing. Ten minutes later, more members of the Pinkham crew arrived at the hut with their radio and fifteen minutes after that the three Pinkham crew who had turned around on the trail called from the parking lot at the base of the Valley Way and said they'd stand by to see if any more people would be coming down the trail. At 11:30 the last two members of the Pinkham group reached the hut and the five waiting in the parking lot were cleared to return to Pinkham.

Five minutes later Peter went to bed, but he did not rest. "You know there's someone up on the mountain and half a mile from the hut who most likely will not survive the night. It weighs on you." Up at the hut, everyone managed to find a bit of space to lie down and see if they could sleep. The crew room was full, the two big bunkrooms were full, there were people sleeping upstairs in the storage attic, there were people sleeping on the dining room tables and on the floor in places where they hoped no one would step on them. During the night the summit observatory recorded winds of 121 mph.

Emily went to bed in her crewroom bunk, but she did not sleep. She kept getting up, she'd go out to look at the night, she'd sit in the kitchen and think, "Could we do it?" There was wet clothing hanging everywhere and draped on every possible spot and she'd feel to see if it was getting dry. She even thought about how many for-sale AMC T-shirts there were — she could hand those around for dry clothes. She listened to the sleeping sounds of the people all around her in the hut, and most of all she kept listening to the constant roaring and rushing of the wind and she thought that sometimes storms just suddenly blow themselves out and she'd stretch to see if she could hear the slightest lessening that might bring hope, but she never heard it.

Stephanie was still with Tavis. "It was hard for me to know what he was thinking. I don't remember much sleep. I was staring out the window into the darkness and holding him and trying to reassure him that he was okay. People were coming in and out and there was the darkness and he was sleeping some. I was whispering to him and murmuring to him in the night, trying to be quiet."

First light came and at 5:55 A.M. Emily radioed Pinkham with a weather report: 42° and wind-driven rain at the hut, and the rescue group up there would be ready to start for the summit in five minutes.

On consultation it was decided to send a carry party of nine to the summit and keep a relief group of five at the hut. Peter reminded the hut contingent that Don should be treated as any person in severe hypothermia: his wet clothes should be removed and replaced with dry insulation, he should be protected from wind and further wetting, and any possible heat loss should be eliminated as far as possible.

Then Peter again made sure that Emily and everyone in her crew remembered the first rule of search and rescue: No member of the rescue group should risk becoming a victim. The litter group left the hut at 7:05 and they found Don Barr thirty minutes later. He was in the trail just below the summit of Mt. Madison and the EMT people determined that he was unresponsive.

It was the second time up there for Lars: "The wind was still blowing pretty good, certainly not as high as the night before, the clouds had lifted and the angle of wind had changed just enough so when we got to the flat place where he was lying it was almost calm. He was just lying there with his hands crossed on his chest." Lars stood off to one side in that small island of quiet air, out of the way of the people tending to Don. It was his first death and he kept thinking that he was the last one to see Don alive, and now this. Then he saw Emily go over and kneel down beside him.

Emily was struck by the way Don lay there on his back with his hands crossed on his chest and she thought that he looked very peaceful and composed; this was such a contrast to what she expected that she almost spoke to him. She saw that his eyes were wide open and looking up into the endless sky, and she thought it was time for his eyes to close. Emily remembered all those death scenes in the movies where someone reaches out with a small gesture and brushes a person's eyelids down as a sort of final benediction, but now she learned that unseeing eyes don't close as easily as that.

The guideline among emergency teams is "Not dead until warm and dead," so this was still a rescue, not a recovery. They put Don Barr in a sleeping bag and added blankets and the weatherproof hypowrap, and they were careful to handle him as gently as they could, because when a person is in extreme hypothermia even a slight interruption can push the heart into crisis. They started down toward the hut with the litter, they were thinking, "Maybe there's a chance." The carry required everything they had — at one point the entire team was knocked down by the wind and they struggled to keep the litter from hitting anything.

Earlier in the morning Emily had sent a radio request for someone to start up the trail with dry clothing for Tavis and Christian, and a speedy volunteer was found for that mission. Tavis was in the kitchen while the crew was getting ready to go up to the summit and Lars was watching him, "I could see in his eyes that he kind of recognized what had happened. But maybe there's still some hope, 'Okay, the rescue crew is going up and they're going to see what's going on.' We explained that hypothermia is one of those things where you can recover. We were injecting a little bit of hope into ourselves, that there is a possibility that he could make it. So I'm sure he was still holding out some hope, but he kind of knew that if his dad had been lying up there all night, things weren't very good."

When Kari Geick was back in the hut after she helped rescue Tavis, she decided that her best part was tending to the domestic routine. Everyone else on the crew was between eighteen and twenty-two years old and they'd been together all summer; she was five years older than the oldest of them, but she was still only a few hours into her career with the AMC. She did understand housekeeping, though, and the hut was still in full operation, so she decided to concentrate her efforts on the dishes and pots and pans and other domestic necessities, and free the regular crew for the difficult tasks rising on every side.

The next morning she was struck by the layering around her. The crew was tending to routine tasks but there was a stunned quality everywhere. Alexei was the cook for this day and he'd finished his part of breakfast some time ago, so he began the usual business of checking out the guests. "It was kind of surreal, taking their Visas and MasterCards at the same time as all these other things were going on." The guests were very quiet as they packed up and most of them changed whatever other hiking plans they had and went down the Valley Way, where they'd be sure of quick shelter.

Traffic was moving up the Valley Way at the same time. There were men from New Hampshire Fish and Game and from the Forest Service and still more from the AMC. Stephanie was devoting all her time to Tavis, but she heard members of the crew saying, "Rich Crowley is coming up — Rich Crowley will be here soon," as if that would change everything and they'd be all right.

Kari heard this, too, and she was impressed and puzzled. Then she learned that Rich was the long-time manager of the storehouse down at Pinkham; he took the hut crew orders and did the food shopping to meet their cooking needs and then packed it into cartons and delivered it to the base of the pack trail, and this day he was coming up with extra clothes for Christian and Tavis. Then he reached the hut and nothing changed. Kari decided that Rich was the person who took care of the hut crews — that's what the storehouse man does, he gets what the hut crews need. So, in the awful strangeness of that morning, it seemed natural that he'd be the one who could set things right.

The crew was amazed to learn that Tavis was only thirteen; seeing his size, they thought he was probably seventeen. They were worried about his day, they imagined the ways he could meet his father being carried in a litter with his face covered, and they worked out a timing to avoid that.

At 8:43 further reserves were alerted in an AMC group staying at Camp Dodge, the old CCC station four and a half miles from the Pinkham Notch headquarters. The litter party from the summit of Madison reached the hut at 9:00, and an hour later Emily called Pinkham and learned that further reinforcements of eleven people from the Forest Service, Fish and Game, and the AMC had started up the Valley Way at 9:15. At 11:15, the litter team started down the Valley Way with MacDonald Barr.

Stephanie Arenalas stayed with Tavis through the night and through the early hours in the kitchen when everyone was up and around and she stayed with him through breakfast. She cooked some things to eat for the various people coming up the Valley Way to help and she kept Tavis occupied while the litter party came past the hut with his father. Finally she and Rich Crowley started down the Valley Way with Tavis and Christian.

Tavis hadn't been saying much during the morning; the crew thought he seemed a bit distant and disengaged, and they tried not to crowd him. Then on the hike down he seemed to be bothered by the clothes that had been brought up for him. There wasn't any underwear and the pants were much too big, so the crew had made a belt for him out of a piece of the rope they use to tie loads on when they're packing supplies up to the hut. He kept talking about the pants as they made their way down the Valley Way and Stephanie realized that she really didn't know what a seventh-grader should say at a time like this.

That trail was originally built as a bridle path with easy grades all the way from the valley to the hut, but that was ninety years ago and now it was severely eroded by the many generations of hikers and the rains and meltwater of all the years. The footway was filled with loose rocks and roots and wet places, and a very severe test for a litter carry.

An hour after the litter party started down, a call went to the valley contingent to start up with relief carriers, and another hour after that three more AMC crew members headed for the Valley Way to help. The combined litter crew reached the Valley Way parking lot at 3:40 P.M. and they were met by an emergency response vehicle from the Androscoggin Valley Hospital. Every resuscitation effort failed and MacDonald Barr was pronounced dead later that afternoon.

Rich Crowley drove Stephanie and Tavis and Christian back to Pinkham Notch in his car and Stephanie went into the AMC building with Tavis. There was a telephone booth near the door and he insisted on calling his mother; then he told her abruptly that his father was dead. Yvonne Barr already knew; she'd had a call from an official source.

Stephanie and Rich thought it was time for Tavis to be alone for a while, so they showed him to a bunk upstairs in the crew quarters. Later that morning Mrs. Barr arrived at Pinkham and she met Peter Crane and Stephanie out near the kitchen. Stephanie tried to explain what had happened and what they tried to do up at Madison, but then she had to walk away from Mrs. Barr. She'd done all she could do.

The Madison crew was in the habit of making a little talk to the guests at suppertime. That evening Lars made a larger talk than usual. He talked about his love for the mountains and his respect for them and he said that people are not infallible, they're fragile up in the mountains and there are times when things go wrong, not as a sacrifice but as a reminder of what can happen. He talked about the cold fronts that come through at the end of August and how people start at the bottom and when they get to the top it's a different world. He told them that they'd come to our nice cozy hut expecting all sorts of amenities and we provide that to you, but you have to get here first. Then he said that one of those times came just the night before...

When he finished, Lars said later, "They were all looking at me." Kari Geick was looking at him, too. It seemed to her that the talk was partly for the guests and partly for himself, that it was his way of finishing up the terrible night of MacDonald Barr.

Three days later Emily was back at Middlebury College; she was on the women's field hockey team and they had a pre-season training camp. Everywhere she turned there was laughter and cries of greeting and hugs of reunion and, "How was your summer?" and, "My summer was really great!" Emily gave them her greetings and her hugs, but she didn't go into much detail about being in charge at Madison Hut.

AFTERMATH

The two climbers who were marooned on Mount Washington were exposed to the full force of the storm on August 24, but when the weather moderated they emerged from their tent and hiked down the mountain without any adverse effects.

About ten years after the death of MacDonald Barr, two women hit heavy weather while crossing the range toward Madison Hut. They were exhausted and felt unable to continue, so they took shelter under a plastic sheet they had with them. The crew at Madison hut heard about them and, remembering the story of MacDonald Barr, they went out along the range until they found the women a mile from the hut, and then the Madison crew insisted that the women get up and hike on to the hut.

Peter Crane stayed with the mountains. The weather observatory on Mount Washington has expanded its work and now runs extensive educational programs on the summit and in its new valley station in North Conway. Peter is director of all special programs for the observatory.

Emily Thayer suffered a severe knee injury two days after the start of the Middlebury field hockey camp and she missed the whole semester. She continued with seasonal work for the AMC for three more years as summer hutmaster or winter caretaker. At this writing her brother Chris is huts manager for the AMC. She married Peter Benson, who followed the Barr emergency on the radio at Zealand Hut, and they have two children. Peter is the New Hampshire Preserves Manager for the Nature Conservancy. Emily has not forgotten MacDonald Barr, "It's always hovering, it's always there." Since then, she has run many guided hikes for mountain visitors.

Alexei Rubenstein worked at the AMC's Greenleaf Hut in the summer of 1987 and had to deal with a fatal heart attack there. Lars Jorrens took advanced EMT training and is now teaching those skills and working full time in wilderness education at Keeping Track, in Richmond, Vermont. He married Jennifer Botzo, who followed the Barr emergency on the radio from Lonesome Lake Hut, and they are raising a family.

Kari Geick stayed with the AMC longer than she expected. The next summer she worked at Carter Notch Hut with Emily and Lars, she worked as a winter caretaker at Zealand Hut and she guided hikes for two summers. Since then she's worked in Alaska, and she spent three years in Antarctica including two winters at the South Pole. Her first day of AMC work is still with her. "It shaped my life. With my mountaineering life, or life in general, I look at what can happen."

There was, for instance, the day in May 1999 when she hiked up the Zugspitz, Germany's highest peak. It's a popular tourist climb, and she and her friend took a return path that led over a snow slope lingering from the winter. It was late in the afternoon, the sidehill fell away steeply, and Kari knew the soft snow of the day would be glazing over and she didn't have the right equipment. She took a long look, weighed the consequences of a slip, and turned back to find another way down.

Tavis Barr has not done much hiking since his father's death. Then in April 1999 he was on a trip to California and spent a day in Yosemite, where he and some friends hiked up the path to the top of the park's signature waterfall. "There were people there who were casually out on their day hike," he said later. "I don't think they'd thought twice about it, they were going up in the same jeans and T-shirts that we were wearing. You can see the top of the falls from the bottom, you can see it's not cold. But I could see that they're not cautious enough. I brought along a down coat and a sweater and a hat and gloves. There was no reason I needed a winter hat and gloves up there at the top, but I still remembered."

CHAPTER SEVENTEEN

THE DEADLIEST SEASON

*T*he last fifty years have seen large changes in the popular view of winter. Cold weather used to be like the mountains themselves, it was something to be avoided, and winter visits to the heights of the Presidential Range were only undertaken by necessity or by impulses that were viewed as borderline eccentricity.

Frederick Strickland reached the summit of Mount Washington in the course of his snow-racked outing in 1849, but he'd been advised not to do it and he did not survive. The old records do not tell of much high-elevation activity until mention of a forward-looking party that tried to climb the Tuckerman Ravine headwall in 1884. They failed.

Two men did reach the summit on December 7, 1885, and they made the climb in the service of a legal dispute of the highest order: ownership of the summit. One of the proprietors of the Tip-Top House disputed the real estate title and a deputy sheriff climbed the mountain to serve papers announcing that the property was under attachment by court order. The summit was unoccupied, but custom dictated that a copy of the papers be physically attached to the property. The sheriff was accompanied on the climb by Benjamin Osgood, the keeper of the Glen House who made the trail to the summit of Mt. Madison that still bears his name.

Necessity was the mother of that climb, many years would pass before the idea of winter climbing as sport took hold, and when Joe Dodge kept the AMC cabins in Pinkham Notch open for the winter of 1927, the centers of civilization in southern New England still regarded them as an outpost on a distant horizon. Nevertheless, Joe accommodated 512 guests that winter and served 1,096 meals, and the sale of supplies and sundries totaled $67.15. Wheeled traffic was infrequent and a summertime picture from 1928 shows why: the highway grade up the south side of the notch looked as if it was paved with boulders. It was not plowed for the first several years of his winter occupancy and it was still a lonely place when plows did come to the notch; Joe's son Brooks remembers that in the 1930s and even in the '40s, whole evenings would pass when he wouldn't hear a single car go by.

Useful winter seasons really arrived after World War II, when the civilian market was flooded with cold-weather equipment developed for the military. Since then, winter equipment has advanced with exponential strides and now there are stores near the Presidential Range where an enthusiast can walk out with $4,000 worth of clothing in addition to a wealth of hardware. Parking lots take the story from there.

On New Year's Day of 1998 I drove "around the mountains" — up through Pinkham Notch, around the north end of the range through Randolph, down the west side to Twin Mountain, around the south end through Crawford Notch, and back up to Pinkham. I stopped at every parking lot that served trails giving access to 4,000-foot peaks and counted cars. The weather had been brutal and the previous night brought temperatures below zero in the valleys and equally threatening conditions on the heights. A generation earlier I would have been surprised to find any cars at all in these parking lots, but on this day I counted 231 vehicles.

I did it again in 1999. The weather was the same, below zero every night for a week in the valleys with several sieges of very high wind, and this

New Year's Day the upper elevations were buried in storm clouds. I made the same stops and counted 289 cars. As in the 1998 inventory, I did not include vehicles with the kind of trailer used for off-road vehicles, but I did count a dog sled with 28-paw drive.

Another new age had already arrived. One summer day in 1988 an accident report was brought down from the Carter-Moriah Range on the eastern side of Pinkham Notch. The terrain up there can be difficult and the day was raw and wet, so a full-scale rescue was laid on. The trouble was discovered to be a hiker who was very much reduced by alcohol, and the evacuation took most of the night. Accidents are accidents, the rescue team was thinking, and a bad fall can happen to the best of us, that's why we always answer the call. But this fellow could not have gotten drunk by accident and his rescue put many people at hazard themselves. So he was cited for reckless conduct and ordered to pay a considerable fine.

This kind of situation is now covered by two statutes. The first one was New Hampshire RSA 576:3 Reckless Conduct, which provides that, "A person is guilty of a misdemeanor if he recklessly engages in conduct which places or may place another in danger of serious bodily injury." This was enacted in the early 1970s, and the commentary attached to the statute explained, "In dealing with conduct that endangers but does not harm others (this) fills an undesirable gap in New Hampshire statutes. If actual harm occurs, then a criminal assault will have taken place. Since, when a person acts recklessly, he disregards a risk he knows of and acts with an indifference to the injury he may cause to others, he is just as culpable when the risk does not eventuate in the injury as when it does. Without a statute of this sort, however, a person whose behavior menaces in this way could be prosecuted only if the harm actually occurs."

RSA 576:3 was later amplified by RSA 631:3, which included the addition proviso that, "If you engage in reckless activity, you may face criminal prosecution. If you fail to heed warnings of authorized personnel, in addition to being criminally prosecuted, you may be required to pay the entire cost of your search or rescue."

The rapidly increasing number of hikers in the mountains combined with increasingly sophisticated rescue equipment, and costs became a serious factor: the New Hampshire Department of Fish and Game alone goes on more than 150 rescue missions a year and spends about $150,000 in their support. The matter of cost recovery came up again and again, but the provisions included in those RSA statutes were rarely invoked in mountain emergencies. Then in December 1999, New Hampshire Fish and Game officials announced that they would take a stricter attitude in billing hikers who required aid.

Several questions arose. Who would define reckless behavior and what standards would be applied? If insurance against such claims was available, as is widely done in Europe, would this become a variant of the cell-phone effect? Would it embolden hikers to take more risks than they usually would?

Few seasons provided as many landmarks on this cultural map as the winter of 1994, when four lethal emergencies developed on the Presidential Range. Just one of them enlisted the help of 204 search and rescue personnel including 32 from the Forest Service, 32 from the AMC, 120 from Fish and Game and other organizations, and 20 volunteers, with the services of Thiokol snow tractors, an ambulance, and a helicopter. The father of one of the victims brought suit against the United States of America for failing to protect visitors in the national forest against hazard.

· DEREK TINKHAM ·
JANUARY 1994

$\mathcal{J}$oe Dodge's legacy is a cluster of buildings at the Appalachian Mountain Club headquarters in Pinkham Notch and the "pack room" is a popular spot, the place climbers gather when they're about to start on a climb, or just returning from one. Thursday evening, January 15, 1994, a young man was holding forth at considerable length on his plans, a four-day traverse along the skyline ridge of the Presidential Range. Another hiker was forcibly struck by how easily he dominated the room and the people there, and how his companion sat by, silent and enthralled.

The speaker was Jeremy Haas, the listener was Derek Tinkham; both college students. Derek had plans. He loved the mountains, he went climbing up here whenever he could, he meant to go on to work as a guide, and he'd gotten a job with the rescue team in Yosemite for the coming summer. His long-time friend Jennifer Taylor often drove him up to the mountains to start a trip and picked him up when it was done.

Their route usually took them through North Conway, twenty miles south of Mount Washington, and Derek would always stop at International Mountain Equipment, a major source of serious gear, advice, and companionship. Jennifer noticed that Derek would let only one person wait on him; no matter how small the transaction or how many unoccupied people were behind the counter, he always waited until a short, compact fellow was free. Finally Jennifer asked her friend why he always waited for that person. Derek explained that the person he waited for was Rick Wilcox, that he was a great mountaineer, that he'd climbed Mount

Everest. Derek admired him tremendously and wanted the kind of life Rick had. Jennifer understood.

What they could learn from Rick Wilcox should also be understood, because it's the key to everything that followed. Rick started with the neighborhood mountains of New England and worked his way up. Now he's made eleven trips to the Himalayas and he knows how very small are the margins which determine not just whether a summit is reached, but whether a climber returns at all.

A Himalayan summit day begins years earlier, when the leader applies for permission to make the try. The planning, the money-raising, the risk to business and family relations, the long trek to base camp, the push higher and higher up the flanks, all increase the pressure to make those last few hundred yards to the summit. That's what we're taught to do; our culture is obsessed with success and climbers are our surrogates, they're the ones who keep pushing upwards.

For Rick Wilcox and his climbing mates, the weather had gone bad just a few hundred yards below the summit of Makalu, fifth highest in the world. They turned around without hesitation. Six days of dizzyingly steep snow climbing protect the summit ridge of Cho Oyo, then there's a very long knife edge and, just below the summit, a small rock wall with a drop of 10,000 feet at the climber's heels. Rick's partner was Mark Richey and he led the first move onto that wall and when he began to drive in the first piton he sensed the brittle quality of the rock. He looked at Rick and, with hardly a word, they turned around. The summit was right there, and they turned around and headed for home, half a world away.

On his fifth Himalayan expedition, the summit of Everest was so still that Rick sat there for an hour. From the beginning, he'd had the feeling that finally, on this trip, it was his turn. The clouds came in that afternoon and Rick's partner kept track of his own descent by noting the curious markers at the top of the world. There are frozen bodies on the summit pitches of Everest, climbers who did not plan as well or who kept pushing when the signs were bad. It's too difficult to take dead climbers down, so they stay there forever and wiser climbers use them as guides.

The hike Jeremy had planned for himself and Derek began Friday afternoon, but, like a Himalayan expedition, the important decisions had been made much earlier. Jennifer had urged Derek to take along a small mountaineering tent, but Jeremy wanted to travel light, so they took bivy bags instead, weather-resistant coverings for their sleeping bags. Jeremy also left his over-mitts at home; he wanted the added dexterity of gloves.

Something else had already been decided, probably years earlier: Jeremy had a tendency to keep pushing. He'd led a climb for the University of New Hampshire Outing Club, and when they returned many of the group complained that he'd kept charging ahead and was not sensitive to their needs. He was told he could not be a trip leader anymore and he resigned from the club. Over the Christmas break he took Chris Rose on a Presidential Range traverse and Chris got so cold that his toes were frozen. The trip Jeremy planned for himself and Derek was the same route as the one that had claimed his friend's toes two years earlier.

The pack-up room where Jeremy held forth at Pinkham Notch was built many years after we set out to rescue the failing hiker on Guinea Day, but other elements have not changed. The weather observatory on Mount Washington is 4,288 feet upslope from the AMC buildings, detailed reports and predictions for the upper elevations are always posted by the AMC, and climbers check them as a reflex before starting up. High winds and extreme cold were predicted for that weekend. Jeremy and Derek started for the base of the Air Line Trail, a popular route departing from Randolph and rising to skyline on the northern end of the Presidential Range.

The trees grew smaller and more dense as they neared timberline. There are openings here, certified as overnight campsites by years of native wisdom. The two climbers stopped in one and settled into their bivy bags; "bivy" means bivouac. As they slept, the weather above timberline, severe enough when they started, grew worse.

The summit observatory recorded -6° at midnight and -23° at 8:00 A.M.; the wind moved into the west and at 8:00 A.M. it was steady in the 40 mph range, not high by local standards, but a west wind rakes straight across the skyline teeth of the 6.5-mile ridge Jeremy and Derek would traverse. They climbed to the top of Madison, then Adams, second-highest peak in the Northeast. It was close to noon now, and they'd been making quite good time.

This section of trail leads down to Edmands Col, a mile of easy going. Derek was having trouble, but Jeremy would go on ahead, wait for him to catch up, then go ahead again. Derek was going slower and slower and he was becoming unsteady on his feet, signs that betray the onset of hypothermia. Edmands Col lies between Adams and Jefferson and the mild descent took many times longer than it would in summer. Hypothermia is not just cold hands and feet; it comes when the cold has bitten right through and the core temperature begins to drop. The body circles up the metabolic wagons to make a last stand against death, blood is concentrated in the viscera, the mind becomes sluggish and the limbs erratic.

At this point, there were three refuges nearby, all below timberline: The Perch is a three-sided shelter, the old cabin at Crag Camp had just been replaced with a snug and completely weatherproof building, and Gray Knob had also been rebuilt and had a caretaker, heat, lights, and radio contact to the valley. The two hikers discussed a retreat to one of them, but decided to continue upward toward the summit of Jefferson. Jeremy's original plan was to go on to Clay Col, a mile and a half away up Jefferson and down the other side; he remembered an ice cave there during a previous trip and his idea was to use it for the second night of this trip.

In the prevailing weather conditions, this was a plan of breathtaking stupidity. Ice caves are ephemeral, what Jeremy had seen two years earlier might not be there at all this year. Even if it was, Clay Col would be a furious torrent of arctic wind and an ice cave was not what they needed. As bad as it was in Edmands Col, it could only be worse in Clay Col, higher and nearer the Mount Washington weather vortex. The two climbers were getting weaker, the storm was getting stronger.

Afterward, Jeremy said the decision to push on was a mutual one. But veteran climbers know that, since Jeremy was the stronger and more experienced of the two, his job was to get Derek down to shelter, any shelter. As Rick Wilcox puts it, "When you climb solo, you only have to worry about yourself, but when you climb with another person,

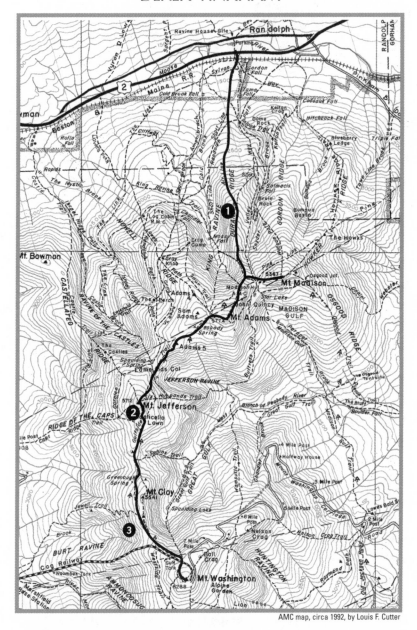

AMC map, circa 1992, by Louis F. Cutter

1 Climbed with Jeremy Haas up Air Line Trail and spent night in Spruce Shelter

2 Up on Air Line to climb Mt. Madison, then across Gulfside Trail to
Mt. Jefferson; Tinkham died on the summit of Jefferson

3 Haas crossed Gulfside Trail to summit of Mount Washington

it's your responsibility to look out for him." In fairness to Jeremy, he was suffering from the same extreme conditions and that might have affected his judgment.

When they got to the summit of Jefferson, Derek collapsed. Having left a tent at home, Jeremy tried to get him into a sleeping bag, then left for the summit of Mount Washington more than three miles away. It was 4:30 P.M., darkness would soon overtake him, the summit temperature had dropped to -27°, and the wind was in the 80s with a peak gust of 96 mph. Jeremy lost his gloves and, having left his heavy overmitts at home, his hands were too cold to let him get at the food and the flashlight he had in his pack. He kept his hands under his armpits as he staggered and crawled along the ridge toward Mount Washington.

Conditions like this do not match normal experience. One year I went up to the summit for Thanksgiving dinner with the observatory crew; the weather was moderate and the climb enjoyable, but the day after the feast the wind rose to 150 mph; the day after that the recording pen went off the chart at 162. In lulls, the observers would climb the inside of the tower to the instrument deck to clear ice from the sensors. I'd go up to help and found a curious situation: Facing the wind made it difficult to exhale, back to the wind made it difficult to get a breath in. Strictly speaking, it was physics, but it felt like drowning in an ocean of air. Purposive effort hardly worked at all, and years later when I saw news footage of people getting hit by police water cannons I thought of that storm on Mount Washington.

Supper on the Saturday of Jeremy and Derek's trip was a noisy meal in the observatory. There was the hammer of an 80-mph wind and cracking sounds from the building itself: the concrete and the embedded steel reinforcing rods contract at different rates. Ken Rancourt and Ralph Patterson were on duty and they were used to this, but now Ken suddenly looked intent; he'd heard a different, more rhythmic banging in the midst of the uproar. He and Ralph traced the sound to a door on the north side of the building: Someone was out there.

A few minutes later Jeremy Haas was inside. He was barely able to talk, but as Ralph checked for the most obvious signs of damage he asked Jeremy if he was alone. Jeremy indicated that he'd left his partner near the summit of Jefferson. The wind peaked at 103 that night and between midnight and 4:00 A.M. the temperature held steady at -40°.

Some newspaper reports described Jeremy's fierce traverse as "heroic." Others had worked out a different calculus of risk and they did not share that view. Prominent in the latter group are the ones who tried to rescue Derek Tinkham.

By 9:00 P.M. the observatory crew had called the valley to report the onrushing emergency, and the message reached the Mountain Rescue Service. Joe Lentini answered, then he and co-leader Nick Yardley put the "A Team" on standby. The first decision had already been made: The combination of darkness and brutal conditions made a rescue attempt that night impossible. It's a difficult but accepted calculation; at a certain point, many lives cannot be risked in a try to save one. At 5:00 A.M., the team left for the base of Caps Ridge Trail, the shortest route up Jefferson.

Conditions were extraordinarily harsh as the eleven team members started up; "We looked," one thought, "like an advertisement for every high-tech equipment company you ever heard of." Even so, Joe Lentini was keeping a sharp eye out for signs of frostbite or falter among his crew. Caps Ridge takes its name from a line of three rocky outbursts heaping up above timberline like the bony spines on the back of some prehistoric monster. Summertime hikers have to hold on up here, and in winter it's immeasurably tougher: The caps are clad in ice, with wind-blown snow in the sheltered parts of the jagged skyline. There's dwarf spruce under the drifts and impossible to see, and when the climbers stepped in the wrong place they'd fall through up to their ribs.

Up past the last cap, Tiger Burns advised Joe Lentini that his feet were getting cold. Knowing that it would only get worse and that a disabled team member higher up would vastly increase their problems, he descended to a sheltered place to wait for the others to return. He was still above timberline, but he was ready.

Tiger's outfit was typical of the MRS team that day: He had many layers of specialized clothing under his weatherproof outer shell. He had insulated bib-pants and parka with a heat-reflective Mylar lining, a balaclava helmet, a pile-lined Gore-Tex hat under the hood, and a scarf and flaps snugging up the spaces around his face. He had polypropylene liner gloves, expedition-weight wool gloves, extra-heavy expedition mitts with overshells, and chemical heaters for hands and feet. In his pack, Tiger had two sets of back-ups for his gloves and mitts, two more hats, another scarf, extra chemical heat packs, and a bivy bag. Unlike most of the climbers, he was not wearing goggles. Instead, as his exhaled breath froze in his balaclava he pinched the woolen fabric into narrow slits over his eyes.

Tiger's big problem was his cocoa. He zipped himself inside the bivy bag, loosened his boots, set the chemical heaters to work on his feet, and reached for his Thermos. Hot as it was, though, and nestled under all the other insulating gear in his pack, the stopper had frozen tight.

Up above, the trail led onto an alpine zone of ice and rough broken rock, with the 1,000-foot summit pyramid of Jefferson rising above it. It was just here that the wind hit the MRS team, a blast so severe that they could communicate only by putting their heads right together and yelling. At 10:00 A.M., Al Comeau spotted a bit of color up near the peak of the mountain.

It was Derek's bivy bag. It was just below the summit and Derek was lying there half out of his sleeping bag. He was wearing a medium-weight parka and it was only partly zipped; his other clothes were barely sufficient for a good-weather winter climb, and his hands were up at his face as if trying to keep away the calamity that fell on him at dusk the day before. There were two packs with sleeping bags nearby, on top of an insulated sleeping pad. Troubling things had happened here, but there was no time for reflection now.

As the team started down, the wind hit them straight in the face. It was -32°, the wind was peaking in the high 80s, and they were barely keeping ahead of it in clothing like the outfit Rick Wilcox had on the top of Everest. In conditions like this, you don't go where you want to go, you go where the wind and terrain let you go, whether your feet and burden like it or not.

Suddenly Maury McKinney pulled up lame. He understood life in high places; in Nepal he'd turned back short of the summit in a winter attempt on 26,504-foot Annapurna. Here on Jefferson he broke through into a hole and the whole of his weight drove his heel down. At first he thought the Achilles tendon had torn, but a brief test showed that the damage was higher up in his calf. In this moment, the rescue party's situation became critical. This kind of injury worsens quickly and in these conditions they could neither leave him behind nor slow to his pace, so they'd have to carry him and leave Derek's body behind.

Then Andy Orsini's eyes froze shut. He and Maury had planned a climb that day, but when they saw the weather they decided to watch the NFL play-offs instead. As it turned out, they made a climb anyway. So Bob Parrot helped Andy cover up completely and Maury leaned against his other side, partly to guide him, partly to relieve his own bad leg. This battered troika made its way down through the ice and rock for several hundred yards until Maury was able to reach in through Andy's wrappings to rub his eyes and melt the ice.

Down below, Tiger Burns was still trying to get at his cocoa. He bashed the top against a rock to loosen it, but only dented the cup. He burrowed into his bivy bag for awhile, then reached out to bang on the Thermos again, but he only succeeded in tearing the handle off. The exercise did warm up his hands so he took off his gloves for a better grip but still no luck; it only made his hands cold again.

When the team reached him, they took their first rest in eight hours of continuous maximum effort. Several times they'd considered leaving the body and saving themselves, but then they thought of Derek's family and how they'd feel if their son was still up there, alone with the storm, and they kept going. Once in the woods, they talked amongst themselves about what had happened. "Bottom line," said Mike Pelchat, "I would never ditch a partner like that."

Later, there was time for reflection. Like many members of the recovery groups, Andy Orsini had instinctively shut out the human qualities of the job in order to get on with it. By Tuesday, this insulation had turned to anger. He had the newspaper account and read that, when asked if he had any regrets, Jeremy had said, "Yes, I wish I'd brought mittens instead of gloves." Andy was so appalled that he called the newspaper reporter to verify the remark. "It's something I have to live with," said Al Comeau, "seeing Derek there... He was a victim of Jeremy's state of mind and over-ambitiousness. That one really bothered me."

• MONROE COUPER AND ERIK LATTEY •
FEBRUARY 1994

    *T*hat winter, Jim Dowd had also been bothered. He was care-taker of the Harvard cabin below Mount Washington's Huntington Ravine and about two miles up from the highway in Pinkham Notch, and it seemed as if practically every climber who came through said he'd read an article about ice climbing in Pinnacle Gully up in the ravine. It was in *Climbing* magazine and it was written by an eager but inexperienced teenager who'd gotten into trouble up there with his friend. The two boys thought the experience was kind of neat and people kept telling Jim they thought it was a great story.

    Talk like this made Jim feel a little sick and he'd made a point not to read the article; when he was eleven years old, his father had died while climbing the next ridge. One of the reasons Jim was working up here was a sense that he'd like to give something back, and he didn't like to hear about people rushing into ill-advised risks.

    While that issue of *Climbing* was current, Monroe Couper and Erik Lattey were planning their own climb in Huntington Ravine. They were friends in New Jersey, both had young families, and both were just getting started in winter climbing. Now they headed for New Hampshire and signed in at the AMC headquarters at 1:30 on Friday afternoon, February 25. The weather forecast for the next day was favorable: high temperatures in the teens, winds on the summit increasing to 40-60 mph. They wouldn't be going to the summit, so it looked good.

    Huntington Ravine has always been place of risk. Monroe and Erik planned to climb Pinnacle Gully, which is just to the right of Odell's Gully, the site of Jessie Whitehead's troubles sixty-one years earlier. They left the Harvard cabin in good season, then they returned —

they'd forgotten their climbing rope. Having retrieved their rope, Monroe and Erik started back up toward Pinnacle at about noon. The weather forecast, however, had been wrong; conditions higher up were deteriorating rapidly. Bill Aughton was the director of Search and Rescue at the AMC camp in Pinkham Notch and he was guiding a trip across the Presidentials that day. He was so struck by the unexpectedly bad weather that he took a picture looking ahead to Mount Washington, then turned his group around.

A climber at the bottom of Huntington Ravine spotted Monroe and Erik in upper Pinnacle Gully at 5:00 P.M. They were not moving well. Guides allow three hours for Pinnacle; Monroe and Erik had been up there for five. The usual turn-around time is 2:30 or 3:00, they were two and a half hours past that and still going up, toward the approaching night.

Going up in ice climbing must be understood conditionally: while one climber is moving, the other stays in a fixed position to tend the rope and belays, the safety margin. Thus, either Monroe or Erik had been almost motionless for half of their time in Pinnacle, absorbing the cold. The overnight lodgers at the Harvard cabin were settling in, tending to their gear and making their various preparations for supper, when someone noticed two packs in a corner which didn't belong to anyone there.

The top of Pinnacle eases over onto the Alpine Garden, well above timberline. This place is a summer delight, table-flat and almost a mile wide, and spread with tiny flowers, dense moss, and delicate sedges. One of the several unique plants that lives here has its growth cells at the base of its stalk instead of the tip, the better to withstand the brutal winter.

This was brutal winter, and as Monroe and Erik felt their way out of the top of Pinnacle, they found only wind-scoured ice and rock. Just above them on the summit, the wind averaged 90-mph between nine and eleven that evening, gusting to 108 at 9:50; by midnight, the temperature had fallen to -24°. A maximum rescue effort was being organized in the valley.

At 6:00 A.M., thirty-three climbers gathered at the AMC headquarters; the plan was to send teams up several climbing gullies of Huntington Ravine and also comb the adjacent area, the most likely places to find the missing pair.

The plan was quickly modified. The climbers were getting into their routes soon after 9:00 A.M., it was -16° at the observatory on the ridge above them, and the wind averaged over 100 mph from 7:00 A.M. until noon with a peak gust of 127 at 9:45. Tiger Burns was working his way up Escape Gully with two partners and he suddenly found himself in midair, blown out like a heavily dressed pennant in the arctic wind, with only one elbow looped through a webbing strap to keep him from a very long fall. Nick Yardley and his partners were the only ones to get above timberline, and that only briefly — they had to crawl down.

After all the teams were back down on the wooded plateau near the Harvard cabin, it occurred to Jim Dowd that Monroe and Erik might have gotten into Raymond Cataract. It's a broad basin between Huntington Ravine and Tuckerman Ravine with a remarkably even contour, no steeper than a hiking trail, and funneling into an outlet nearby. Jim was thinking that Monroe and Erik might have made a snow cave in Raymond Cataract. They might still be there, probably unhappy, but safe.

Jim and Chad Lewis started up into the Cataract. Snow drifts in heavily here and it almost avalanched on them. Jim had a grim sort of chuckle: Al Dow had died in an avalanche near here during another winter search mission and there's a plaque honoring him on a rescue cache in Huntington Ravine. Jim was thinking that if this slope let go they could just add "d" to the name on the plaque to remember himself.

Their hopes lifted when they found boot tracks, but they turned out to be from Nick Yardley and his partner, descending. Other than that, there was only a fuel bottle and a pot lid, found in the floor of the ravine. They were on top of the snow, so they couldn't have been there long; they'd probably been blown loose from someone higher up. Jim and Chad made a last visual check up Pinnacle and saw nothing. Then they looked at each other and said, at almost the same moment, "They're still on the climb." Privately Jim thought, "Damn, we missed the boat. We were looking in the escape routes." He imagined the climbers thinking, "We need to get out of here and the direction we're going is up." First lessons in climbing teach people to climb, not escape. Monroe and Erik had kept pushing upward.

When Jim got back to the cabin that evening, there were the usual number of recreational climbers in for the night, but the usual banter was missing. "Everyone was looking at me with these big eyes, like, 'What happened to those guys?'" Jim had gone through their packs earlier to see if he could get an idea of what they had with them by seeing what they'd left behind. He'd also found two steaks, so now, after the long day of work trying to find the missing climbers, he cooked their steaks for his own supper.

Early Monday morning the teams started up again. The summit temperature was steady between -13° and -15° at 5:00 A.M. the wind peaked at 128 mph, just after 8:00 A.M. it touched 124. Ben Miller was with a group climbing Odell Gully. Ben had the longest association with Mount Washington: his father worked up there for thirty-nine years. Himself a climber of long experience, Ben knew the mountain and its habits as if it were his backyard.

Ben's group reached the intersection of Odell with Alpine Garden and found a cleavage plane — lying flat, Ben felt that if he put his head up, the wind would simply peel him off the snow. Working his way up over the crest, he saw others on the Garden fighting through the wind, their ropes bowed out into taut arcs. Rick Wilcox and Doug Madera went up the ridge above the right wall of the ravine. This place has no difficulties for a summer hiker, but when Rick wasn't totally braced against his crampons and ice axe the wind would send him sprawling along the ground. There was a 2,000-foot drop thirty feet away.

As soon as Al Comeau came over the crest of South Gully he saw someone there in the sun. As with Derek Tinkham, Al was the first one to reach the victim, but now he faced the moment all rescue climbers dread — it was someone he knew. Al recognized Monroe Couper, a climbing student he'd had the winter before, a musician of unusual talent and sensitivity, a person Al remembered with great affection. Not seeing Erik Lattey, Al went back down the top section of Pinnacle to see if he'd gotten stuck there.

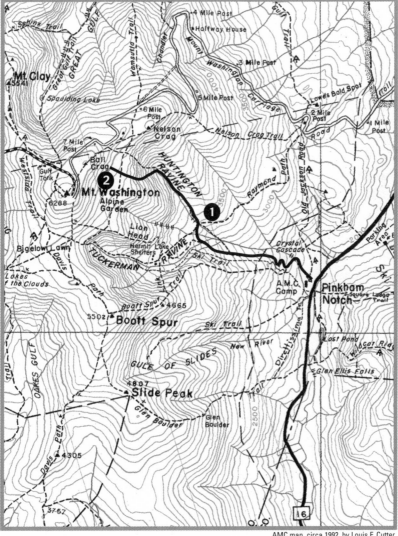

AMC map, circa 1992, by Louis F. Cutter

1 Up Tuckerman Ravine Trail and across Huntington Ravine cut-off
to spend the night in Harvard Cabin

2 Up Odell Gulley, they collapse and die on Alpine Garden

A few minutes later, Brian Abrams saw a huddled knot of color in the lee of some rocks and, thinking it was another member of the rescue team, he made his way over through the fierce blast of weather and lay down close beside a man in a blue outfit; it's a mountaineer's way of getting a bit of shelter in extreme conditions above timberline. The man was leaning toward an open pack and his gloves were off; apparently he was getting something to eat. He didn't seem aware of Brian's presence, then the rescuer realized that the man providing his shelter was dead.

Al Comeau did not find any sign of Erik Lattey near the top of Pinnacle Gully and when he got back to the plateau he found Brian Abrams and some other members of the rescue team and they took stock of the situation. They realized that Monroe had died in the act of trying to make something hot for himself and his friend. Erik was nearby, lying face down in the rocks with his arms outstretched, heading toward Monroe. It looked as if he'd tried to find an escape route Saturday evening, then gone back for his partner.

This was a tough one. Members of the climbing community had little sympathy for Jeremy Haas, but Monroe and Erik had tried to do things right, they'd taken climbing lessons from the best in the business, and in their last moments they were trying to take care of each other.

The bodies were finally recovered on Tuesday. Then, after three days of almost continuous effort, the teams gathered for a debriefing down at AMC headquarters. An official from the Forest Service offered to arrange psychological counseling for anyone who felt the need, but there were no takers. The consensus was that they'd rather have the Forest Service arrange steaks and beer. This was, after all, volunteer work.

• CHERYL WEINGARTEN •
MAY 1994

$\mathcal{T}$uckerman Ravine is a sort of twin to Huntington Ravine, a left-hand punch into the side of Mount Washington by the same primordial giant that made Huntington with his right. The surrounding topography is a little different, though, it has the effect of an immense snow fence, and the drifts pile into Tuckerman all winter long. By spring, snow has banked up against the headwall 150 feet deep, and skiers come from all over America to hike up from the highway and test nerve and technique on some of the steepest skiing anywhere on the planet. "Going over the Lip," making the vertiginous plunge from the higher snowfields down into the bowl, is a major rite of passage. In fact, going up over The Lip can be as scary as most people would want. It's not like climbing a slope in any familiar sense — it's more like climbing a thousand-foot ladder. There's always a line of steps kicked into the snow at the right side of the headwall, and as the slope steepens the surface of the snow gets closer and closer to the front of the bended knees. Darwin is in charge of safety here; skiers usually stop climbing up at the point dictated by thoughts of skiing down.

Darwin was not with me the first time I skied down over the Lip. I'd climbed an alternate route to take the mail to the crew at the summit observatory; not only that, but fog came in on the way down. There are several major choices of route: Gulf of Slides and Raymond Cataract both end at the same place in the valley and are far more accommodating to nerve and technique. I planned to ski down with someone from the observatory, trusting him to navigate on my youthful and somewhat tremulous behalf.

Being above timberline, on snow, in fog, is like being inside a milk bottle: It's a whiteout with no visual references at all. At best you're lost; at worst you totter with vertigo and nausea. As we skied down, my increasing speed told me the slope was steepening, and even though years of hiking had taught me the terrain in mapmaker's detail, it was fair-weather mapmaking. I asked where we were and heard, "The Lip is right down there." In this case, the whiteout was my friend, and I made my rite of passage over the Lip mainly because I couldn't see well enough to be scared.

Not everyone skis, and a good spring day will also bring out hikers who enjoy the cushiony surface underfoot, the bright sun, and the spectacle. On May 1, 1994, Cheryl Weingarten and her friends Julie Parsons, Anna Shapiro, and Nick Nardi, arrived at the foot of the trail in Pinkham Notch and started up toward the ravine. They were all students at Tufts University near Boston and the plan had taken shape at a concert, and there was not very much experience in the group; Nick had the most, he'd climbed Mount Washington twice before and he'd done some other hikes in the White Mountains and some in the Alleghenies. This day they were wearing clothes suitable for an unthreatening spring day on Mount Washington, but they had no crampons or any other equipment that would help them on high-angle climbing.

Matthew Swartz and a friend were starting up, too. They were good skiers and well-versed in ravine days, and they'd come over from the University of Vermont. The next day Matthew posted a report on the Internet. It began, "Tuckerman's 5/1 We hiked thru some rain to get to HoJo's in 1 hour 15 minutes. Trail in decent shape, some snow etc but no creeks opening yet. Rain stopped at HoJo's and we went on, many people turned back.... Maybe 30-50 people in the bowl all day. We climbed the Lip and up into the snowfields, there was still quite a bit (of snow) up there. The connector over the Lip into the bowl was pretty solid with crevasses opening on both sides. Water is running pretty good over the rocks now. Saw two people lose it in the Connector and do endos over the falls and cartwheel over the crevasses all the way to the bottom of the bowl. They were extremely shaken and a bit bruised but very lucky to be alive. The Connector (the Lip) should be carefully navigated, unless it loosens up a bit." That is, the top of the headwall was not corn snow, it was frozen snow.

Nick Nardi and his three friends were right in Matthew Swartz's tracks coming up from Pinkham, then Anna Shapiro stayed in the ravine to ski and the others headed for the summit. The weather was not enjoyable; fog was right down on the ground and they could see only fifty or one hundred feet and, as Matthew Swartz noted, this is why so few skiers had decided to come up from Howard Johnson's. Nick and Cheryl and Julie kept going up the ladder of steps that skiers had kicked into the snow at the right side of the ravine.

Trouble was already with them, though; fog had come in, and they couldn't see the larger picture. Caution is largely determined by vision — out of sight, out of mind. They reached the summit and Nick signed the register at what he called "the mall," and then they started down the same way they'd come up.

Conditions were dreary. At 3:00 P.M. the summit weather observatory recorded fog with light to moderate rain and intermittent ice pellets in the air. Nevertheless, the three friends had fun sliding down in the soft snow of the upper, milder terrain. They were on my youthful track exactly, but they didn't have my guide; with no horizon and no shadows, slope and detail disappeared in a wash of gray. They paused near the signs marking a trail junction above the ravine and briefly debated which way to go. Nick had one idea, Cheryl and Julie had another. There wasn't much difference — a little more to the left or a little more to the right — and they decided to take the women's inclination.

As the season advances, the snowpack in Tuckerman Ravine turns to ice and behaves exactly like a glacier; it pulls away from the rocks on the headwall and crevasses open up in the surface, and the ice becomes slightly plastic and follows gravity downhill. Robert Underhill was a notable AMC activist and this glacial effect had always interested him, so late in the snow season of 1939 he surveyed a line straight across the floor of the ravine and set a line of stakes there. He surveyed the stakes again in July and found that in the twenty days of his experiment the center of the snowpack moved thirteen feet farther downslope than the edges, true glacial behavior.

As the springs days grow warmer a tremendous amount of snow melts above the ravine and runs out over a flat rock at one side of the Lip, then plunges down the headwall behind the icy snow that's pulling away from the rocky headwall.

Julie was in the lead as the three friends hopped and slid, then she and Cheryl dropped onto their backsides and began to slide down the slope feet first. The angle gets so steep so fast here that it passes beyond reason and suddenly Julie slid onto the beginning of the waterfall. With a lunge, she got hold of a bit of dwarf spruce and stopped herself. Then Cheryl slid past her and out of sight.

With extraordinary courage and presence of mind, Julie held onto her tiny bit of safety. Nick had not been sliding and he was thirty or forty feet higher up the slope when he heard her screaming. He got down to where he could see her and realized that she was unable to move, she was frozen with fear. He called down and tried to reassure her, he told her to give him one step and it was a long time before she was able to do that. Then he coaxed her again, he told her to give him another step, then another step. This way, Julie pushed and crawled her way back up the dizzying slope to where he was.

Neither of them knew where they were on the headwall and they didn't know where Cheryl was, only that she was farther down. Nick thought that if they went to their left, looking uphill, they could meet up with her by going "around the cliff," as he put it later. As they tried to collect their wits they heard voices off to one side. They called, made contact, and crossed the fog-shrouded slope toward the voices. They found skiers who said they were heading down themselves, and the skiers led the way through the fog.

Not really knowing where they were, Julie and Nick probably hadn't realized that the footstep ladder they'd come up was right beside them when Julie pulled herself off the ledge. It was right there, just a few steps away on the other side of the Lip. Though forbiddingly steep, it was still the easiest way down. The skiers they now joined were heading for the Chute, so scary, so vertiginous a run that many veteran ravine skiers have never attempted it and have no plans to do so. Incredibly, Julie and Nick got themselves down this drop of ice and rock and snow that many climbers would hesitate to attempt without full equipment.

They didn't find Cheryl when they got to the floor of the ravine, and they didn't know where she was. Cheryl had grown up as the kind of girl who was ready for anything. She was bright and active and very popular, and she had an endless zest for life; she'd been studying in France and only recently she'd survived a head-on crash in Morocco. Knowing Cheryl's eager enthusiasms, her parents sometimes worried about her.

Now they got a call from the White Mountains. Brad Ray was the veteran forest service supervisor for Tuckerman Ravine and by Sunday evening he'd pieced together the sometimes contradictory details and realized what had happened: Cheryl had gone over the waterfall below the flat rock and been carried down behind the snowpack.

After Nick and Julie had made their way down The Chute, they'd gone to the Forest Service shelter and found Chris Joosen, who was posted there as the Forest Service technician, more popularly known as the snow ranger. He didn't remember seeing them earlier in the day and this struck him as unusual; he always tried to remember the faces of people who talked to him. There were only a few people in the ravine that day because of the weather, and he didn't remember seeing this party. It occurred to him that if he had, he would have advised them not to go on up into the ravine with the summer hiking gear they had. Now Nick Nardi told him that one of their friends was missing — she'd slid down the slope above the bowl and they couldn't find her.

Chris got as much information as he could from Nick and Julie, and he realized that they did not have a clear idea of where they'd been on the slope, only that Cheryl Weingarten had slid down out of sight. Brad Ray was the senior snow ranger in the ravine, a man with thirty years experience there, and he'd already gone down the trail to Pinkham and on to his home in Gorham. Chris called him and Brad directed him to begin a search-and-rescue mission with Lewis Baldwin, the other member of the crew at the AMC Hermit Lake Shelter.

The two of them started up toward the headwall, checking the holes and crevasses as they went, and it was almost dark by the time

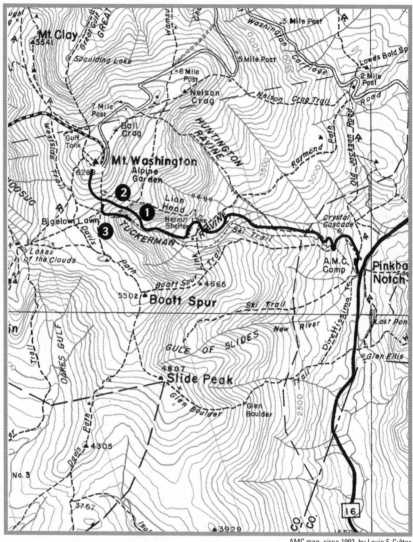

AMC map, circa 1992, by Louis F. Cutter

1 Up Tuckerman Ravine Trail, up snowslope in ravine to summit
2 Cheryl slides over Lip into crevasse on the headwall
3 Other two descend headwall by the Chute

they had climbed up to the crevasse below the waterfall. They rigged their ropes there and Lewis belayed Chris over to the edge of the crevasse. The day had been warm and rainy and there was a tremendous volume of water coming down, so Chris was already soaked by the spray when he was still twenty feet from the edge. Even more troublesome, the roaring was so loud that he and Lewis could barely hear each other when they shouted. Chris shouted down into the crevasse and he got no response.

Then they climbed up above the waterfall and Lewis put Chris on belay again and he worked his way down toward the crevasse. Then he saw sliding marks in the icy snow and they looked as if they'd been made by a person sliding feet first on their backside. Still on belay, Chris worked his way down beside the tracks to about eight feet from the point where they disappeared over the edge into the waterfall. Their line would carry the person who made them straight into the edge of the crevasse.

They couldn't do anything more, so they went back down the headwall, checking other crevasses as they went. Back at the Forest Service shelter, they called Brad Ray again and talked the situation over. Brad told them that the volume of water was too large for any useful work, they'd have to wait until early morning, when the volume would be much smaller and someone with immersion gear could be lowered into the crevasse. Then Brad called the Weingartens and told them that the situation was very serious.

By now a call had also gone to Rick Wilcox in North Conway. He talked the situation over with other lead people in the rescue network and they agreed with Brad Ray's decision, they knew that by the time a group was in position to do anything up in the ravine it would be very late in the evening, extremely dangerous for the rescuers, and almost certainly too late for Cheryl Weingarten.

By 6:00 A.M. the next day, a combined team of Forest Service, Fish and Game, AMC crew, Mountain Rescue Service, and Androscoggin Valley Search and Rescue had gathered at Pinkham. They had a wetsuit and scuba equipment in addition to their more usual ropes and security devices, and when they reached the top of the headwall they found the situation they expected: the temperature on the upper slopes of Mount Washington had fallen to 17° overnight and the chill had slowed the melting and greatly reduced the volume of water. They rigged 300 feet of ropes and anchors, then Jeff Gray of Fish and Game put on immersion gear and was lowered into the crevasse. When he was about sixty feet down he found Cheryl Weingarten.

They brought her to the surface and carefully wrapped her in thermal barriers and secured her in a Stokes litter and belayed her down the headwall. Even though it was clear that she'd suffered terrible injuries and was partly frozen, they took the million-to-one chance and Mike Pelchat began cardiovascular resuscitation with oxygen. They continued with this as they carried her out of the ravine, put her onto a snow tractor at the Forest Service shelter, and went on down to the highway. The combined rescue forces devoted 204 man hours in their attempt to help Cheryl and more than fifty radio and telephone calls had gone through the communication center at AMC headquarters, but when Dr. Sterns met them in the valley he determined that Cheryl's neck was broken and she was dead.

That waterfall forms every spring and a trace of it usually remains in summer, just to the left of the hiking trail as it rounds up over the top of the headwall. Habitues of the ravine call that place Schiller's Rock to remember Dr. Paul Schiller, a skier who died after sliding over the waterfall and into the crevasse forty-five years earlier to the month, week, day, and hour.

AFTERMATH

*I*n April of 1997, Leonard Weingarten filed *Weingarten v. United States of America*. He claimed damages for the wrongful death of his daughter and for the loss of her society and comfort.

There were sixteen charges in the first claim, among them that the "Forest Service by and through its employees was charged with the duty to preserve and protect the area of the White Mountain National Forest and the safety of persons lawfully on the property under its management." And "the defendant breached its duty to the plaintiff's decedent by failing to warn through posting of signs, orally, or in some other manner of inherent dangers on its property which (it) knew or should have known existed; in failing to post warning signs, barriers and/or fences around an eroded area of said property which was dangerous and which reasonably could be foreseen to be a site where injury or death could occur." And "The defendant's failure to warn of the existence of or to barricade the entrance to said chasm was a substantial factor in causing plaintiff's decedent to fall into said chasm." And "the foregoing resulted solely through the culpable conduct of defendant and with no negligence on the part of plaintiff's decedent contributing thereto."

The federal government based its defense on several grounds. One was found in the doctrine of sovereign immunity, a position that descends from the elder days of royal rule: "The United States, as sovereign, is immune from suit unless it has expressly consented to be sued." This led into questions of the court's subject matter jurisdiction.

The defense also argued matters of liability found in New Hampshire's recreational-use statutes. "An owner, occupant, or lessee of land, including the state or any political subdivision, who without charge permits any person to use land for recreational purposes or as a spectator of recreational activity, shall not be liable for personal injury or property damage in the absence of intentionally caused injury or damage." And "An owner, lessee or occupant of premises owes no duty of care to keep such premises safe for entry or use by others for hunting, fishing, trapping, camping, water sports, winter sports or OHRV — hiking, sightseeing, or removal of fuelwood, or to give any warning of hazardous conditions, uses of, structures, or activities on such premises to persons entering for such purposes."

More specific entries are found in the sixteen-page declaration of Brad Ray, who at that time had served as a snow ranger in the ravine for more than thirty-eight years. "As lead Snow Ranger, I have responsibility for managing Tuckerman Ravine consistent with the policy goals of the U.S. Forest Service. As Lead Snow Ranger, the Forest Service leaves me with authority to accomplish that responsibility by using my professional judgement and discretion. Nothing in the statutes, regulations, or Forest Service policies dictate particular actions that I must follow in the handling of hazards, warning the public of those hazards, or managing public safety issues in the Ravine. The *Forest Service Handbook*...provides more detailed guidance on things that I, or any other Forest Service official, should take into consideration in managing the Forest's trails. It does not set forth specific steps or actions that I am mandated to take.... Nothing in the Trail Management Handbook mandates specific actions that I, or any other Forest Service official, was required to take in the handling of a safety hazard such as the waterfall crevasse.

"In particular, the Forest Plan establishes that the Pinkham Notch Scenic Area is to be managed as a semi-private, non-motorized recreational opportunity spectrum class area — a predominantly natural environment — to be managed with minimum on-site controls. For such an area, although restrictions on the use of the area may exist, they are to be subtle restrictions.

"With regard to the Backcountry Undeveloped Areas, which would include Tuckerman Ravine, the management emphasis generally will be placed on protecting the natural resources first and the quality of the human experience second. Thus, in managing the Pinkham Notch Scenic Area as a semi-primitive, non-motorized area, we are to emphasize protection of resources in a manner such that this protection takes priority over the quality of the human experience in using the area.

"Thus, in managing Tuckerman Ravine, I and other Forest Service personnel are to balance issues of public safety associated with the use of the Ravine against the policy goals of protecting or maintaining the Ravine in its natural condition, maintaining a recreational opportunity that has minimum on-site controls, and making the Ravine available for multiple public uses.

"Over the years, and long before Ms. Weingarten slid into the crevasse, I have been concerned about the dangers presented by the waterfall cravasse when it opens up each Spring. For that reason, even prior to 1994, once the waterfall crevasse opens, the Snow Rangers have listed the presence of crevasses on the Avalanche Bulletin and have specifically noted its existence in other literature. But in addition to providing such warnings, prior to 1994, we considered whether we should take steps regarding the waterfall crevasse. In the end, however, for a variety of reasons, I concluded that the best approach to safeguarding the public in a manner consistent with the Forest Service's policy goal for the Pinkham Notch Scenic Area and Tuckerman Ravine has been to continue to provide warnings about the crevasse through the Avalanche Bulletin and other literature, as well as through personal contact with the public. These decisions were ones that, in accordance with Forest Service policies, were within my discretion and exercise of judgement.

"Among the options that we considered, and rejected, prior to Ms. Weingarten's death, was to provide some warning at the site of the waterfall by erecting crossed bamboo poles. Crossed bamboo poles are a well-established means of signaling trail closure or danger to skiers. However, I ultimately concluded that taking such a step would not be effective, would be dangerous, and would lead to a situation potentially contrary to the policy goals of the Forest Service. For example, at that time of the year, snow often melts in the Ravine at a rate of three to four feet every one to two days. Bamboo poles are eight feet long and usually are planted with at least four feet sticking out above the snow. With snow melting at the rate it does, the bamboo poles usually would fall down at least every other day. To maintain the warning, I would have to direct a team of two individuals, diverting them from other responsibilities, to reset the bamboo poles at least every other day. I determined that, in view of the limited benefit likely to be gained from the poles, I could not afford to divert those other snow rangers from their other tasks.

"Moreover, another consideration in my judgement was that it would be dangerous to send those rangers repeatedly to that location to reset the poles. Because of the snow melt and the river, one of the risks in that area is of undermined snow. As one team member belayed down to reset the poles, that individual would be at risk of falling through the snow and over the Headwall. I determined that I was unwilling to expose the rangers to this risk in view of the very limited benefit I expected from the poles. A significant factor in my decision against using poles to mark the crevasse was that I was convinced that it would not be effective. On those rare occasions that I have tried crossed bamboo poles in the area above the waterfall, I have seen individuals go right up to the poles, putting themselves at great risk because of the undermined snow. When questioned, it became clear that they did not know what crossed bamboo poles meant, instead indicating that they thought the poles marked the trail location.

"In addition, although we have considered erecting a fence above the waterfall, any fence would be directly contrary to the policy goal of maintaining the Ravine in its natural state. For example, during late April and early May, the snowpack above the waterfall is often 20 feet deep. For a fence to remain standing, especially given the pressures and movements of the snowpack, it would have to be drilled into rockface. That means, to be visible and effective, any fence would have to be at least 24 feet tall, so that it would stick out above the snow. Moreover, to withstand the pressures of the snowpack and the winds found at the top of the Ravine, the fence would have to be constructed of essentially girder-like material. In the Summer and Fall, that would mean that the Ravine would be marred with a 24-foot tall girder-like fence. Because the existence of such a structure would obviously contravene the Forest Service's stated policy goals for the Ravine, I rejected it.

"For similar reasons, I rejected the idea of placing signs above the waterfall, warning of the crevasse's presence below. For example, to be readable from a safe distance, a sign would have to be quite large, again marring the pristine landscape with its presence. Placing a reasonably sized sign itself at a safe distance from the edge of the Headwall would mean that it would be very easy to miss the sign in the large expanse above the Headwall. As a result, to be effective, I considered that we would have to place multiple signs around the perimeter of the Headwall-waterfall area. Again, I considered that this would be contrary to the goal of maintaining the Ravine in its natural condition.

"Finally, in considering any of these means of marking the crevasse site, I considered the fact that there are many other locations within the Ravine that are equally dangerous to users of the Ravine. I concluded that, if I marked or barricaded this particular location, I would start the Forest Service down the road of needing to mark or barricade those other dangerous locations as well. If the Forest Service marked or barricaded all those locations, Tuckerman Ravine would be a sea of signs and fences, giving its multiple dangers and risks. Because the policy goal for the Ravine is to maintain it in its natural state, I concluded against marking or barricading the crevasse.

"Another available option was to close the areas above the Headwall to any use once the crevasses open. In 1994, and now, there comes a time each Spring when I close the Lip and the Tuckerman Ravine Trail in the Lip area to all use. I use my professional judgement and discretion to determine when to close the Lip and that section of the Tuckerman Ravine Tail, taking into consideration the historic uses of the Ravine, the feasibility of enforcing the enclosure, and the policy goal of promoting self-reliance by users, providing recreational opportunities, and using minimal on-site controls. As a result, I do not close the Lip until, in my professional judgement, I conclude that a good skier or hiker can no longer safely negotiate the Lip, going up or down. At this time, the hiking trail, which traverses above and close to the Lip, is considered too dangerous, as a fall on the steep snow will result in a slide into rocks or crevasses. . . . Because, in my judgment, a good skier or hiker could still safely negotiate the Lip, I had not closed the Lip on May 1, 1994.

"As a result, to further the Forest Service's policy goal of minimizing man-made intrusions or changes to the natural environment of Tuckerman Ravine, I developed a general policy of not marking natural hazards that routinely exist or appeared annually, especially in the upper areas of the Ravine. Thus we do not mark the waterfall crevasse, protruding rocks, or high-water trail crossings. These hazards are obvious, and readily apparent to the users of the Ravine. In addition, in determining what, if anything, we should mark, we take into consideration the location of the hazards and, therefore, the users most likely to encounter them. Users who go over the Headwall into the Lip area tend to be more experienced individuals who try to be prepared and knowledgeable about the risks they will encounter."

Judge Paul Barbadoro heard the case in February 1999, and several points in his twenty-page ruling bear on the larger question of the public in the wilderness. One of the clauses chosen to support his motion mandates that the Forest Service, "conduct all management activities with full recognition of the appearance of the forest, realizing the importance to society of a natural landscape distinct from the man-made environment otherwise dominant in the East." The judge also noted that "the Forest Service is free to engage in a balancing of competing policy interests," and cited a ruling that the "Park Service is not obliged to put public safety concerns above the policy of preserving the historic accuracy of a landmark."

Noting Brad Ray's decision not to erect crossed poles because of the danger to his staff and the limited effectiveness and the risk to visitors who often approach the poles, the judge wrote that, "It is precisely this type of policy balancing that Congress intended to protect. That Plaintiff disagrees with the Forest Service's ultimate decision is of no import to the discretionary function analysis."

Citing a precedent in a Park Service judgment, the judge wrote that, "Faced with limited resources and unlimited natural hazards, the [National Park Service] must make public policy determination of which dangers are obvious and which dangers merit the special focus of a warning brochure or pamphlet. The Forest Service cannot possibly warn the public of every danger associated with skiing and hiking in the Ravine. To do so would not only cut into limited financial resources, but could also have a limited public safety benefit — too many warning brochures and pamphlets would invariably reduce the impact of the individual warnings to the public."

In concluding, Judge Barbadoro wrote, "I find that the defendant's decision not to barricade or post warnings of the waterfall crevasse was a discretionary act susceptible to policy judgements and, therefore, was the type of discretionary government action Congress intended to protect. Accordingly, I find that this court lacks jurisdiction to hear Plaintiff's claims as they are based on acts or omissions of the government which fall within the discretionary function exception to the Federal Tort Claims Act. Thus, I grant Defendant's motion to dismiss and dismiss Plaintiff's claims for lack of subject matter jurisdiction."

· SARAH NICHOLSON ·
JUNE 1994

*T*he last Mount Washington death of the 1994 winter was in June. As the sun climbs toward summer it loosens the ice that forms on the ledges lining the ravine at the level of Schiller's Rock. It's on just such lovely days that the greatest number of skiers come up, and long practice has endowed a citizen's early warning system: when the telltale crack is heard, the cry "ICE!" goes up. Sound carries well in this vast acoustic focus, everyone hears the call, and everyone looks up the slope.

On June 4, Sarah Nicholson looked up and saw a car-sized block of ice sliding and bounding down toward her. Gravity is also on the side of the skier, and a quick escape left or right downslope almost always avoids the danger of falling ice. But this block was breaking into fragments, and it wasn't clear which way led most quickly to safety. It's a familiar sidewalk dilemma: step left or right to avoid the collision? Sarah's moment of hesitation broke the heart of her friends, and brought the list of mortality on the Presidential Range to 115.

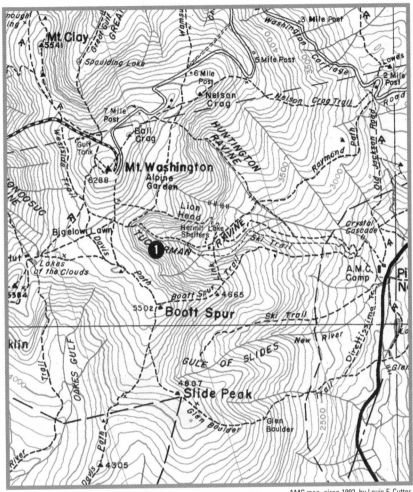

AMC map, circa 1992, by Louis F. Cutter

1 Only known that she was killed by falling ice on the left side
of Tuckerman Ravine

ACKNOWLEDGMENTS

*T*his book began in the mind of Mel Allen, the long-time features editor at *Yankee Magazine*. I'd written a number of pieces for Mel, all in the manner of pleasant reveries. Then he asked for an article on the terrible winter of 1994 on the Presidential Range. I wrote it and Mel said, "That's a good job of reporting." I understood that he was damning with faint praise. Then he said, "I want to hear voices, I want to hear your voice." I rewrote the piece and it ran in the February 1995 issue.

It drew a large and often touching response from the readers, and some rang unexpected bells. There was, for instance, the letter from Richard Moran, of Port Ludlow, Washington. He'd grown up in Whitefield, New Hampshire, and his father delivered dairy goods to the Tip-Top House, and sometimes young Richard rode up with him. Mr. Moran went on to tell about a winter episode when four hikers were trying to reach the summit by way of the cog railway track; the weather went against them and three of them died. The bodies were brought to an undertaker in Whitefield and the survivor married the nurse who attended him in the Whitefield hospital, thus launching the favorite story of the winter in that remote mountain town.

Mr. Moran said he remembered that vividly, but he wondered why it was never listed in the roster of fatalities on the Presidential Range. I wrote back and told him of childhood days when we'd go into the AMC building at Pinkham Notch and head straight for the death list posted on the wall. Father would stab the list with his finger and say, "There's something missing here — three fellows froze to death on the cog railway trestle. That must have been around nineteen-hundred and thirty." More than fifty years would pass before Mr. Moran confirmed my father's sense of history.

Most of this book was found in ancient texts. The library in Gorham, New Hampshire, has one of the very few collections of *Among the Clouds* known to exist and I'm most grateful to Ida Bagley, Valerie LaPointe, and Judy Blais for putting up with my interruptions; the cabinet holding the bound issues of the old summit newspaper is right behind their desk. The town libraries in Berlin and Jackson, the state library in Concord, and the Dartmouth College library in Hanover were valuable sources, other documents were found in the federal court records and the state supreme court library in Concord. The archives of the summit and valley stations of the Mount Washington Observatory were both abundant and essential, and I owe a very large debt to the staff members who abided my many interruptions and, especially, to Sean Doucette, the staff computer specialist who rescued many photographs from their faded old age.

I must also thank Howie Wemyss and Brian Bennett, managers of the Mount Washington auto road, for their kindness, Adelina Azevedo Axelrod for her research help in Providence, Rhode Island, and my brother John for his tales of life on the summit.

Living memories of the accidents began with Brad Washburn, man for all seasons and all ages on Mount Washington and a principal in the rescue of Jessie Whitehead in 1933. Sixty-six years later he was a tireless help to me and made many minute corrections to the text. Nancy Fielder and Hartie Beardsely and his sister Mary Fenn helped with the story of Jeremy Pierce. Fred Stott was on the crew at Madison Hut when

Joe Caggiano died in 1938 and Fred is still doing yeoman service with the AMC. Paul Turner also contributed memories of that ill-fated hike.

Sam Goodhue provided details of the elder days on the Mount Washington Volunteer Ski Patrol, and my own inability to throw anything away preserved the stories Kibbe Glover gave me twenty years ago. He embodied an entire chapter in the long story of Tuckerman Ravine, he retired to live at Pinkham in his old age, and now he is sorely missed by everyone who knew him.

The account of Philip Longnecker and Jacques Parysko drew on the memories of Paul Dougherty, George Hamilton, and Mack Beal. The story of the terrible night that took the life of MacDonald Barr could not have been told without the very generous help of Peter Crane, Emily Thayer Benson, Kari Geick, Lars Jorrens, Alexei Rubenstein, Stephanie Aranalas, and Yvonne and Tavis Barr. None of their memories were easy.

The original *Yankee Magazine* article appears with some additions as the last section in this book. It was written with the help of Rebecca Oreskes and Brad Ray of the Forest Service, Ralph Patterson of the observatory, Bill Aughten, Jim Dowd, Brian Abrams of Fish and Game, and Rick Wilcox, Nick Yardley, Joe Lentini, Maury McKinney, Mike Pelchat, Al Comeau, Tiger Burns, and Ben Miller of the local rescue teams.

Finally, I must thank Brooks Dodge for his memories of growing up at the AMC camp in Pinkham Notch, for the use of his irreplaceable collection of Joe Dodge's papers and photographs, and for no end of help in a variety of writing projects over the years.

APPENDIX
DEATHS ON MOUNT WASHINGTON
1849-1999

1. October 19, 1849:
Frederick Strickland, 29, Bridlington, England, died after losing his way in an early storm.

2. September 14, 1855:
Lizzie Bourne, 23, Kennebunk, Maine, died of exhaustion and exposure in stormy weather.

3. August 7, 1856:
Benjamin Chandler, 75, Wilmington, Del., died of exhaustion and exposure near the summit.

4. October 4, 1869:
J. M. Thompson, proprietor of the Glen House, drowned in the flooded Peabody River.

5. February 26, 1872:
Pvt. William Stevens, U.S. Signal Service, died of natural causes on the summit.

6. June 28, 1873:
Pvt. William Sealey, U.S. Signal Service, died in Littleton July 2 of injuries received in a slideboard accident on the Cog Railway.

7. September 3, 1874:
Harry Hunter, 21, Pittsburgh, Pa., died of exhaustion and exposure. His remains were found six years later.

8. July 3, 1880:
Mrs. Ira Chichester, Allegan, Mich., was killed when a coach overturned on the Carriage Road.

9. July 24, 1886:
Sewall Faunce, 15, Dorchester, Mass., killed by the falling of the snow arch in Tuckerman Ravine.

10. August 24, 1890:
Ewald Weiss, 24, Berlin, Germany, left the Summit House to walk to Mt. Adams. He was never found.

11. June 30, 1900:
William Curtis, 63, New York, NY, died of exhaustion and exposure in a sudden storm near the Lakes of the Clouds.

12. Allan Ormsby, 28, Brooklyn, N.Y., hiking with Curtis, died 300 feet from the summit.

13. August 23, 1900:
Alexander Cusick, employee of the Cog Railway, was killed while descending on a slideboard.

14. September 18, 1912:
John Keenan, 18, Charlestown, Mass., a surveyor, wandered off the cone of Mount Washington; he has never been found.

15. August 5, 1919:
Harry Clauson, 19, Boston, Mass., was killed descending the Cog Railway on an improvised slideboard.

16. Jack Lonigan, 21, Boston, Mass., killed with Clauson.

17. November, 1927:
A woodsman named Harriman drowned in Jefferson Brook while following his traplines.

18. April 1928:
Elmer Lyman, Berlin, N.H., froze to death while attempting to walk through the unplowed Pinkham Notch Road.

19. December 1, 1928:
Herbert Young, 18, Salem, Mo., died of exhaustion and exposure on the Ammonoosuc Ravine Trail.

20. July 20, 1929:
Daniel Rossiter, Boston photographer, was killed when the renovated old engine Peppersass was destroyed on the Cog Railway.

21. July 30,1929:
Oysten Kaldstad, Brooklyn, NY, was drowned in Dry River, Oakes Gulf, on a fishing trip.

22. September 18, 1931:
Henry Bigelow, 19, Cambridge, Mass., killed by a falling stone while rock climbing in Huntington Ravine.

23. January 31, 1932:
Ernest McAdams, 22, Stoneham, Mass., froze to death while making a winter ascent.

24. Joseph Chadwick, 22, Woburn, Mass., died with McAdams.

25. June 18, 1933:
Simon Joseph, 19, Brookline, Mass., died of exhaustion and exposure near the Lakes of the Clouds Hut.

26. November 11, 1933:
Rupert Marden, 21, Brookline, Mass., died of exhaustion and exposure in Tuckerman Ravine.

27. September 9, 1934:
Jerome Pierce, 17, Springfield, Vt., drowned in Peabody River.

28. April 1, 1936:
John Fowler, 19, New York, NY, died of injuries after a 900-foot slide down the east side of Mount Washington.

29. May 23, 1936:
Grace Sturgess, 24, Williamstown, Mass., died of injuries from falling ice in Tuckerman Ravine.

30. July 4, 1937:
Harry Wheeler, 55, Salem, Mass., died of a heart attack on the Caps Ridge Trail on Mount Jefferson.

31. August 24, 1938:
Joseph Caggiano, 22, Astoria, NY, died of exhaustion and exposure on the Gulfside Trail near Madison Hut.

32. June 9, 1940:
Edwin McIntire, 19, Short Hills, NJ, was killed by a fall into a crevasse in Tuckerman Ravine.

33. October 13, 1941:
Louis Haberland, 27, Roslindale, Mass., died from exhaustion and exposure on the Caps Ridge Trail on Mount Jefferson.

34. April 7, 1943:
John Neal, Springfield, Mass., suffered a fatal injury while skiing the Little Headwall of Tuckerman Ravine.

35. May 31, 1948:
Phyllis Wilbur, 16, Kingfield, Maine, was injured while skiing in Tuckerman Ravine; died on June 3.

36. May 1, 1949:
Paul Schiller, Cambridge, Mass., died while skiing on the headwall of Tuckerman Ravine.

37. February 2, 1952
Tor Staver, injured in a skiing accident on the Sherburne Trail; died in Boston Feb. 5 of a fractured skull.

38. August 23, 1952:
Raymond Davis, 50, Sharon, Mass., died of exposure after collapsing above the headwall of Tuckerman Ravine, from a heart condition.

39. January 21, 1954:
Philip Longnecker, 25, Toledo, Ohio, buried in an avalanche during a Tuckerman Ravine camping trip.

40. Jacques Parysko, 23, Cambridge, Mass., died with Longnecker.

41. February 19, 1956:
A. Aaron Leve, 28, Boston, Mass., killed by avalanche in Tuckerman Ravine.

42. September 1, 1956:
John Ochab, 37, Newark, NJ, died from a fall on Mt. Clay.

43. June 7, 1956:
Thomas Flint, 21, Concord, Mass., died from a fall and exposure on Mt. Madison.

44. May 17, 1958:
William Brigham, 28, Montreal, Canda, killed by icefall in Tuckerman Ravine.

45. July 19, 1958:
Paul Zanet, 24, Dorchester, Mass., died of exposure on Crawford Path.

46. Judy March, 17, Dorchester, Mass., died with Zanet.

47. August 22, 1959:
Anthony Amico, 44, Springfield, Mass., died of a heart attack near the top of Tuckerman Ravine.

48. June 2, 1962:
Armand Falardeau, 42, Danielson, Conn., died of exposure near the summit of Mt. Clay.

49. September 12, 1962:
Alfred Dickinson, 67, Melrose, Mass., died of exposure near the summit of Nelson Crag.

50. April 4, 1964:
Hugo Stadmueller, 28, Cambridge, Mass., killed in an avalanche while climbing in Huntington Ravine.

51. John Griffin, 39, Hanover, N.H., died with Stadmueller.

52. May 3, 1964:
Remi Bourdages, 38, Spencer, Mass., suffered a heart attack in Tuckerman Ravine.

53. March 14, 1965:
Daniel Doody, 31, North Branford, Conn., killed in a fall in Huntington Ravine.

54. Craig Merrihue, 31, Cambridge, Mass., killed with Doody.

September 6, 1967:
The following people died in an accident on the Cog Railway:

55. Eric Davies, 7, Hampton, N.H.

56. Mary Frank, 38, Warren, Mich.

57. Monica Gross, 2, Brookline, Mass.

58. Shirley Zorzy, 22, Lynn, Mass.

59. Beverly Richmond, 15, Putnam, Conn.

60. Kent Woodard, 9, New London, N.H.

61. Charles Usher, 55, Dover, N.H.

62. Mrs. Charles Usher, 56, Dover, N.H.

63. January 26, 1969:
Scott Stevens, 19, Cucamonga, Calif., killed in a climbing accident in Yale Gully, Huntington Ravine.

64. Robert Ellenberg, 19, New York, NY, died with Stevens.

65. Charles Yoder, 24, Hartford, Wisc., died with Stevens and Ellenberg.

66. February 9, 1969:
Mark Larner, 16, Albany, NY, died of injuries sustained in a slide on Mt. Adams.

67. Summer 1969:
Albert R. Tenney, 62, died of a heart attack on the Crawford Path between Mt. Webster and Mt. Jackson.

68. October 12, 1969:
Richard Fitzgerald, 26, Framingham, Mass., died of head injuries sustained in Huntington Ravine fall.

69. November 29, 1969:
Paul Ross, 26, South Portland, Maine, died in a light-plane crash on the south-west slope of Boott Spur.

70. Kenneth Ward, 20, Augusta, Maine, died with Ross.

71. Cliff Phillips, 25, Island Pond, Vt., died with Ross and Ward.

72. March 21, 1971:
Irene Hennessey, 47, died in a light-plane crash above Huntington Ravine.

73. Thomas Hennessey, 54, died in the same crash.

74. April 24, 1971:
Barbara Palmer, 46, West Acton, Mass., died of exposure near the Cog Railway base station.

75. August 28, 1971:
Betsy Roberts, 16, Newton, Mass., drowned in the Dry River.

76. October 1971:
Geoff Bowdoin, Wayland, Mass., drowned in the Dry River.

77. May 17, 1972:
Christopher Coyne, 21, Greenwich, Conn., died in a fall in Tuckerman Ravine.

78. September 23, 1972:
Richard Thaler, 49, Brookline, Mass., succumbed to a heart attack while hiking on Mt. Adams.

79. August 22, 1973:
Peter Winn, 16, Bedford, N.H., died of head injuries while skiing in Tuckerman Ravine.

80. August 22, 1974:
Vernon Titcomb, 56, Santa Fe, Calif., died in a plane crash above Gray Knob during a thunderstorm.

81. Jean Titcomb, 53, died in the same crash.

82. December 24, 1974:
Karl Brushaber, 37, Ann Arbor, Mich., died of a skull fracture in Tuckerman Ravine.

83. October 23, 1975:
Clayton Rock, 80, Massachusetts, died of a heart attack near the Lakes of the Clouds.

84. March 26, 1976:
Margaret Cassidy, 24, Wolfeboro, NH, died from injuries suffered in a fall in Huntington Ravine.

85. May 8, 1976:
Scott Whinnery, 25, Speigeltown, NY, died of injuries sustained in a fall in Hillman's Highway.

86. July 12, 1976:
Robert Evans, 22, Kalamazoo, Mich., died of injuries sustained in a fall in Tuckerman Ravine.

87. February 14, 1979:
David Shoemaker, 21, Lexington, Mass., died of exposure after a fall in Huntington Ravine.

88. Paul Flanigan, 26, Melrose, Mass., died of injuries after falling with Shoemaker.

89. August 21, 1980:
Patrick Kelley, 24, Hartford, Conn., died in a fall in Tuckerman Ravine.

90. October 12, 1980:
Charles LaBonte, 16, Newbury, Mass., died after a fall into a brook near the Ammonoosuc Trail.

91. October 13, 1980:
James Dowd, 43, Boston, Mass., died of a heart attack on the Tuckerman Ravine Trail.

92. December 31, 1980:
Peter Friedman, 18, Thomaston, Conn., died while ice climbing in Huntington Ravine.

93. August 8, 1981:
Myles Coleman, 73, Wellsville, N.Y., died of a stroke on the summit of Mount Washington.

94. January 25, 1982:
Albert Dow, 29, Tuftonboro, N.H., died in an avalanche while searching for two lost climbers.

95. March 28, 1982:
Kathy Hamann, 25, Sandy Hook, Conn., died of head injuries in a fall while climbing in Tuckerman Ravine.

96. May 25, 1982
John Fox, 47, Shelburne, Vt., died of a stroke in Tuckerman Ravine.

97. January 1, 1983:
Edward Aalbue, 21, Westbury, NY, died after a fall in Huntington Ravine.

98. March 24, 1983:
Kenneth Hokenson, 23, Scotia, NY, died after a fall down the icy cone of Mount Washington.

99. March 27, 1983:
Mark Brockman, 19, Boston, Mass., died after a fall on Mount Washington.

100. July 30, 1984:
Paula Silva, 22, Cambridge, Mass., died in an auto crash at the base of the Mount Washington road.

101. August 22, 1984:
Ernst Heinsoth, 88, Burlington, Vt., suc-cumbed to a heart attack on the summit of Mount Washington.

102. July 21, 1985:
Marjorie E. Frank, 25, Randolph, Mass., committed suicide by asphyxiation on the Valley Way Trail to Mt. Madison. Her remains were found nine years later.

103. March 15, 1986:
Basil Goodridge, 56, Burlington, Vt., died of a heart attack on the Castle Trail, Mt. Jefferson.

104. April 5, 1986:
Robert Jones, 53, Bridgton, Maine, died of a heart attack on the Tuckerman Ravine Trail.

105. August 24, 1986:
MacDonald Barr, 52, Brookline, Mass., succumbed to hypothermia in a summer snowstorm on Mt. Madison.

106. June 30, 1990:
Edwin Costa, 40, Manchester, N.H., died while skiing in Great Gulf.

107. October 2, 1990:
Jimmy Jones, 34, Texas, died in a plane crash.

108. Russell Diedrick, 24, died in the same crash.

109. Stewart Eames, 27, died in the same crash.

110. February 24, 1991:
Thomas Smith, 41, Montpelier, Vt., died while ice climbing in Huntington Ravine.

111. January 27, 1992:
Louis Nichols, 47, Rochester, NH, died of exposure on Cog Railway Trestle.

112. August 12, 1992:
George Remini, 65, Efland, NC, died of a heart attack in the Alpine Garden.

113. January 15, 1994:
Derek Tinkham, 20, Saunderstown, RI, died of hypothermia on the summit of Mt. Jefferson.

114. February 26, 1994:
Monroe Couper, 27, New Jersey, died of hypothermia while ice climbing in Huntington Ravine.

115. Erick Lattery, 40, New Jersey, died with Couper.

116. May 1, 1994:
Cheryl Weingarten, 22, Somerville, Mass., was killed by a fall into a crevasse in Tuckerman Ravine.

117. June 4, 1994:
Sarah Nicholson, 25, Portland, Maine, died of injuries from falling ice in Tuckerman Ravine.

118. October 8, 1994:
Ronald Hastings, 63, Grantham, N.H., died of a heart attack on the summit of Mount Washington.

119. March 28, 1995:
Chris Schneider, 32, Pittsfield, Vt., fell while skiing in Hillman's Highway, off Tuckerman Ravine.

120. January 5, 1996:
Alexandre Cassan, 19, Becancour, Quebec, died in an avalanche on Lion's Head.

121. February 3, 1996:
Donald Cote, 48, Haverhill, Mass., fell on Lion's Head Trail while hiking.

122. February 25, 1996:
Nicholas Halpern, 50, Lincoln, Mass., died of hypothermia while hiking near Mt. Pleasant Brook on Mt. Eisenhower.

123. March 2, 1996:
Robert Vandel, 50, Vienna, Maine, died in a fall while climbing in Pinnacle Gully, Huntington Ravine.

124. March 24, 1996:
Todd Crumbaker, 35, Billerica, Mass., died in an avalanche in the Gulf of Slides.

125. John Wald, 35, Cambridge, Mass., died in the same avalanche.

126. September 21, 1997:
Steve Carmody, Danbury, Conn., died in a fall over the Lip while hiking on the Tuckerman Ravine Trail.

127. Summer 1999:
A person driving up the Auto Road died of a heart attack.

128. October 30, 1999:
Douglas Thompson, 68, Hanover, N.H., collapsed and died near the summit of Mt. Madison.

ABOUT THE AUTHOR

Nicholas Howe's family first went to the White Mountains as "summer people" in the mid-1880s. As a youth he spent long summers in the mountains and later worked for the Appalachian Mountain Club for four years, serving mainly on the crew at Madison Hut on the Presidential Range, and as a muleskinner. After graduating from college he moved to Jackson, New Hampshire, where he continues to live.

A journalist since 1977, Nick spent twenty years as a contributing editor and feature writer for *Skiing Magazine*. He has been a feature writer for *Yankee Magazine* since 1983, and his 1995 feature "Fatal Attraction" was a runner-up for a National Magazine Award. His work also has appeared in *The Old Farmer's Almanac*, *Backpacker Magazine*, *Outside*, and several anthologies.

Nick began playing jigs and reels for traditional dancing in 1961 and he continues to hike in the White Mountains while working on his next book, *The Hiker's Companion: Tales of the Trail and Other Useful and Curious Aspects of Life in the White Mountains* (Appalachian Mountain Club Books).

ABOUT THE
APPALACHIAN
MOUNTAIN CLUB

Since 1876, the Appalachian Mountain Club has promoted the protection, enjoyment, and wise use of the mountains, rivers, and trails of the Appalachian region. The AMC believes that successful, long-term conservation depends on first-hand experience and enjoyment of the outdoors. The AMC is a nonprofit organization whose members enjoy hiking, canoeing, skiing, walking, rock climbing, bicycling, camping, kayaking, backpacking, and working together to safeguard the environment.

ALSO AVAILABLE FROM AMC BOOKS

A Journey North:
  One Woman's Story of Hiking the Appalachian Trail

Forest and Crag:
  A History of Hiking, Trail Blazing, and Adventure in the Northeast Mountains

Into the Mountains:
  Stories of New England's Most Celebrated Peaks

Logging Railroads of the White Mountains

North Woods:
  An Inside Look at the Nature of Forests in the Northeast